ZAMBONI RODEO

Jason Cohen

ZAMBONI RODEO

Chasing Hockey Dreams from Austin to Albuquerque

GREYSTONE BOOKS

Douglas & McIntyre Publishing Group

Vancouver/Toronto/Berkeley

*This one is for my dad, even if he thinks a
hockey game should only last two periods*

It is also dedicated to the memory of Larry "Duck" Friddle

Greystone Books
A division of Douglas & McIntyre Ltd.
2323 Quebec Street, Suite 201
Vancouver, British Columbia
Canada V5T 4S7
www.greystonebooks.com

National Library of Canada Cataloguing in Publication Data

Cohen, Jason
Zamboni Rodeo

ISBN 1-55054-813-1 (cloth)   1-55054-945-6 (paper)

1. Austin Ice Bats (Hockey team) 2. Hockey—Texas. I. Title.
GV848.A87C63 2001   796.962'64'0976431   C2001-911205-X

Library of Congress Cataloging-in-Publication data is available.

Editing by Brian Scrivener
Cover design by Peter Cocking & Jessica Sullivan
Text design by Peter Cocking
Cover and interior photographs by Darren Carroll
Printed and bound in Canada by Friesens
Printed on acid-free paper ∞
Distributed in the U.S. by Publishers Group West

We gratefully acknowledge the financial support of the Canada
Council for the Arts, the British Columbia Arts Council, and the
Government of Canada through the Book Publishing Industry
Development Program (BPIDP) for our publishing activities.

CONTENTS

Introduction   *1*

1   The Best Little Motorcoach in Texas   *7*

2   Game Called on Account of Fog   *19*

3   Sleepless in Hell Paso   *33*

4   Requiem for the Girndog   *49*

5   Way Up and Down the Swan River   *65*

6   Thanksgiving   *79*

7   The Ivory Tower Line   *89*

8   Forecheck. Backcheck. Paycheck.   *107*

9   Just Trying to Capture the Spirit of the Thing   *127*

10   Big Stick, Little Cojones   *141*

11   The Changing of the "C"   *153*

12   Laying Down the Law   *171*

13   This Shoe Is Made for Stomping   *179*

14   Shot Through the Hart   *193*

15   Playing Out the String   *203*

16   The Real Season   *211*

Epilogue: Instant Karma   227

Afterword: "The Kid" Stays in the Picture   234

Appendix: Where Are They Now?   239

Acknowledgments   246

Photo Identification   249

INTRODUCTION

A GOAL IS A SOUND the crowd makes.
It can happen any time, in any part of the rink—wood, flesh and
vulcanized rubber whooshing at 90 miles an hour, too fast to com-
prehend completely—but the fans can always spot a developing
play. The puck is knocked loose and there's a hopeful, hesitating
murmur: *Aah-aaah-aaaaah* . . . Is a defenseman out of position?
Will a long pass give a winger the jump? Is there time, space, opportunity? The volume rises: *Mmmhhh!*

And more often than not it ends there, with a whiff or a save or
a muff or a miss, 8,000 people choking out their disappointment:
Ohhhh . . . ! That's what you get for loving a game where so much
of the really great action revolves around the times that someone
doesn't score.

Until somebody does. Goals are all the more exciting for their
scarcity. Built-up tension flies free in a great exhalation, the puck
a needle popping thousands of breathless balloons. Guys in
sombreros jump and dance, stodgy suits slap five and toddlers

scream—who cares if they don't know why—as everybody stomps and shouts to the *de rigueur* strains of Gary Glitter's "Rock 'n' Roll, Pt. 2." C'mon, you know the words: "HEY! HEY!"

Down on the ice, six men put on an emotional display that would make Robert Bly proud, hugging, shouting and flashing the biggest smiles you'll ever see, teeth and all. Reconstructive dentistry has come a long way. This is what the fans pay for and the athletes play for. Especially these guys, career minor leaguers who live and work in conditions that are easily trumped by anyone with a union card or a passing grade on the civil service exam. But longshoremen don't have this moment. Clerks don't get to hear this sound.

I can't get enough of the sound. In this postmodern age, the things that used to define community—neighborhoods, family, politics, religion, popular culture—are more fragmented than ever, a spin cycle of slightly overlapping social interactions that don't carry any universal meaning. Pro sports is no less tarnished an institution—its highest levels are commercialized and overpriced, and plenty of right-thinking people plain don't care. But being a fan—and having something in common with thousands of other fans—can still provide little unifying moments of grace. The sound of a hockey goal is an almost-magical expression of communal energy. I guess that's why I've conspired to hear it so often, thousands of times in the past five years.

The funny thing is, I had to move all the way from Pennsylvania to Texas to do so.

I was born in 1967, the same year as the Philadelphia Flyers. Hockey is my regional birthright.

I never played; though it's hard to believe, coming from a professional writer, I wasn't much of an athlete. And since my childhood was spent about 70 miles north of the city, I was oblivious to Philadelphia's bounty of covered outdoor rinks, as well as the fact that every Stanley Cup–crazed kid was learning how to skate.

Still, I can remember, barely, mimicking the 1975 Flyers–Buffalo Sabres finals with an orange street hockey ball in my garage. I can recall more clearly the souvenir glasses my family had, picked up with the purchase of a tank of gas (which wasn't so easy to come by, what with the energy crisis) at a local service station, the Flyers logo and the Stanley Cup on the front, the names of all those Broad Street Bullies on the back. I was at the Spectrum for one of the Edmonton Oilers' visits in the 1980s, and in 1989 I sat in a parked car in Evanston, Illinois, listening to a staticky transmission of Patrick Roy shutting down an unexpected Flyers playoff run. That conference finals game wasn't on TV, not even cable, so I had to drive a few blocks from my apartment to get a nighttime signal from the Philly AM station.

I moved to Texas a year later. The Flyers were awful. Hockey still wasn't on American TV much. The Stars came to Dallas in 1993, but I wasn't about to drive three hours just to see Shane Churla.

That was then. These days, I drive to Dallas several times a year during the regular season and have attended most of the playoffs during the Stars' recent glory years, driving up and back the same day without thinking twice. I watch as many Flyers games as my satellite dish will let me. From October to June, just about every Friday and Saturday of my life is taken up by hockey. And it's all because a dead-end, bush-league, just-for-the-fun-of-it minor league team came to Austin in 1996.

The Ice Bats, they were called—an intriguing novelty, to be sure. The incongruity of hockey in Texas was an irresistible hook. But when I went to the first home game in team history, it was as if Austin had been starving for frozen action all this time. People showed up wearing bat wings. Dozens of obvious non-natives were decked out in the full spectrum of NHL jerseys, with a certain orange-and-black number 88 (this was just six months after the Legion of Doom was first assembled) the most common outfit.

With teams also based in El Paso, Amarillo, Waco and Bell County, it was easy for me to convince the editors of *Texas Monthly*, a statewide general-interest magazine in the vein of *Vanity Fair* or *Saturday Night*, to let me go out in this world. I soaked up the atmosphere of practice, which happened to take place at a local mall. I sat in the locker room during a game in Central Texas, chatting with the players who'd already been kicked out for fighting. And I joined the team on a 14-hour bus ride to Albuquerque, New Mexico.

By the time I finished the article, I felt as if I'd stumbled on a secret culture—one that I could root around in for a lot longer than 5,000 words. All I could think was, here's a story that's never been told. Even obsessive hockey fans are mostly focused on the big-time, whether it's NHL stars, junior prospects or the hometown kid who earns a U.S. college scholarship. Very few people realize that literally hundreds of other players, an overwhelming majority of whom are Canadian, exist in this alternate universe of teams, agents and coaches.

That universe spreads from New York to Michigan to Colorado to Alaska, but obviously the idea of Texas hockey was particularly bizarre. Games were played in buildings that had "No Shearing" areas. Fans wore goalie masks decorated with Longhorns. One of Austin's first season ticket holders, Mike Rice, was a cowboy who'd actually ridden bulls competitively on the same patch of ground the Bats now skated over.

Minor league hockey also loves a gimmick. When you are selling an unfamiliar game to casual fans in nontraditional markets, any exposure is a godsend. So when I asked the team to grant me unfettered access for the entire season, I knew it wouldn't be a problem. One of the owners thought I should pay them for the privilege, but I soon brought him up to speed on both journalistic ethics and freelance writer finance.

And that was it. For six months, I hung around the Austin Ice Bats. I couldn't quite keep up with the players on either skates or barstools, but they tolerated me well enough. The ones who'd been there when I wrote the *Texas Monthly* article knew I understood the sport. It also helped that in my regular journalism career, I'd written about the likes of Courtney Love and Matthew McConaughey. The guys seemed flattered that I'd want to spend so much of my professional time on the likes of them. In my mind, they were just as colorful and complicated.

I hope you'll think so too. This book is about hockey, but it's also about passion, about loving a certain way of life so much that it becomes your life, about chasing hockey dreams to a place as strange as Texas not because they might come true, but because the chase itself is so much fun, even the grubby parts. "Playing for the love of the game" may be a sports cliché, but most of the hockey players in this book never accomplish anything truly remarkable as pros. To some, this makes their efforts seem forlorn. To me, it makes them more inspiring.

one

THE BEST LITTLE
MOTORCOACH IN TEXAS

IN MOTION it's quite a sight, this hurtling metal cylinder of red, white, yellow and blue, tricked out with team logos from bow to stern, shuttling its heroic cargo from rink to rink and state to state. Making a getaway from an opposing arena it becomes a moving target, weathering a fusillade of jeers, curses and obscene gestures, anything short of rotten fruit. Sometimes, a spirited group of young women will come into view, happy to greet the bus's occupants with a smile, a wink, a patch of flesh—and not just midriff. Mostly, though, the Bat Bus spends six months and too many days in a row passing through the middle of nowhere, only to arrive in a place that barely meets the definition of somewhere.

All of that, however, is when the bus is moving. Right now, it isn't going anywhere. It's October. 4:30 A.M. Nine hours earlier the puck dropped in Lake Charles, Louisiana, marking the first exhibition game of the season, Ice Bats vs. Ice Pirates. Five hours earlier, 20 hockey players hit the Players Island Casino dinner buffet, possibly the nicest road meal in minor league history. A few of them scored preseason bonuses at the blackjack table.

Now everyone's asleep, oblivious to the fact that the bus has been sputtering along at 20 miles per hour the last couple of miles. It whinnies to a halt at the side of a rainsoaked two-lane highway in Ellinger, Texas. Ellinger, 274 citizens strong, is a country town that has escaped development, just a dot on the map between Austin and Houston to most folks.

The groggy souls who notice the stoppage in play chalk it up to the driver's tiny bladder, or his jones for coffee, or both. No need to dwell on the way he wanders around the well-lit but unmanned Texaco station without any purpose. Surely it's too soon to wonder how many cabs might have to travel from Austin—nearly two hours northwest of here—to get everyone home.

Guys wander off the bus. Ellinger's entire retail district—pretty much all of Elllinger, in fact—lies before them. But neither the Texaco nor Hruska's Instant Shopping across the parking lot is available for relief or sustenance. A nearby puddle does the trick for the former. The scent of frying bacon suggests the latter will be ready when the convenience store greets its early-rising farmer clientele with biscuits and breakfast sandwiches at five o'clock.

The Ice Bats can wait until then. They aren't going anywhere.

Brian Fairfield believes otherwise. He's already under the bus, tinkering.

"I like this guy," Chris Morque, a returning veteran who will captain this Ice Bats squad, says of the 19-year-old rookie netminder. "He can stop the puck, and he can tell us what's wrong with the bus."

Freckled and strawberry blond, with a face that's destined to get carded well past 40, Fairfield is, quite literally, fresh off the family farm in Omemee, Ontario.

It took about two seconds for the boys on the bus to saddle Fairfield with the nickname "Tex." The youngster showed up in Austin ready to two-step, already outfitted with the hat, the neatly pressed Wranglers and a couple of fancy western shirts.

Tonight's vestment is fancy enough that Fairfield peels it off before embarking on his mud-splattered journey to the innards of the bus. The driver lays out triangular hazard markers, wielding a flashlight while the goalie does the real work.

"Get out from under there before you get your country ass run over!" someone shouts.

But Fairfield knows what he's doing. On the farm, when he wasn't delivering calves and such, he messed about with tractors and plows. He understands the workings of a diesel engine.

"If he gets us out of here, he makes the team," medical trainer Eric Seeber suggests.

Breakdowns are a bummer, but the Bats are not particularly fazed by their predicament. Rookie Jason Rapcewicz rode a train from Hamilton for 40 hours to get a tryout. He is, as the cliché goes, just happy to be here. Chris Morque *has* been here, more times than he can remember. When he and Andy Ross and Mike Jackson played for the Memphis River Kings, their bus would fritz out after a couple of hours and the players would hitchhike back to the city they came from, setting up camp in the lobby of the hotel they'd just checked out of—the team wasn't about to spring for another night of rooms.

And while it might be wet, it's still 60 degrees Fahrenheit. The last time Tim Findlay had to wait around for roadside assistance he was in Sudbury, Ontario, where a February night at 30 below might be considered idyllic. A hotshot sniper for the Windsor Spitfires of the junior Ontario Hockey League, Findlay arrived in Austin this morning from Detroit, where he spent four weeks with the Vipers of the International Hockey League (IHL), the best league you could be in if you're not surefire NHL material. The Vipers wanted to stash Findlay with their AA team in Flint, Michigan, for more seasoning, but neither the warm fuzzy feeling Flint has had ever since the movie *Roger and Me* nor the exciting prospect of ten-hour bus rides to Thunder Bay was enough to keep him there when Ice Bats coach Jim Burton called.

Findlay's Western Professional Hockey Leage (WPHL) career is just three hours old, but he already wants to know who won the scoring title last season. Told the answer—Chris Brooks, with 45 goals and 65 assists for the Amarillo Rattlers—the rookie, who found tonight's action to be a little slow but also chippy enough that he plans to wear a visor in future games, nods calmly. "I'll have to take a run at that," he swaggers.

By now it's 6 A.M. Brian Fairfield has figured out what the driver probably knew all along but didn't want to confess to the irritated hockey players. The bus is out of gas. With diesel engines you can't just fill 'er up.

If one more thing could go wrong, it would be this: at 6:35 the rain begins to fall again, hard. Fortunately, the back-up bus lumbers down Highway 71 at that very moment. The players drag their gear onto the new bus, and 10 minutes later, as the sights of LaGrange (former home of the Chicken Ranch, a.k.a. the Best Little Whorehouse in Texas) fly by, the sun is up and the Bats are back to sleep.

So—first day of the season, new team, new coach, new bus— it's a good thing hockey players aren't superstitious! Jim Burton tries to put an optimistic spin on the ordeal.

"This is a good sign," the coach reasons, displaying a glass-half-full optimism that should serve him well in certain postgame interview situations. "It means it won't happen again."

The team pulls into the parking lot of the Chaparral Ice Center at 8 A.M., just in time for morning traffic. Practice is in four hours.

THE LAST TIME Jim Burton parked his butt on the Bat Bus, he was at least a dozen rows back, hunched over a makeshift table with the rest of the boys, cards in one hand and a spit cup in the other. "Burty" was the elder statesman of the '96–'97 team, a former IHL great who came to the "Wiffle" as a possible prelude to coaching.

As last year's captain, Burton was already like a coach. By the middle of the season, most Ice Bats players figured he'd take over the job from the team's part-owner Blaine Stoughton, a former NHL star who'd be the first to admit he didn't become a minor league mogul so that he could run daily 10 A.M. practices.

But while Burton's ascension was no surprise, actually seeing him in the jacket and tie is an adjustment. When Burty was *like* a coach, you could open a beer in front of him, and the Ice Bats, a party team in a party town, frequently did. When this year's players assembled in a conference room at the Austin Airport Quality Inn for the first official team meeting—a nuts-and-bolts orientation about housing and paperwork, just like the first day of camp or school—Burton's most notable admonition was "Pick your spots when it's a good time to go out."

In addition to transforming himself from the cool older brother into a more credible authority figure, Burton has to make the transition from on-ice ability to off-ice empathy. It's an article of faith in every sport that the best players don't make the best coaches, because they didn't have to learn things the hard way. Guys with unusual physical gifts or innate instincts have trouble explaining things to guys who don't—and most players, especially in the minors, don't.

Burton is definitely a natural, right down to his boyish face and thick, clean-cut waves of golden hair. A native of Brantford, Ontario, Burty didn't quite have the same chops as his childhood pond-hockey comrade, a fellow by the name of Wayne Gretzky. At one tournament, Burton can remember playing in front of 17,000 people. Wayne was 11 years old. "I think we won by about 25 goals," Burton recalls.

But as a member of the IHL's Fort Wayne Komets, Burton was honored as the league's most valuable defenseman three times. And while starring for Klagenfurt of the Austrian Elite League, he was able to take advantage of a distant blood tie to represent that country at the 1994 Olympics.

During his year as an Ice Bat, Burton was the class of the WPHL, putting up 68 points in 52 games despite gimpy knees that finally forced him to hang up the skates.

Whatever challenges loom, the 35-year-old rookie coach is eager to meet them. Burty is known as a good teacher and a straight shooter, qualities that, along with his connections at every level of the game, make him a terrific recruiter. That's important, because career minor leaguers are constantly retiring, moving up or going elsewhere in search of more ice time or an extra 50 bucks a week. In the WPHL, every year is a rebuilding year.

Nine Ice Bats are back from last year's squad, but the remaining

11 slots are going largely to youngsters. The Bats spend the early days of training camp with just half a team. Some guys are still trying their luck at higher levels. Troy Binnie, the team's best player in the second half of last season, is at home in Toronto dealing with a family crisis. No one is saying it out loud, but it's likely the "crisis" boils down to the fact that once the season starts, Binnie will barely get to see his wife and son. If the Bats brass have a problem with that, they can try to get 50 goals out of someone else.

In the meantime, the team fills the holes however it can. Blaine Stoughton's brother, 41-year-old assistant coach Gerald, suits up for the first scrimmage, using the occasion to have a mock brawl with his ex-roommate, 22-year-old Ryan Anderson. Team co-owner Paul Lawless also makes an appearance. An NHL journeyman and IHL star who, like Burton, played for the Bats last season and, also like Burton, struggled with both injuries and advancing age, "Lawly" lasts about one period before he staggers off the ice, huffing, puffing and grinning. Andy Ross shakes his head in mock disappointment.

There are also several rookies who, whether they know it or not, are probably taking up space until a warmer body arrives. Rapcewicz hopes to brawl his way onto the roster. Burton personally scouted Jay Hutton, a tough six-foot-three defenseman who, in the coach's own words, "can't skate," but might be able to hang on as the seventh guy. (The team only dresses six defensemen on any given night.) Keith O'Brien is a recent Princeton graduate who came to Austin to work for a local software company.

Tim Findlay and Ryan Pawluk arrive on the fourth day of camp, just in time for a quick morning skate before the bus ride to Lake Charles. It being an exhibition game, a sleepover isn't in the budget. The team will leave Austin at 11 A.M., arrive in Lousiana 90 minutes before the 7:30 game and head home afterward. Before the bus departs, the Bats' radio voice and public relations guy, Mark Martello, pops by to get vital stats on the new arrivals.

"A buck ninety-five," he says to the six-foot Findlay, confirming his weight. "215?" he shoots back at Pawluk, who at roughly the same height is huskier and more muscled than his friend, but not by that much.

Martello is usually the guy who makes the pick-up at Blockbuster before a road trip, but the game isn't on the radio, so he won't be coming. Blaine Stoughton, however, has brought along a copy of *Fargo*, which he hasn't seen. "It makes fun of where I'm from," Morque, a North Dakotan, notes, though he likes the film. Several players chime in with their rendition of Fargo-speak, not that their Canadian accents are that far from it in the first place.

Later, the team will watch, well, what else would they watch on the first day of the year but the movie about the only guy in the history of hockey to take off his skate and stab someone with it? It will not be the last time *Happy Gilmore* is shown on the bus this season.

"Back on the old iron lung," Stoughton sighs. He settles in for the afternoon with his cell phone (the Bats need players, and Stoughton still holds the job of general manager) and a blanket that must belong to his daughter or wife. It is strewn with kitty cats: orange, gray, tortoise shell, calico, tiger stripe, white . . . every variety except unlucky black.

"Burty stole my seat," Stoughton gripes. "I'm in second class." Tradition puts the head coach in the very first row on the right, with other nonplayers nearby. The hierarchy continues all the way to the back—rookies in the first few rows, new veterans in the middle, returning players like Morque, Andy Ross and Ryan Anderson at the rear.

Anderson, nicknamed "Kid," is a blond-mulleted, babyfaced bruiser who won the team's "Rabid Bat" award last season for collecting the most penalty minutes. He is only a second-year pro, however, so the older guys ruminate on his proper place in the pecking order.

"He's not a veteran," Morque decides.

"You're an old grouch, Morque," the Kid answers. "I don't want to play with you."

"Play with me?" Morque says. "Who's going to teach you defense?"

Gray Line, the bus company the Ice Bats used last season, is no longer operating in Austin, so Star Shuttle has taken over. The worst part of that situation is the loss of the old driver, a guy named Cowboy, who never missed a game, home or away, and was always at the rink door to tap the guys for luck before each period. He also decorated the bus, adorning the driver's side window with a little orange-glowing, battery-powered Bat that he lit up whenever the team won a game, an homage to the University of Texas' practice of illuminating its famous Tower after every Longhorn win.

Even before enduring what will turn out to be an unfortunate first journey on the new bus, the players do not have many good things to say about it. It has only three little TV monitors (the old one had six bigger TVs), and the seats are all in a row, like a regular Greyhound, whereas the players prefer that several rows be turned 90 degrees, creating a lounge area for card playing and more comfortable sleeping.

On the bright side, Andy Ross observes, "The shitter is nicer."

The bus leaves for Lake Charles at 11:05, which for the Ice Bats is a remarkably accurate approximation of 11. Not for the first time, Burty expresses his amazement at Gunner Garrett, the team's equipment manager, who occupies the first row on the left. He's seen Gunner do his thing a million times, but this is his first close-up look.

What Gunner does is sleep. Sitting up, head back, pillow between his face and the window, he sleeps and sleeps and sleeps and sleeps. If the trip is three hours long, Gunner needs three hours of sleep. If it's 10 hours long, Gunner can stay unconscious for the duration. If the bus stops for lunch, Gunner will wake up, eat and konk back out without warning. When an older player teases him about it, Gunner is quick to strike back. "I sleep for five hours on the bus. You sleep for three hours after we get to the rink," he says.

Besides, the 55-year-old former minor league goalie earns his naps with all those late nights and early mornings, doing laundry and maintaining sticks and skates. "This bus will add 10 years to my life," Gunner speculates before nodding off. "It has seatbelts, so I won't slide forward."

Burty wonders out loud if it's okay for him to use the aisle seat in Gunner's row as a footrest.

"I did that all the time," Stoughton says, "but he always pushed me away when my feet got too close to his crotch."

Around 2 P.M. the bus stops in Houston for lunch, settling on a versatile suburban strip on the west side of town that features a Pappadeaux's, a Pappasito's, a Fuddrucker's and a Macaroni Grill. Most guys opt for the latter establishment, pasta carbo-loading being the pregame ritual of choice for most. The waiter brings out a basket of bread with a plate of olive oil for heart-healthy dipping. "You don't see that in Peterborough," Jay Hutton says, before discovering that he doesn't care for the taste. Kyle Haviland does—he ends up pigging out on the bread before his salad and spaghetti come. Another player might worry that he'd lose a step during the game, but Haviland is a tough, immobile, crease-clearing defenseman and enforcer. He doesn't have a step to lose.

Andy Ross ends up at Fuddrucker's, where he enjoyed a nice plate of lemon pepper chicken. This information is made public because "Roscoe"—the nickname goes all the way back to *The Dukes of Hazzard*—has been getting teased about his diet since he showed up in the morning with a bag full of McDonald's.

"Wait, Roscoe needs some potato chips," Stoughton had cracked when the bus stopped at a convenience store. The truth is Stoughton and Burton have been pleased with Ross's training camp conditioning so far, but because he's a smoker and has been known to enjoy a libation or two, they ride him hard. They understand him all too well. Burton happens to be the other guy pacing outside the bus when it's time to light up, and there's little doubt that when Stoughton was in the NHL, he was also a "play hard, play hard" kind of guy. When Stoughton played in the NHL, everyone was.

By the time lunch is finished it's 3:30 P.M., and the bus is on the wrong side of Houston, right in time for early rush hour. Thanks to the ensuing traffic jam, the team is still at least 60 minutes away from Lake Charles at 5:30.

"We're playing tomorrow, right?" Gunner, who has woken up to navigate, says.

In fact, not only is the game tonight, but it's at 7 P.M., not 7:30. The Ice Bats are comically late.

At 6:20 the bus whizzes past the oil refineries and into downtown Lake Charles, which consists of two neon pink–and–teal–

colored casino boats and one generic shiny glass building. It's a muggy, 65-degree night, but outside the arena a group of kids are playing in a pile of snow—the telltale sign of a nearby Zamboni. The players change into their khakis and golf shirts on the bus. They're supposed to be out on the ice for warm-ups, sticks bent and taped, skates sharpened, pads and sweaters on, in just 10 minutes.

"Don't ever touch those cases," Gunner tells the bus driver when he attempts to offload some gear. "I got the rookies for that." The rookies aren't quite sure what to make of the Gun Man yet—he maintains a gruff, laconic demeanor that puts the fear of God in them if they do the wrong thing. "I don't carry skates, son, I just sharpen them," he tells one naif. And "If you don't put your sticks in the right place, you can take 'em to the bench yourself."

Garrett is also a profane, prolific and unprovoked insult machine. "Roses are red, violets are blue, [insert player's name here] looks like a bucket of shit," he'll say as he sets up the coffee machine. On the bench, Gunner yaps louder than the players.

Tonight's game is fairly meaningless, but there is a subplot, and its name is Bobby Wallwork. Wallwork was the Ice Bats' player/ assistant coach and leading goal-scorer last year, but after some fractious and mutually bullheaded negotiations with Stoughton, he fled for Lake Charles, where the team also got him started on a real estate career. Some of his closest friends are Ice Bats. Many of them played together before in Memphis and Muskegon, Michigan. Wallwork was the guy who brought everyone together in Texas for the inaugural season.

When the bus pulls in, "Wally" is waiting. He has a hug for Ryan Anderson and happily braces himself for Gunner's greeting. "Just what I thought: afraid to play," Garrett says, eyeing Wallwork's street clothes. In fact, Lake Charles is sitting seven of its best players tonight so they can give the ice time to less proven commodities. Before returning to his new team's locker room, Wallwork makes sure his buddies realize exactly how little he misses Austin. "Check out the talent in the stands," he gloats, gesturing at the wide assortment of exotically beautiful Louisiana gals.

This will be the first night of hockey for Lake Charles and its civic center. The game isn't even open to the public, just boosters, advertisers, corporate sponsors and other local dignitaries. Sixty-five miles away the team in Lafayette, which plays in another league, draws 10,000 people a night, so hopes are high for this market. The visiting locker room isn't finished—the lavatory consists of two toilets, sitting there wide open, like some sort of conversation pit—and the home team doesn't have its uniforms. Most of the players wear plain yellow or white jerseys, but there are more training camp aspirants than shirts, so a few guys sport generic "NHL" practice sweaters.

While the players guzzle Powerade, Jim Burton puts on a sportscoat and ponders who to start in goal. As the incumbent, Chad Erickson assumed he would get the initial minutes, but that does not turn out to be the case. Erickson tells Burty that advance notice would be appreciated next time. "Goalies like to know," he explains.

Burton, half grudgingly and half sincerely, invites Chad to help him out with any other useful pointers.

"Rookie coaches," Erickson grumbles. "Gotta break 'em in."

The team quiets down for Burton's first official locker room address. "There's two things I dislike," he says. "One is negative talk—backstabbing, complaining on the bench. The other is, you can't play for me if you're lazy out there. You don't have to go retarded all the time, but don't be lazy. Short shifts. Have fun.

"And if you wanna show me something," he adds, referring to the rough stuff, "show me in the third."

Exhibition game rules state that if you fight twice, you're automatically ejected. But fighting is pretty much what the night's about, much to the delight of the "coon-ass" crowd. Coon ass is a term of endearment that specifically describes Southern Louisianans. As in, "You ain't got no crazy fucking coon-asses like us in Texas!" So says Brad Downs, a slightly tipsy fan who leads "Let's Go, Ice Pirates" cheers all night.

"I'm trying to pump 'em up," Downs explains, adding that he thinks the fights are the best part.

"We like the fights," Brad's friend Beau Diamond clarifies, "because we don't know the damn rules."

That will come in time. Between periods, the Pirates put on a demonstration of how icing works. When Kyle Haviland uncorks a slapper that sends the blade of his stick flying over the crossbar, Gunner can be seen explaining to a bench-side fan how the stick's construction makes that possible. Ordinarily, Gunner's encounters with opposing fans are less civilized. "When they fool with me, they're unarmed," he says of would-be hecklers.

Tonight there is more fighting than icing. Over the course of the evening, seven different Bats drop the gloves, including Jason Rapcewicz, who'd been taken aside by Burton before the game and told to stir it up at least once. "Scrapsy" also scores a goal, but that's of little consequence compared with his skirmish, an ill-tempered, verbiage-rich tiff that leaves onlooker Ryan Anderson chuckling appreciatively, as if remembering a long-ago time when he too was prone to such youthful indiscretions.

Anderson gets his turn, though. In the third an Ice Pirate calls him out with this simple taunt: "All you Western Canada boys are pussies."

"So I went after him," Anderson says. "I'd be lying if I said I didn't enjoy it."

Brian Fairfield plays well between the pipes. His counterpart Erickson does not, much to the amusement of his teammates. But the veteran goalie is happy to play along. "I handled it like a girl," he says of a textbook wraparound chance, joking that he let it by on purpose so the aspiring Ice Pirate who took the shot would have a better chance to make the team.

Mike (a.k.a. "Jake") Jackson also has a big night, earning himself the "Gordie Howe hat trick"—a goal, an assist and a fight. But the stars of the evening are Jake's new linemates, who each lit the lamp, while also assisting on his score. "Those two kids that just came—number 8 and number 9," Anderson says, referring to Findlay and Pawluk. "They're gonna be great players. I don't even know their names."

two

GAME CALLED ON ACCOUNT OF FOG

HOCKEY IN THE 1990s could be summed up in two words: "Go South!" Once upon a time, the movie *Slap Shot* made a doomed, desperate joke out of the notion that a minor league club might set up shop in senior citizen–rich St. Petersburg, Florida. Twenty-five years later, hockey has indeed flocked to the lower half of the United States like a gaggle of geriatric snowbirds. The NHL has put franchises in Miami, Nashville, Atlanta and, yes . . . Tampa–St. Pete. Meanwhile, the league relocated teams from Minneapolis, Quebec City and Winnipeg to such hallowed hockey havens as Dallas, Denver and Phoenix, respectively.

But the biggest hockey explosion was at the minor pro level, where, at its apex, there were seven leagues and more than 100 teams between the United States and Canada. Although this blast of activity began to fizzle (along with the rest of the U.S. economy) in the year 2000, Texas still has more pro hockey than any other place in North America—13 minor league franchises and one NHL team as of May 2003.

The Ice Bats play at what's considered to be the AA level, a tier below the American Hockey League (AHL) and the International Hockey League (IHL), the latter of which went under, with six of its teams transferring to the AHL, at the end of the 2000–01 season. In 1997 those two outfits, with approximately three dozen teams between them, served as direct pipelines to and from the NHL. As a general rule, the AHL developed the most glimmering prospects, while the IHL, which had fewer affiliated teams, nurtured younger players who might fall a hair short of The Show, as well as older players who'd already been there and weren't going back.

The East Coast Hockey League (ECHL) is the granddaddy of the current AA circuit—it began in 1988 and as recently as 1992 still had the category to itself, with just 15 clubs. That number has swelled as high as 30, with a majority of the teams south of the Mason–Dixon Line and nearly all of them connected with an NHL parent. (Goalie Olaf Kolzig of the Washington Capitals, who backstopped the Hampton Roads Admirals for parts of two seasons, is the league's poster boy for upward mobility.)

The remaining leagues, including the Western Professional Hockey League (WPHL), exist mostly for their own sake. While the NHL's America First! progression is an understandably emotional topic for fans north of the 49th parallel, U.S. minor teams are a different beast. These clubs give small to medium-sized American communities an experience roughly akin to supporting a Canadian junior team, in the process creating hundreds of jobs for young men whose hockey lives would otherwise be over. Middle-aged former NHL grinders, can't-miss prospects who did, twentysomething bush-league lifers, rookies spurned by the NHL draft—it is now possible for a player to eke out a half-decent living playing the game he has loved since toddlerhood, so long as he's willing to leave behind Canada, New England or the Great Lakes for Texas, Louisiana or Mississippi. The low minors also provide new opportunities for players at the end of their careers, allowing them to stick around in coaching, front office or rink management jobs.

Texas's status as a hockey Mecca is a fairly recent development, but the game is not a total stranger to the Lone Star State. Back in the 1970s, Gordie Howe and his sons skated for the Houston Aeros of the World Hockey Association. At various times between the late 1960s and the early 1980s, the old Central Hockey League (CHL) tried its luck in Amarillo, Fort Worth and Dallas. In the mid-1970s, the semi-pro Southwest Hockey League camped out in Amarillo and El Paso. In the fall of 1992, a resurrected CHL got the puck rolling again in Fort Worth and San Antonio, while the Aeros returned to Houston as an IHL team in 1994.

Dallas also had a CHL team, but the NHL froze out the Freeze when the Minnesota North Stars headed down Interstate 35 in 1993. Five seasons later, the Dallas Stars corralled the Stanley Cup for Texas, making Mike Modano and Derian Hatcher as beloved as Troy Aikman and Emmit Smith in some circles. The Stars' impact goes well beyond spectator sports: since the team came to town, the number of high school hockey squads in the Dallas–Fort Worth Metroplex has risen from four to 40. Since 1990, Texas has gone from a place that had just a few dozen youth and adult recreational teams to a state with more than 350 of them.

The WPHL was the dominant force on the Texas landscape. It began in 1996, when former coach Rick Kozuback teamed up with three Vancouver-based entrepreneurs—financial planner Nigel King and Boston Pizza founders George Melville and Jim Treliving. They'd been thinking about starting an ECHL franchise somewhere in Texas but soon upgraded their sporting ambitions to encompass a whole new league.

Kozuback, who'd manned the bench for the British Columbia Hockey League (BCHL) Penticton Knights and the Western Hockey League (WHL) Tri-City Americans, had finished his coaching career as an assistant with Phoenix of the IHL. Having become familiar with the American Southwest, he saw it as a vast, uncolonized territory filled with folks whose sporting interests—NASCAR, football, bull-riding, pro wrestling—were a natural fit with the kind of action minor league hockey offers. Market research showed that many of the Texas towns under consideration were demographically similar to Southern cities where hockey was already thriving. And because of university allegiances and high school football traditions (to say nothing of long-held grudges and regional prejudices), natural rivalries were already in place across the state.

The first season featured five Texas teams (Amarillo, El Paso, Waco, Central Texas and Austin), as well as one in Albuquerque, New Mexico. The New Mexico team was originally owned by NHLers Joe Murphy and Bernie Nicholls, along with baseball pitcher John Wetteland. Former NHLers Andy Moog, Kevin Lowe, Darcy Rota and Pat Quinn were some of the league's other investors.

The Austin franchise was originally going to be dubbed the Outlaws, but the more inventive Ice Bats, named for the famously large colony of winged beasties that resides under the city's Congress Avenue Bridge, prevailed. Borderline silly names are an esteemed minor league tradition. The ECHL's marquee team in Lafayette, Louisiana, is the Ice Gators. The people of Greenville, South Carolina, cheer on the Grrrowl, and there used to be a club in Georgia called the Macon Whoopee—with a fig leaf logo, no less. The most outrageous name of them all, however, might have been Waco's, at least in the eyes of the local Baptist community (that is, all of Waco), which believed "Wizards" has a Satanic connotation.

Hockey was an instant hit in Austin, a city of half a million people (with a metro area twice that size) that loves its University of Texas Longhorns above all but has been hankering for pro sports— any sport, at any level—for years. Until the Bats came along, Austin was the largest city in America without a professional sports franchise. In the time it took the Bats to find a building, strike a deal, build an ice plant and open for business, three different groups tried and failed to bring minor league baseball to the area.

The Ice Bats averaged more than 6,000 fans a night in their first season, with an occasional 8,000-plus sellout. Albuquerque, the league's other big market, put up similar numbers, and three of the four smaller cities held their own with crowds of 3,000 or 4,000 people a game. All told, just under a million people spent a night out enjoying WPHL action that first year. The league's slogan, "We Play Hockey Loud," is an appropriate evocation of the fan support. It also serves as a suitable description for the style of play, which is wide open in terms of both offense and fisticuffs.

Between the trickle-down from the Stars and the state's large contingent of Northeastern and Midwestern transplants, the league had a good base of experienced hockey fans to build on.

Each team went out of its way to explain the game to newcomers, distributing flyers that explained everything from how the ice is made to why a play would be offside (though not as many are; the goals-minded league allows the two-line pass). Glossaries of hockey terms ("back check," "headman," "one-timer") were also provided. One team, the Central Texas Stampede, even had a page of "basketball to hockey translations." Some were illuminating ("point" equals "top of the key"), some unnecessary ("court" equals "rink") and a few simply confusing. If "halftime" equals "intermission," it's no wonder several thousand fans hit the exits after two periods of the first-ever Stampede game: they didn't realize there was still more hockey to be played.

By the end of its first season, the WPHL had approved the addition of three more Texas teams (San Angelo, Odessa–Midland and, in direct competition with the CHL, Fort Worth), as well as three in Louisiana. Ultimately, the league would hit a peak of 18 teams. It had 13 in the spring of 2001, when the WPHL merged with the CHL and yielded to the other circuit's more hallowed title.

But despite the trials of specific markets and the disappearance of the WPHL name, in the larger sense Texas hockey has been a huge success. Really, that isn't so surprising. Where better for a rough-and-tumble frontier sport filled with well-mannered hotheads, a blue-collar work ethic and prodigious snuff-dipping? Culturally and socioeconomically speaking, it's possible the only difference between a little town in Alberta and a little town in West Texas is the weather.

Which, admittedly, is no small difference. It's safe to say an account of hockey in Red Deer has never included the phrase "It was a dark and stormy night." At least, not when the game is played indoors.

THE ICE BATS' PRESEASON is meant to end with a rematch against the Ice Pirates, this time at home in the Travis County Expo Center (a.k.a. "The Bat Cave"). It's a big, drafty old barn that was built to showcase livestock and farming equipment, not Zambonis and Canadians. During the course of the first season, the team was regularly booted out in favor of tractor pulls and cattle auctions, leaving them to practice at a local shopping mall, the undersized ice sheet conveniently located between the Pay Less shoe store and the Glamour Shots photo booth. But at least the mall is climate-controlled—more than you can say for the Cave, where January games leave Austin fans griping about the cold instead of appreciating the winter weather's effect on ice quality.

The weather in October, on the other hand, is worth getting grumpy over. The Bats and Pirates are barely through the first shift when rising body temperatures and the sultry climate combine to bathe the rink in fog and perspiration. Forget pond hockey—this is *swamp* hockey. The goaltenders develop a new appreciation for the expression "You can't stop what you can't see." The guys with face shields need wiper blades. Every play is a no-look pass. The red line's a cherry Slurpee. And since the laws of physics dictate that steam rises off the jungle floor, the folks in the stands are seeing even less than the ice-level participants. All that's missing is a creepy old guy on the concourse intoning "Stay off the moors!"

"I've never seen anything like that," defenseman Corey Fletcher will say after the game. "I'm used to rinks where you can see your breath because it's so cold."

Play is stopped several times over the course of the first period in an attempt to puncture the soup. The players circle the rink, trying to stay loose, pairing off to chat with members of the other team like it's some kind of couples skate. Finally, between periods, Pirates coach Dennis Maruk refuses to bring his squad back on the ice. This infuriates Austin management. But the Bats players are siding with Maruk, especially after co-owner Daniel Hart pops into the locker room with a bit of useless, meant-to-be-funny advice. "Don't sweat," he tells them. "Don't breathe."

The way the players see it, money is taking precedence over common sense, no big surprise in minor league hockey, which Chris Morque calls "the most corrupt sport in the world except for prizefighting." Since there's no chance of making up a meaningless exhibition contest, the Austin brass would rather get through the night than offer up thousands of ticket refunds. Never mind that the game is unwatchable and ice conditions aren't safe. "If I hurt a knee on that slop, I'd sue," Kyle Haviland says.

Eventually, league officials get involved and a settlement is brokered. Play is stopped for good midway through the second period and concluded with a shootout, which is how tie games are settled during the regular season. A few disenchanted season ticket holders end up canceling their orders, while the Bats give everyone in attendance a coupon good for tickets to a future game. And the owners shell out the dough for a couple of dehumidifiers.

Despite the fog, the new players still get a taste of the fans, who were named the best in the WPHL during the first season, a tribute to both their enthusiasm and Austin's league-leading average of 6,239 a night. "It looks like it's gonna be a great place to play," Tim Findlay says. "They have their fun in the stands, and they seem like they know a lot about the game. I was surprised, actually. I didn't think a city in Texas could support a pro hockey franchise."

After four exhibition games and 13 days of training camp, the Ice Bats roster is more or less set. The first line returns Andy Ross on the right side of Brett Seguin, with Troy Binnie promoted from number-two center to number-one left wing. The second line has Findlay at center, with Ryan Pawluk on one wing and traffic cop Mike Jackson on the other. Jeremy Thompson heads up the third unit, which has undergone an impromptu makeover. During the preseason Jason Rapcewicz managed three fights, four stitches and one bloody jersey, but that wasn't enough to postpone his trip back to Hamilton. Filling his spot is Chris Haskett, a six-foot-one, 220-pound rookie who decided at the last minute to bail out on his OHL over-age year. Another late addition is Darrin MacKay, who as a Waco Wizard last season scored 10 of his 21 goals against the Ice Bats.

Ryan Anderson, Kyle Haviland and Chris Morque return on defense, with Morque wearing the "C." The new arrivals are rookies Corey Fletcher and Jay Hutton and second-year pros Jeff Kungle and Ken Ruddick. An eighth blueliner, rookie Steve Jones, joins the team just in time to show off his street clothes at the season opener.

Christian Soucy, a former Chicago Blackhawks prospect on loan from the IHL Aeros, is the starting goalie. This does not necessarily please Chad Erickson, who was ready to be alone at the top after serving equally with former NHLer John Blue in the previous season. Brian Fairfield also makes the cut, there to work his butt off in practice and take over as back-up if and when Soucy gets beckoned to Houston.

While you'd like to think a hockey team's roster is purely the product of available talent, locker room chemistry and the proper distribution of on-ice roles, league policies also play a part in determining the Ice Bats' makeup. Each team gets 14 work visas, so six of the players have to be either U.S. citizens, U.S. green-card holders or Native North Americans. A player who doesn't need a visa will sometimes make the team over a more talented player who does. In addition, every club has to carry at least four rookies—players with 30 games or less of pro experience—as the WPHL attempts to position itself as a developer of rising young talent, rather than a collection of aging mercenaries.

The league has also instituted a new salary structure. In its first season, the WPHL had a salary cap with three "star" exemptions, allowing general managers to open up their checkbooks for proven players who might otherwise avoid an unproven league (in Texas, for God's sake!). But that system was easy to abuse, so a hard cap of ten thousand dollars per week has been instituted. Talk inside the locker room is that Blaine Stoughton asked most of the returning players to take pay cuts; the ones who wouldn't found themselves playing elsewhere.

Now the minimum salary for a player is $350 a week; a few guys in the league will still command four figures. Lodging is part of the deal. This year the Bats are housing the players in the Riata, a fancy suburban apartment complex owned by Dallas Cowboys owner Jerry Jones. Jim Burton, one of the higher-paid "stars" last year, foresees a problem that the league elders probably didn't think of. "With the salary cap," the coach laments, "no one on this team will be able to play poker."

Of course, Burton can still cover his bets. "You must have gotten some kind of bonus," Chad Erickson teased at the second exhibition game, after noticing the coach was wearing a different jacket-and-tie combo than the one he'd sported the first night.

"Nope, you've seen 'em all," Burton replied. "This and the horse hair."

Burton feels pretty good about the way things are going. Making the transition from player to coach has been no trouble at all . . . well, except for that one moment during the second exhibition game.

"I was leaning over talking to Ryan Anderson and I actually jumped over the boards," Burton says with a laugh. "As soon as my feet hit the ice I realized what I'd done. So, yeah, some habits die hard. But training camp is so busy, with the two-a-days and the meetings and the road trips, I haven't even had time to think about playing. I'm really enjoying what I'm doing. I'm having a good time."

"If we work half as hard as Burty played, we'll be all right," Ryan Anderson says. "He'll probably be on a lot of the guys' asses so that we're doing it, and that's all right too."

All told, Burton's squad features 13 veterans and seven rookies. Stoughton says this relative youth has more to do with the product on the ice than the color of his balance sheet. "If you spend a little more money and you end up winning, you get your money back," he reasons. The general manager says that because of age, injuries and exhaustion, last year's team of well-traveled pros didn't live up to its potential. "This year we're going to concentrate on younger kids. I don't know if we're going to be as successful in the regular season, but come playoff time, if these guys develop, the young legs will prevail."

Tim Findlay and Ryan Pawluk are the owners of the most important of those legs. "We won't be calling them the second line for long," Bats color commentator Danny Foreman suggested after the first exhibition game.

In its first season the WPHL had plenty of talented and experienced players, but the two youngsters from Windsor boast a slightly different pedigree. They are among the first big-ticket rookies to cast their lot with the nascent league. When Findlay was 18 he skated on the same line as Peter Forsberg at a Colorado Avalanche training camp, and last season he finished things up with the Syracuse Crunch of the AHL. Pawluk, a major junior player since the age of 14, only came to Texas after final cutdowns for the Canadian National Team. Last year in the OHL, playing against NHL first-rounders like Joe Thornton and Manny Malhotra, Findlay racked up 82 points and Pawluk tallied 84.

Pawluk, whose dark hair, delicate cheekbones and generous eyebrows suggest a Mediterranean Ethan Hawke, was once rated by the Central Scouting Bureau as a fifth-round draft pick. But the modern NHL places a huge premium on size, and Pawluk taps out, he allows, at five-eleven and three-quarters.

Also, his OHL career did not go exactly as expected. A native of St. Clair Beach, Ontario (just north of Windsor), Pawluk left home as a high school freshman to play for Kitchener. "Going to juniors at such a young age was really tough," he says. "It beats you down a little bit. You get in a bad situation with a team, you're away from home, you don't know any better. Then you have a bad year and everyone gets on you."

In other words, Kitchener wasn't much fun. He averaged just 23 points in his two full seasons. After spending the tail end of one campaign and the start of another with Peterborough, he finally joined Findlay on the hometown team halfway through 1995–96 and found his groove, scoring 40 points in 36 games.

On the hour-long bus trip to the Bats' regular-season opener against Central Texas, Pawluk is all anticipation. As a 10-year-old skating in on imaginary goalies in the backyard rink, he never envisioned his first professional game would take place in a region that's best known for the Luby's cafeteria where George Hennard gunned down 22 people in 1991.

But there's no trace of sour grapes on Pawluk's part—just a sense of possibility. He spends the ride skimming a copy of the diet book *The Zone*. Playing hockey without the proper nutrition, he says, "is like trying to drive a car with no oil." He gorged on protein in the off-season, eating two cans of tuna a day to help his muscles through long sessions of weight work and plyometric drills. His focus is singular. "I want to have a career as an NHL hockey player," he says. "This is a stepping stone."

Even an IHL career wouldn't be so bad. Tim Findlay is still talking about his Viper experience—the team has its own plane, you stay in Hiltons rather than Super 8s, and if you really make a go of it, you can earn an annual salary in the low six figures, complete with a 401K plan and full medical benefits, for seven months' work.

That Pawluk and Findlay are here at all is a tribute to Jim Burton's tirelessness. He spent the summer on the phone, massaging agents and romancing parents, combing the higher-level leagues for leftovers and the junior circuits for hidden gems, working 20 years of hockey connections every which way he could. In Pawluk's case, Burton played against his agent, goaltending guru Rick Heinz, in the IHL in the mid-1980s. The Ice Bats would need an IHL carrot to land the kid, but that wasn't a problem either. Canadian National Team honcho Andy Murray was happy to put in a good word for Pawluk with his pal Dave Tippett, the coach and general manager of the Houston Aeros. Perhaps it's a coincidence, but Burton also took a flyer on another Heinz client, a certain raw, Stetson-wearing freckle-faced teenage goalie.

"I didn't know too much about the WPHL, to be honest," Pawluk says of his decision to join the Bats. "They don't say too much about it back home, so I was a little worried—it could have been like a rec league for all I know.

"Jim was the deciding factor," Pawluk continues. "He's so goddamn nice on the phone. He makes you feel comfortable, he answers all your questions, he doesn't bug you. He seemed to me like a 'players' coach.' They're down-to-earth, they tell you the way it is, they'll never lie to you, they don't scream, they don't play head games. That's the kind of guy you want to play for."

Not to mention that Pawluk got his best friend and favorite center in the bargain. As he describes it, "Tim got sent down to Flint, but he didn't like it there. Jim called him, Timmy called me, me and Timmy talked, here we are."

"Jim found me in my hotel room in Detroit," Findlay says. "I had been released probably 20 minutes earlier, so I'm sitting there thinking, *Geez, I need somewhere to play.* It was just a little bit of luck." Findlay spent one day with Flint, then went home to repack, swapping his sweaters and long underwear for a wardrobe more appropriate to Texas.

Twenty-four hours later he was in Lake Charles, putting the puck in the net with Pawluk, just like he's been doing since they were kids. The Pawluk family rink was the envy of southwestern Ontario, set on a natural creek with lights on both sides and seven-foot snowbanks for boards. Pawluk's dad would shovel the rink before he'd shovel the driveway, and the two boys lived on that frozen creek, going for hours at a time even when it was 20 below zero. "I remember Tim came over one morning," Pawluk says, "and when his mom came to pick him up at night we were still playing."

"We're fortunate to have them," Burton says of the duo. "I had thought that going pro for the first year, this might be a good fit for them, that since they know each other they might be a bit more comfortable. I spoke to both of their parents. Obviously they're concerned about the young guys' welfare, and they thought it'd be a great thing. They're like salt and pepper, always together."

THE BAT BUS pulls into the Bell County Expo Center parking lot and is directed to a space that's nowhere near the players' entrance. There's a horse show in the exhibition hall next door, and those trailers have priority. Next week, it'll be a gun show.

The Ice Bats–Stampede rivalry is akin to the University of Texas Longhorns–Texas A&M Aggies split. Despite its proximity to upscale, free-thinking, somewhat liberal Austin, Bell County is a bastion of farm-town conservatism, with a huge chunk of its population coming from the Fort Hood military base.

At a game here last season, Bats fan Nicole Chastain brought along a sign that made up in bluntness what it lacked in elegance: it read "You Suck." Similar sentiments can be found at hockey arenas across the country, but Chastain found herself confronted by one Deputy Lynce, Bell County Sheriff's Department. He very courteously informed Chastain that she had three choices: stop holding up the sign, let him confiscate the sign or, if she wanted to fight about it, "we could go down to the jail and talk." Yet somehow, the "ASS BITES" banner held up by one of the home fans completely escaped Deputy Lynce's hawkeyes.

Nothing so heated happens on this night, on or off the ice. With Houston Aeros coaches Dave Tippett and Dave Barr watching, Findlay and Pawluk both score goals in the opener as Austin rolls. It's only one game, but Barr thinks Pawluk showed something. "You can see where he's making two moves and the Central Texas guy is only dealing with the first one," he says.

The evening's unlikely focal point turns out to be Jay Hutton, a rookie blueliner with broad shoulders and Eric Lindros looks. The similarity ends there. Whereas a player like Ryan Pawluk is all skills and no size, Hutton is the opposite: big and raw and slow afoot. He is trying to break into the pros after attending Sir Sandford Fleming College in Peterborough, Ontario, not an institution known for churning out hockey players.

In some ways, Hutton is very small-town. Unfamiliar with the egregious policies of hotels and motels, he dialed home direct one afternoon, and couldn't believe it when he got stuck with a $124 phone bill. But the 22-year-old also has an iconoclastic side. He not only lists Marilyn Manson as his favorite musician but also demonstrates a more nuanced understanding of Manson's shtick than most punk rock kids are capable of expressing. "The whole point of Marilyn Manson is that he promotes individualism, not imitation," Hutton says. "He's not saying everyone should wear makeup."

Training camp has been a bit of an adventure for the longshot D-man. "In our own zone it's like a blur out there," he marveled after his first exposure to the professional game. He's trying do the simple things: keep the crease clear and not get burned one-on-one by faster, savvier, more experienced players. Being six-foot-three, he's also supposed to welcome the rough stuff. When one of his major penalties for fighting wasn't properly noted on the official score sheet, Hutton is mildly distressed. "They better not screw that up," he worries. "Those are the only stats I got."

Not so. Hutton's first moment in the spotlight against Central Texas is not a good one, as he takes a four-minute penalty early in the game. But instead of giving up a goal during the lengthy power play, the Bats get a lucky shorthanded score. Looking to simply sweep the puck out of the zone, Ken Ruddick's pass caroms off the boards and into the empty net as the Stampede goalie tries to play the dump-in. A few minutes later Hutton finds himself trailing Brett Seguin on a two-on-one, cruising into the Stampede zone. All Hutton has to do is come along for the ride while the Bats' finest playmaker lays it on his stick blade, and that's what happens. The Bats take a 2–0 lead en route to an easy 5–2 win. "I was surprised as anyone else," Hutton says of his goal after the game.

He'll be traded to Waco within the week.

three

SLEEPLESS IN HELL PASO

THE BRIGHT WHITE BANNER hangs high above the middle of the rink, perched comfortably between the Stars and Stripes and the Texas Lone Star. Its message is neither flippant nor boastful but, rather, a simple statement of fact: "El Paso Buzzards. 1997 WPHL President's Cup Champions."

To the veteran members of the Austin Ice Bats, it could just as easily read "Welcome Back, Losers!"

"I can't even look at it," Andy Ross says.

It's only the sixth contest of the season, but the Bats enter El Paso County Coliseum juiced up like it's the middle of April. No use pretending this is "just another game." Ross knows the Buzzards wouldn't have beaten Central Texas in last year's WPHL finals were it not for the cooperation, one round earlier, of an ailing, disheveled and all-too-compliant Ice Bats squad.

Austin went 8–1–1 against El Paso during that regular season. But when it really mattered, the Bats played dead and the Buzzards picked the carcass clean, starting with a 7–2 Game 1 blowout in which the victors tallied three shorthanded goals, one for each period. The fans here may have been new to hockey, but they understood how devastating that was. "GET A PENALTY, SCORE A GOAL," the signs taunted in subsequent contests. When the Bats lost Game 2 in overtime after blowing a 5–3 lead, their spirit shattered. Austin was eliminated in six.

Game 5 of the series was the last time the Bats skated in this building. On that night the team played its best, gutting out a last-stand 4–3 victory in an Easter Sunday overtime thriller, the game-winner coming from an unlikely duo of penalty-prone "plumbers." Having scored the biggest goal of his life here, Jeremy Thompson might be the only Ice Bat who's happy to be back.

"I still can't believe I was open," he says to Ryan Anderson, who, for his part, is equally incredulous that he managed to spin around at the blueline and keep the puck onside before chipping it to his teammate in the slot. "I wasn't ready to go lay shingles," he said at the time, though in the end, Anderson's heads-up play only kept him from his summer job in Manitoba for 48 more hours.

Talk has turned to the creaky bodies and advancing age of last year's squad when Jim Burton happens by. "And man," Thompson says, not missing a conversational beat, "our D was *really* old."

As the Bat veterans chew on the bitter root of memory, El Paso bench boss Todd Brost is shaking in his shoes at the thought of Austin's present lineup.

"We are definitely going to have our hands full with the Ice Bats," Brost writes in the "Coach's Corner" handout that fans receive with the game program. "In my opinion the Ice Bats could be the top team in the entire WPHL right now. It's going to take a great effort and tremendous concentration to keep them in check."

"That guy's a head case," Jim Burton says when I bring the program to his attention. "Don't let the guys see it," he adds, which suggests that it isn't *Brost's* head he's worried about.

The El Paso coach's scouting report is not entirely gratuitous. Austin has rattled off five straight wins in this young season, making the Bats one of the league's two undefeated teams. The secret is out on Tim Findlay and Ryan Pawluk, both ranked among the WPHL's top five scorers. Two nights ago against Amarillo they combined for five goals, including a Findlay hat trick.

Burton takes a seat for warm-ups, focusing most of his attention on the other team. The Buzzards' Coors Light–sponsored pregame jerseys don't have numbers on them, which makes it harder for rival coaches to determine who's who and which line is which. On the other hand, Burton still hasn't memorized all the name-number combos of his own players—Andy Ross and I help him fill in a couple of blanks on tonight's lineup card—so it probably doesn't make much difference.

At around seven minutes to game time Burton stomps out his post–warm-up, pre–face-off cigarette and climbs the rubber-matted stairs to the coliseum's second-floor visitors' locker room. The dressing area is actually two separate spaces: a little one for the defensemen, and a bigger one containing forwards and goalies. The coach spots his captain outside the first room and accosts him.

"Morque," Burton says. "Write me up for a five-dollar fine."

Chris Morque is genuinely surprised. "What'd you do?" he asks.

"No one should look this good."

All 20 players cram into the second room. Burton mentions El Paso's speed and reminds his forwards that it's a small rink, so "any shot is a good shot." Then he tells them how "Brosty" says they're the best team in the league.

"I don't like that fuckin' guy," Burton says. Heads nod. The message is clear. *Let Brost blow smoke up our ass, it's not gonna puff us up. And we're still gonna win the game.*

It's doubtful Burton harbors actual personal dislike for his opposite number. But there's no question the guy genuinely rubs him the wrong way. It's a matter of style. Burton is a straight-shooting, calmly gesturing, kind-but-firm sort of leader. He swears a lot, but only rarely does he raise his voice. He's a rookie coach with a young team, and a big part of his job is teaching. Mark Martello says he has learned more about hockey from five of Burty's practices than he did all last season with Blaine Stoughton in charge. Burton is all about doing the right thing, about icing a team that plays the game correctly, win or lose. Hard work and proper fundamentals are, to him, just as important as the final score.

Which isn't to say Todd Brost is deficient in any of those areas. Privately, Burton concedes that he's an excellent coach. But Brost is closer to the Scotty Bowman archetype, the sort of coach who doesn't hesitate to wield mind games, manipulation and the occasional temper tantrum to get results. The right results—a mere 29 years old when he took over the Buzzards, Brost won the whole enchilada his first time out.

The Bats don't need to be reminded of that any further. But when the team takes to the ice at the prescribed 7 P.M. game time, the building goes dark. It's El Paso's third home appearance of the season, but last year's championship hype has not yet reached its sell-by date. Instead of a national anthem and a face-off, the Bats players and El Paso fans are regaled with footage from the Buzzards' postseason run. These "highlights" consist mostly of various Buzzards putting pucks past Chad Erickson, as well as various Buzzards fighting various Ice Bats.

When the video ends, cheerleaders shimmy, spotlights swirl and a red carpet is rolled onto the ice. Each member of the home team gets a personal introduction, the players bursting through a big inflatable cartoon buzzard that forms an arch above the rink door.

It's a tacky display. It's discourteous, like showing someone pictures of a party he wasn't invited to. It's also bad sportsmanship, putting the Austin players in a situation where all they can do is stand around, teeth clenched, muscles tightening.

It's an impeccable psyche job.

Jeremy Thompson brushes it off with a wisecrack.

"All I saw," he says, "was me throwing lefts."

Ryan Anderson isn't so glib. "Bad enough I had an ache in my gut coming back here—because I hate them so much," he says. "Then they pull that bullshit. No class."

The Bats' anger only confirms that the ceremony had its intended effect. Brost knows there might be a few scabs left on Austin's confidence from last year's rivalry. Why not pick at 'em? Maybe it gets the Buzzards a win tonight, or maybe it nurtures something bigger, the sort of institutional mystique that lingers in the minds of sports fans for generation upon generation. "Oh yeah . . . we always have trouble with El Paso," Ice Bats followers could be saying 20 years from now.

When the puck finally drops, the gamesmanship seems to be a factor. The Bats are tentative. With five minutes left in the first period El Paso wins a face-off in the Austin zone, and Brent Scott's release is quicker than Chad Erickson's butterfly. It's the first time the Bats have trailed in a game all season.

Of course, it's possible the players are tired. It's their third game in three nights, and simply getting to this point was an adventure.

THE SAGA BEGAN yesterday in San Angelo, before the Bats' game against the Outlaws, when the trusty Bat Bus repeated its opening-night performance—this time, the battery went kaput.

"Never in my whole career have I had to switch out a bus twice in three weeks," Gunner Garrett complained. San Angelo residents looking for a cab during Friday rush hour were out of luck— at 5 P.M. most of them were at the Inn of the Concho motel, ferrying 19 hockey players and a half-dozen support personnel over to the civic center.

Fortunately, San Angelo is only 200 miles from Austin. By 11 P.M. Friday night the Bats have in their possession a 4–3 win, a hundred dollars' worth of Domino's pizza and a replacement bus. Soon everyone is out cold save rookie Chris Haskett, who's pondering the oil-black West Texas night while studying the names of nearby towns on a borrowed road map.

Six hours later the bus pulls into the driveway of the El Paso Marriott, which, with its combination of indoor hallways, room service and a sports bar, is probably the nicest hotel in the league.

Mike Jackson is the first player to get his room assignment. He slides his key card into the lock and turns the handle, only to be greeted by the sight of two very large, very surprised offensive linemen bolting upright from their beds. The Bats' block of rooms has been given to the Arkansas State Indians, in town for a game against the New Mexico State Aggies in nearby Las Cruces. (In addition to sharing its southern border with Juarez, Mexico, El Paso is just a few miles east of the New Mexico state line.)

The desk clerk tries to explain. Somehow the Marriott was

under the impression the Bats were checking in later on Saturday, rather than at six in the morning, which, in the strict parlance of hotel billing, counts as Friday.

Accommodations are eventually secured and the guys scatter to get whatever sleep they can. Most of them, having snatched four or five hours on the bus, will grab another three or four, wake up for a pregame meal and then squeeze in a few more Zs and a light snack before it's time to play.

At 4 P.M., Troy Binnie is at the bar, drinking coffee and watching the tail end of Saturday's college football smorgasbord. On the big screen, the University of Texas is getting pasted by Colorado. Back in Austin, many of the same people who go to Bats games will be rethinking New Year's Day bowl game plans and screaming for coach John Mackovic's head. Binnie contents himself with the game action. As a Canadian, he can't be bothered with the minutiae of regional rivalries, Big 12 conference standings and bowl formulas. And as an American who can be, I'd have to say he's better off.

An Ottawa native whose perennial five-day stubble accentuates his raven hair and Gallic mug, Binnie came to Austin last season one-third of the way in, immediately establishing himself as one of the league's most dangerous forwards. He's a pure goal scorer, that rare player who's a threat to light the lamp every time he enters the offensive zone. If he'd been in the WPHL all year he would have notched 50 goals and a spot on the All-Star team.

As is often the case with guys who know where to put the puck, he has the ego to match his stat sheet. Last year, just minutes after the Bats were eliminated in the playoffs, an Austin newspaper reporter asked Binnie, who was far and away the Bats' postseason MVP, if he felt badly that his line hadn't scored more goals. Somehow the writer had mistaken him for Andy Ross, who'd had a less productive series.

"I'm Troy Binnie," he informed the chastened journalist. "I had 10 points in six games. I was the top scorer on the team." And he hadn't even seen that night's score sheet yet.

Six months later, like everyone else, Binnie is unhappy he had to take a pay cut, though for him it's mostly a matter of principle.

With an off-season contracting business and a wife who works as an attorney in Toronto, he certainly isn't riding buses across Texas to pad his mutual fund account.

The desire to get out of bed every morning and do the thing he's loved most for so long is beginning to wane. Now there's a competing desire: to get out of bed every morning (or evening, or middle of the night) and be with his two-year-old son, Mitchell. He feels the conflict inside, and there's pressure from his wife as well. Having chased his hockey dreams to the edge of 30, Binnie is what he is: an elite player at this level who's not going to make it to the next one.

So if his focus is shaky, that's to be expected. He's also a half-step short in terms of both physical conditioning and the flow of his game, partly because he got a late start in training camp and partly because Burton has him at a new position. The Bats have no other proven sniper to fill the void left by Bobby Wallwork, so Binnie's been shifted from second-line center to first-line wing. He's not pretending to be happy with the change.

On paper, the combination of Binnie with center Brett Seguin, the WPHL's best playmaker, and Andy Ross, a point-per-game power forward, is positively drool-inducing. Ross has even moved to the left side, leaving Binnie to man the flank that carries fewer defensive chores. But though they were teammates for two seasons with the Ottawa 67s just a half-dozen years ago, Binnie and Seguin don't have rapport, either on or off the ice.

Hockey-wise, the problem is there's two of them, but only one puck. Both of them want it, albeit for different reasons. Binnie's a high-octane forward who prefers to create his opportunities one-on-one. Hit him with a breakout pass at the blueline (or, in the WPHL, the redline) and he'll do the rest. Seguin is a master passer, a guy who patiently maintains possession until he gets a read on the other team's defensive coverage. Then, *whoooosssh*—like a basketball point guard, he pops the seam and hits the open man for a gift-wrapped scoring chance. If Binnie can adjust his style to take advantage of Seguin's largesse, he will have no problem putting up the numbers he's accustomed to.

In the meantime, the second line is taking the pressure off. To Binnie, Tim Findlay and Ryan Pawluk must seem like Ghosts of Hockey Past. He knows what it's like to be an OHL hotshot. He remembers being 21 and cocky-hopeful, the way you feel invincible with skates on and ingenuous the rest of the time. He understands how life can veer unexpectedly, depositing you in places like Texas or Central Michigan instead of Madison Square Garden or the Montreal Forum.

In the NHL, one of the great draft-day clichés is when the general manager tells his city's assembled media "[So-and-so]'s defense needs work, but we feel he's got a chance to play in this league." If the player in question improves his positional game and keeps on scoring, he just might become a household name. Another player might embrace defense and checking completely, realizing it's his only chance to make it, never mind how many bantam records he broke in Comox. Then there are the players you never hear from again, at least not on *Hockey Night in Canada* or *Sports Center*.

Binnie had two 30-goal seasons in Ottawa, where, in addition to Seguin, his teammates included Chris Simon, Grant Marshall and Chris Therien, all of whom went on to steady NHL careers. The Minnesota North Stars took Binnie in the 10th round of the 1990 draft, but he wasn't a major prospect. Binnie has decent size (six-foot-one, 200 pounds), reasonable speed and the kind of offensive instincts that can't be taught. But no one has ever accused him of being the most defensively sound player, or the most generous with the puck, or the most willing to fight through traffic.

All players come with baggage of some kind; all eventually find a level where the team is willing to carry it. Binnie cut short his final campaign with the 67s to go to Europe. He stayed there another year, then lit out for Dallas, where he strung together three spectacular seasons in the Central Hockey League. When the relocation of his former NHL parent put the Dallas Freeze out of business, he bounced around the other three AA leagues, then became an Ice Bat.

On the road, Binnie rooms with Andy Ross because Ross is also a smoker. A few hours before every game, the two forwards are stationed outside the locker room, sucking down nicotine on a couple of metal folding chairs. Occasionally, the same blowtorch that's used to bend the stick blades gets put to use as an impromptu lighter. The two wingers also smoke after warm-ups and between periods. Burty would love to make them stop, but he himself would probably puff away on the bench if he could, so what is he supposed to say?

Though Andy Ross's love of a good time makes him something like a minor hockey version of Joe Namath, he is still one of the Ice Bats' hardest workers and least likely success stories.

Ross is a native of Philadelphia's Olney neighborhood, just a few minutes from the suburb where I attended high school. But unlike me, he took up hockey at the height of Flyers fever. Roscoe's Russian immigrant grandmother Lisa put him on double-runners at the age of five; by six he played competitively, spurred on by father Ron, a carpenter and construction worker who was then getting involved in the business of the game. He has since had a long career as a hockey scout, most recently bird-dogging for the WHL Spokane Chiefs.

Dad's scouting report on the player he knows the best? "He's not the best-looking kid in the world," Ron says. But seriously, folks . . . "He has great size, very good hands, he's strong along the boards and in the corners," the elder Ross continues. "His skates aren't as quick as they should be, that's the thing that always held him back. He always said he had heavy boots."

At 16, Roscoe made the decision to focus on the game, leaving his Stateside schooling behind to play juniors in Quebec. In addition to his hockey career, Ross's time with the Hull Olympiques gave him an unexpected proficiency in French. And his dad still carries around a snapshot of Roscoe with Wayne Gretzky, the Olympiques' owner at the time.

He may not be a role model off the ice, but Roscoe leads by example on it. He led the WPHL in power play goals last year, which meant taking a lot of whacks in front. And if his speed hinders him some on defense, you can still see him trying on the backcheck, his cheeks puffed out and beet red as he stretches his aerobic capacity to its nicotine-hindered limit.

"He's worked hard," his father says. "He never really took things for granted. He's going on eight years pro, so he must be doing something right."

Today Roscoe is still napping, which is why Binnie's at the bar. But it's not surprising to find him alone in any case. At 29, Troy is the second-oldest Bat (after Mike Jackson) and the only parent. He isn't really one of the boys. Back in Austin he has his own apartment—a perk that's usually reserved for veterans whose wives or girlfriends live with them—and while he shares his teammates' affinity for golf and water sports at nearby Lake Travis, he eschews the Austin bar scene for Blockbuster nights and long-distance calls.

He is more than happy to play the part of cranky elder statesman. During juniors Binnie spent two springtimes in street clothes with the IHL Kalamazoo K-Wings, so he calls himself an "eight-year pro." On the bus, he invokes seniority to control the video selections. The other day he even overruled Burty, who wanted to watch *Tin Cup*. He also nixed my suggestion of *North Dallas Forty* because "I don't like old movies." He prods Brian Fairfield, who sits across the aisle from him, to stick to his window seat so "an old man" can have some extra legroom. Contrary to the general pecking order, Binnie sits the furthest up front of any player, close to Burty, with whom he has more in common—age, marriage, fatherhood, cigarettes—than his teammates.

Tonight, Binnie hopes to take advantage of this kinship. The team is spending two nights in El Paso before heading to Amarillo. He plans to buy Burton however many beers it takes to make sure tomorrow is practice-free.

What Binnie doesn't know is the coach has already earmarked Sunday as a day of rest. Sure, there's a power play to work on and defensive positioning to go over and new players to integrate, but when you're in the middle of a road trip spanning eight nights, four cities, and 40 hours on the bus, R&R is just as crucial.

Burton doesn't share this information with his players, however. Better to let them think that any chance they have for relaxation depends on how well they play against the Buzzards.

IT'S A FINE THEORY. Rather than allow El Paso's early 1–0 edge to flatten out their road-weary asses, later in the first period of Saturday night's game the Bats reanimate with gusto.

It starts with Tim Findlay whizzing down the left side in pursuit of a dump-in. His trip to the corner earns him a solid *thwack* from the defenseman. He crumples, but the ref isn't buying his dive. Keith Moran, who has just joined the team as the 11th forward and is getting a look-see in Mike Jackson's place tonight, goes after the puck and the man, returning the favor on Findlay's behalf. As Moran completes his check, Ryan Pawluk swoops behind the net and taps the puck to his buddy Findlay, who's back on his feet and right at Buzzards goalie Chris Gordon's welcome mat. It's a speedy, hard-working goal with just 31 seconds left in the period.

"That's one," Findlay says as he pops out the rink door. The rookie center has embraced the role of go-to guy right from the get-go. But after scoring three times on Thursday against Amarillo, he didn't find the net at all in San Angelo; the Outlaws made his line their focal point, hounding and pounding them the whole game long. Troy Binnie says "the kids" need to stand up for themselves a little. When you're a star player, sometimes you flop for the penalty and other times you let a teammate take out your trash. But to truly earn respect, especially as a newbie, you've got to do a little hacking of your own. "If someone sticks their ribs, they have to stick back," Binnie says.

This is especially true because Findlay and Pawluk both wear visors, which, in old-time hockey culture, is the equivalent of painting a bull's-eye on your sweater. Veteran Darrin MacKay is the only other current Bat who sports one. "Until they make robot eyes, I'll be wearing the shield," MacKay says.

El Paso's "Buzzards' Nest" is a colorful, high-spirited and rambunctious place. Sure, hockey towns with bilingual residents are nothing new, but the Buzzards faithful might be the first group of fans whose second language is Spanish. "Tu Cairns," one sign proclaims, proving that bleacher eloquence is the same in any tongue: it translates as "You Suck." The Nest is also the loudest in the league when it comes to the increasingly ubiquitous "Hey Goalie! You Suck!" call-and-response.

The rink's temperament reflects the city, which lies hard against the Mexican border and is a balance of vibrant Hispanic culture and troubling crime and poverty, of beautiful desert mountains rising to the north and greasy smog creeping from the south. Mariachis and low riders have been featured in between-periods promotions. Behind one goal judge there's a hot tub, in which the winner of a daily sports radio contest gets to steam and shrivel in the company of a "Buzzard Bikini Girl." Every night the team picks out the dirtiest car in the lot and gives its owner a free wash. Sadly, it's not for the H&H Car Wash and Coffee Shop, an El Paso institution that allows you to chow down on some of the city's best Mexican food (even Julia Child says so) while your ride gets buffed.

Initially the fans here celebrated goals by tossing tortillas (the staler the better, in order to achieve maximum distance and velocity) to the ice. However, even hardened, the *masa* (corn) flour left a residue, so, as with the famous flying octopi of Detroit, the practice is now discouraged. The policy has been respected, but fans and management haven't seen eye to eye on other things. Last year, even as the team enjoyed its championship run, there was a clash over tailgate parties. Apparently the company in charge of concessions viewed the parking lot cookouts as competition. According to one reveler, management sent out spies every 30 minutes to see if anyone was drinking beer, which would give them the legal right to shut things down.

El Paso is also known for its announcer, a Brooklyn-bred high school principal who seems to pattern his persona on the cafeteria troublemakers he cracks down on in regular life. Paul Strelzin is a famously active presence, the public address equivalent of a third-line pest. He sparks loud "Let's Go Buzzards" chants before each face-off and has been known to lead the crowd in Marty Robbins' "Adios Amigo" when opposing players are ejected from a game. While he was announcing for the University of Texas at El Paso, Strelzin's antics prompted the Western Athletic Conference to ban announcers from cheerleading. Ten years ago he was ejected from an El Paso Diablos baseball game when he blasted Linda Ronstadt's "When Will I Be Loved?" (with its opening lines of

"I've been cheated/been mistreated") to express his displeasure with the umps.

He has already lined up a target for tonight. "The fabulous Gunner is back," he intones. "He's 76 years old, which is also his waist size." But Strelzin is just the undercard at this game. He can sit back and relax. Tonight, there's a professional rabble-rouser on the premises.

He would be Quebec City native Claude Scott. One part musician, one part cheerleader and 10 parts shameless clown, Claude the Happy Trumpeter, a.k.a. Claude the Mad Trumpeter, is the hardest-working man in hockey. Horn in hand, he moves from section to section all night long, pumping up the crowd with repeated stanzas of "Charge!" (before key face-offs) and "Pop Goes the Weasel" (when the home team gets a power play), while honoring regional tastes with a rendition of "Tequila." He also hangs on the rinkside glass like a monkey.

But his best routine is an attempt to rattle Chad Erickson. First he gets the fans to scream "Hey Goalie!" while he puts a poster of some bombastically bosomed Pamela Anderson type up to the glass. When that doesn't work, he pulls out another poster: a Backstreet Boys-ish collection of shirtless dreamy teenage hunks.

"CLAUDE BLOWS," a sign in the arena reads. Scott has been here before. He's been everywhere. The Happy Trumpeter has plied his trade for 26 years, traveling six days a week to 200 games a season in 18 different leagues, from Red Deer to Wisconsin to Buffalo to Texas. If you happen to catch the right NHL match-up on the tube you'll hear his trumpet above the ambient crowd noise. He was a fixture in Edmonton during the dynasty years.

"Seeing people laugh is what I enjoy," Scott says. But his favorite memory is the time he accompanied an Edmonton pee-wee team to a tournament in Calgary. They won their game, and Claude was just chilling out for the rest of the competition when the supporters of another team approached him.

"They asked me if I could cheer their little boys because they were down 7–0 after two periods," Scott says. "I said, 'Okay, but I don't think it's going to do any good.' I started playing at the beginning of the third, and when the little kids saw me, they started dancing on the ice. They threw their sticks in the air and said 'We have Claude Scott, the trumpeter from the Edmonton Oilers, and he's cheering for us.' "

The kids won the game 10–7. "When they got the trophy, they brought it to me," Scott remembers. "That was the best feeling. It just hit me in the heart."

Happily for the Ice Bats, Claude has no such magic tonight. Findlay, true to his prediction, gets another goal in the second. El Paso answers, and it's a 2–2 game when the referee makes a rare judgment call. He cites an El Paso player for hooking, but also sends off the victim, Austin's Rob Hartnell, for unsportsmanlike conduct—taking a dive (an infraction that has since become more common, in both the NHL and the minors).

The teams go four on four and Troy Binnie makes his bid for Sunday furlough, using a Sher-Wood instead of a bar tab. As Seguin leaves a blueline drop pass Binnie drives to net, arriving just in time to gather up the point shot rebound and flip it in, arms raised high in celebration of the 3–2 lead.

Then the Buzzards do something you're not supposed to do *once* in a game, let alone twice—give up a goal in the final 60 seconds of a period. Chris Haskett's score drains the life out of the arena, and it's a 4–2 Bats lead.

In the locker room before the third, the team is loosey-goosey. Despite the fortuitous result, Hartnell is peeved about his unsportsmanlike penalty. "Worst call I've ever seen in my life," he says. "Why call it?" As far as he's concerned, the ref's a control freak who still hasn't gotten over getting cut from Junior B. "Nobody grows up wanting to be a referee," he smirks.

Kyle Haviland massages his legs and laments the shoebox-like sleeping conditions he endured on the bus last night. He blames Ryan Anderson's inconsiderate reclining habits. His gripe gets a laugh, and the laughter spurs him into doing Joe Pesci's "How'm I funny?" bit from *Goodfellas*.

"Twenty miles to go," someone yells, bringing focus back to the task at hand. In the third period the Findlay line socks the game away when Keith Moran picks up a turnover at the edge of the neutral zone and skates it in. Moran hits the slot and fumbles briefly, which just makes it harder for the Buzzards' netminder to read the play as the winger recovers and softly sweeps the puck beyond the line. His first professional goal, unassisted, in his first professional game. Though the Buzzards manage a couple of late goals, Andy Ross adds an empty-netter and the Bats end up with a 6–4 win.

Afterward, the team is still pissed about the mind games. Last year's pain cannot be eased by an early-season win. "I'd rather beat 'em when it counts," Kyle Haviland says.

Haviland would be hard-pressed to find fault with anything else about his year to date. He and Morque have been teamed with the Findlay line, so the combination of their defense and the rookies' strong two-way game has given Havs a gaudy plus/minus rating, with a couple of assists to boot. Haviland didn't score a goal until the final game of the season last year, but he's already got one of those as well. Most importantly, Haviland has never been on a team that started its season with a winning streak—not even to 2–0.

"Best start I ever had," he says. "Every night it gets better."

four

REQUIEM FOR THE GIRNDOG

BACK AT THE MARRIOTT, the waiter is laying out rolls for the deli tray when official word comes down. Shreveport has lost. At 6–0, Austin is the last perfect team.

A celebration is in order. The Marriott kitchen might be closed—hence the cold cuts, arranged in advance by Burton. But the bar is open. With tomorrow off, the players have carte blanche to hang out, do nothing and knock back a beer or four.

Since training camp, the daily activity's been constant—two-a-days, medical exams, photographs, paperwork, exhibition games, moving into apartments. Then, without a hiccup, the season arrived: opening night on the road followed by three home games, with plenty of practice and promotion in between. Last Sunday was spent signing autographs for several hundred enthusiastic Cub Scouts. Another day was devoted to a "golf scramble" with fans and corporate sponsors.

Downtime on the road is actually downtime. It belongs to the players and no one else. Longnecks in one hand, sandwiches in the other, the Bats spread out across the little tables and, in some cases, get to know each other for the first time. Darrin MacKay and Chris Haskett have only been around since the first day of the season. Keith Moran and Rob Hartnell officially joined the team when they boarded the bus to San Angelo.

Hartnell is a major acquisition. A WHL veteran from Rocky Mountain House, Alberta, he was one of the WPHL's most notable inaugural-season performers. Unfortunately, the pint-sized center was noticed not just for his 86 points, but for the fact that he scored them on two different teams, having come up on the wrong end of a gutsy Todd Brost trade. Just weeks after representing El Paso in the All-Star game, Hartnell was shipped to Waco in exchange for Marc Hilton, a bona fide number-one defenseman. Hilton was a big part of El Paso's championship run. Waco was the team El Paso overtook to make the playoffs.

If that wasn't a big enough slap in the face, Hartnell had to listen to the innuendo. "That deal was a classic case of addition by subtraction," people would whisper. Or "You don't win championships with one-way players," a reference to the fact that at the time of the trade, Hartnell's 60 points were accompanied by a negative plus/minus rating. Or "You don't dump a point-per-game forward unless there's a problem in the room."

Hartnell admits that the main problem was his salary. The player, who acts as his own agent, says Brost sweet-talked him into taking a flyer on the unproven league for 500 bucks a week. It was less than he wanted, but after three seasons in the ECHL his options were limited. He accepted the offer, with one caveat: he would have the right to renegotiate at any point in the season.

When he got to El Paso and compared figures with teammates and opposing players, Hartnell felt fleeced. "Guys were saying, 'What are you doing?' " he remembers. "There's no salary cap, people are making a thousand dollars, 1100 dollars a week. Here I am first or second in the league in scoring, and I'm making squat."

Just before Christmas he stopped by Brost's office and presented him with a list of comparable WPHL stars and their much higher weekly takes. Brost wasn't exactly thrilled to see him, but a deal's a deal. "I told him, Brosty, you were a player once," Hartnell says. "Any time you get a chance to market yourself you have to."

I knew you weren't going to come up to me and say, 'Hey, are you ready to renegotiate?' "

The two men managed to reach a mutually satisfactory number, but, Hartnell says, "I knew it left a sour taste in his mouth. I could just tell." When Brost decided to sacrifice a top forward to get Hilton, he didn't have to spend a lot of time studying his roster. He went with the guy who, from his point of view, was in his office asking for a raise instead of wondering how to help the team win more games.

When the season ended, Hartnell took an equally hard line with Waco. The WPHL, like all nonaffiliated leagues, does not have a labor agreement. Contracts aren't guaranteed, medical benefits are limited, and there's no true free agency. At the end of each year a player can go to any other league, but if he wants to stay in the Wiffle he's indentured to his former team.

This exclusive negotiation period lasts until December. Hartnell, unable to come to terms with Waco and not particularly interested in being there anyway, caught a plane to Rome. If the Wizards failed to trade or renounce him, he could spend the winter playing hockey in Italy. Not too shabby. If it didn't suit him, he could sneak back into the WPHL by New Year's.

Waco caved. And because the Wizards had no leverage, the Bats acquired Hartnell for almost nothing. After a handful of games in Italy and enough snapshots to fill a photo album, the center returned to Texas.

As an Ice Bat, Hartnell will have ample opportunity to repair his reputation. He doesn't have a choice, really. His salary is no great shakes, and as the third-line center, he won't be scoring like he did last year. No matter. Austin is where he wanted to go. He's eager to be part of the team. "I'd give up 85 points to be on a winning squad," he says.

Tonight in El Paso, as the former local, Hartnell plays cruise director, leading his new mates over to Bombardier's, the Buzzards' favored watering hole. Considering the temptations an energetic young man can succumb to in these parts, it's a safe, sensible choice. More than a few Ice Bats are already acquainted with Juarez, which, like all Mexican *fronteras*, has its fair share of illicit activities and "exotic" entertainment (only a tiny percentage of which involves donkeys).

The good news is, if you happen to leave "Boys' Town" with more than just a memory, penicillin is easy to come by. Mexico is a haven for pharmaceuticals, especially ones that require prescriptions in the States. Last year, just before the playoffs, two Buzzards players were caught reentering the United States with a carload of steroids. The WPHL did not have a drug policy at the time. It does now.

Said policy is enforced by random but very infrequent testing, for everything from marijuana to steroids to masking agents to Sudafed. Yes, Sudafed. The seemingly benign decongestant contains ephedrine, which is sold on its own as "herbal speed" and also serves as a building block for more potent uppers.

Hockey players have a longstanding affinity for the little red pills. "Coffee and a couple of Sudafeds," Troy Binnie cracked before one exhibition game. "Breakfast of champions." "Sudys" have become a controversial topic at the Olympic level—the Games test for it, but the NHL does not. The IOC bans Sudafed completely, whereas the WPHL is only looking for levels that indicate abuse. Despite the policy, several players still favor ephedrine-and-caffeine-based Mini Thins for a pregame boost.

As far as anyone knows, the WPHL does not test for Jell-O shots, so the guys at Bombardier's don't have anything to worry about. The rivalry is put aside as Buzzards and Ice Bats alike partake of cheap beer, friendly conversation and the attention of female hockey fans. One player takes me aside and deems his behavior in the bar to be off the record, but not because of women—he's chewing tobacco, and his significant other doesn't know about the habit. Meanwhile, the alcohol-fueled gyrations of a couple of Ice Bats on the dance floor give new meaning to the term "mobile defenseman."

Chris Morque introduces Chris Haskett to Buzzard Trent Eigner, with whom he'd fought, reluctantly, during the third period of the game. "Eigs was just padding his PiMs," Morque teases. Morque, Eigner, Buzzards goalie Chris Gordon and Todd Brost all played together for Huntington of the ECHL. Morque says that, despite Burty's distaste, he thinks Brost is a great guy and a great coach.

Chris and Chris shared a taxi over from the Marriott, and they haven't quite recovered from the driver, your basic chatty Cabbie from Hell. Listening to him jabber on about seeing Van Halen at the Coliseum was painless enough, but when he tried talking hockey, things went really sour. Haskett is irked that the guy tactlessly implied that minor leaguers aren't "real" hockey players.

The hack's idea of a "real" hockey player? "Gordie Hull."

Haskett will be hysterical about that one for days. *Gordie Hull*, he'll murmur to himself. *They're not going to believe that one back in Lucan. Gordie Hull!*

SUNDAY AFTERNOON is for sleeping, watching football, the casino, the track, the mall, the laundromat, the movie theater. Brian Fairfield spends it in the gym.

The rookie is a good and dutiful soldier, sure. But lest he be accused of not having any fun, keep in mind that he has yet to see a single minute of game action. He needs the exercise.

When Burton cleared out a roster spot for the developing goaltender, he may as well have issued him a jersey with "USE ONLY IN CASE OF EMERGENCY" sewn on the back. Fairfield is the back-up to the back-up, on call for the times when Christian Soucy is summoned to Houston.

It has already happened. After starting the first two games and sitting out the third in favor of Erickson, Soucy joined the Aeros. He got the nod in convoluted, trickle-down fashion: an injury to Los Angeles Kings second-stringer Jamie Storr forced L.A. to bring up Aeros goalie Frederic Chabot, so Houston, having already lost another 'tender, Petr Skudra, to the Pittsburgh Penguins, called up Soucy.

Fairfield hopes this means his turn will come. He's thinking maybe Thursday in Odessa—the expansion team isn't likely to present much of a challenge, and with a home game Saturday, just 24 hours after coming off the road, Erickson might benefit from a breather. On the other hand, he allows, "Chad shouldn't stop playing as long as he's hot."

In the meantime, Fairfield can take comfort in the fact that he's got his veteran partner beat in one department: giving the maximum effort in practice. "It's all I've got right now, so I do work hard at it," he says.

Fairfield's hometown of Omemee, Ontario, is a rural community of fewer than 2,000 people near Peterborough. It's where Neil Young spent his formative years, and Young's dad, journalist and Hockey Hall of Famer Scott, still has a place there. Fairfield's parents are farmers, but it's not a full-time vocation—his mother is a nurse, his father a police officer.

Most goaltenders don't like to admit as much, but they usually end up in net for one of two reasons: either their older brother made them do it, or the other kids were better skaters. Fairfield owns up to the latter origin. "I guess I didn't like the skating part of being a forward," he says. "But I've learned the hard way that maybe I should have stayed a forward. Goaltending is not all that easy."

That lesson has come courtesy of the OHL—twice. Last year, Fairfield couldn't catch on in major juniors, so he spent the season with the Junior A Caledon Canadians. This year, he was supposed to play for Erie. When he made an early exit from the Otters' training camp, an associate of agent and goaltending guru Rick Heinz pointed him toward Austin.

"It was a bit of a gamble," he says. "You have to pay your own way. I bought a $750 plane ticket on a whim and a prayer. I made the team, so it worked out."

A month ago, Fairfield had never even left Ontario. Now he's so far from Canada that Mexico is but a mile away. At 19, he's a professional hockey player.

FAIRFIELD ALMOST GETS his chance, and a night sooner than he'd hoped. In Amarillo, the Rattlers jump out to a 4–1 first period lead, and the rookie finds himself half wishing for a comeback, and half wondering if a blowout would force Burty to hand him the mop. Instead, the Bats crawl back into the game with an impassioned second period. But that's all. The Rattlers cruise through the third and win it, 7–4. The Bats' unbeaten streak is over.

Jim Burton takes the blame. He asked the team to play a passive, defense-first style, and the Amarillo forwards ate it up. "It wasn't their fault," Burty says. "It was just a tactical error. Kind of a goof by a first-year coach. I instructed them to play a certain way, they did, and it wasn't the right way. Live and learn."

After Burty finishes with the press, a little girl approaches. "Are you a hockey player?" she asks.

Burton says he's the coach.

She amends the question: "*Were* you a hockey player?"

"For 16 years," he says. The girl looks up at him, amazed—it's a length of time she can't even imagine. She assures Burton that despite losing to Amarillo, "the Ice Bats are still a good team."

The players know that. "Hey, you can't go 68–0," says Ryan Anderson. "It was good for us—we were getting cocky."

"Ride her 'til she bucks ya," adds Jeremy Thompson.

Chad Erickson is less philosophical. He refuses to acknowledge a teammate's obligatory "Good game" on his way to the shower. Outside the locker room he knocks over a garbage can, leaving a trail of tape balls and paper cups as he marches to the bus.

Chris Morque is pissed off at the ref, an old nemesis from the CHL who, Morque claims, was expelled from another league for allegedly gambling on games. In the first period, Morque took a minor penalty and then, before he could even get going, a 10-minute misconduct for complaining. If he didn't already have a history with the ref, the misconduct probably wouldn't have happened.

Back at the Quality Inn, it's another Domino's night. The Waffle House next door is open 24 hours, but several players already dined at this landmark of the American South when the bus got in last night. WH's famous hash browns—"scattered, covered and smothered," which means with cheese and onions, for just $1.19—went down great at the table, but not so great the morning after.

The Domino's delivery guy is a little overwhelmed by the order, so Andy Ross collects all the money and distributes the pizzas room-to-room. Not everyone is around. Rob Hartnell and a couple of other guys were last seen at Farley Coliseum, easing the sting of defeat in the company of several Rattlers cheerleaders.

Morning comes, and the team returns to Amarillo's rink for practice. Burton knows the boys are wound a little tight, a combination of pressure from the winning streak and disappointment from the loss. He makes sure the team is on the ice, then he disappears.

The Bats let loose, recharging their mental batteries with a raucous hour of four-on-four. Left to their own devices, with no system and no second-guessing, everyone's flying around as if Gunner had put helium in their skates, giddily embracing the sense of play that made them want do this for a living in the first place. And if that's not enough motivation, Ryan Anderson has put up a trophy for the winning side, a true *objet d'art* fashioned out of black tape, two stick blades, a hairspray can and a popcorn box.

The "just us kids" environment means the razzing never stops. "Here comes Forsberg," several people yell as Findlay bears down in the slot. "Ooohh, how'd that stay out," Ross teases after a feeble shot. "Send that puck Federal Express—it'd be faster."

Roscoe gets it as good as he gives. Whoever he's out with is automatically dubbed "The Booze Line." Rob Hartnell, helmetless, with hair that doesn't quite reach his shoulders, is "Goldilocks." Ken Ruddick is "Hollywood."

Nobody gets it worse than Ruddick. The nickname describes both his movie star cheekbones and his narcissistic ways. The season is only seven games old, but the offensive defenseman has already revealed himself to be a stat whore. The other night he complained to Martello that he was not properly credited with the second assist on an empty-net goal.

"If the league would correct my stats," Ruddick says, defending himself, "I'd be one of the top two D in scoring."

It's too bad, then, that an official scorer isn't present for the shinny session. "First three assists to Ruddick," Roscoe teases after one tally. Then, when Ruddick himself puts one in, "Goal! Number 24. Assist, number 24. Second assist to Number 24."

"If there's ever a chance for someone to get 2,000 points in a year, it'll be Kenny," Roscoe says. Later, Ross will spot Ruddick using Burty's cell phone. "Hey Hollywood, tell Kozuback I said hi," he taunts.

All of his vanity might be tolerated if Ruddick didn't come up short in other areas. A top rookie for the ECHL Louisiana Ice Gators last season, the Hamilton, Ontario, native has the typical rushing defenseman's tendency to get too fancy at too great a defensive cost. But worse than that, he's soft.

Even Burty knows it. "He's gotta learn the pro game," the coach says, meaning that what Ruddick could get away with at Wilfrid Laurier University isn't going to fly here. "He's got such good wheels that he's gotta make the play, whether he's gonna take a hit or not. If he doesn't, he won't get respect from me or the players."

If Ruddick wants to improve, he has come to the right place. Jim Burton was exactly the player Ruddick needs to become— preferably soon, since he's Burton's replacement on the roster. Burty knew how to pick his spots, didn't shy away from contact and still put up numbers so gaudy that it didn't matter if the off-ice officials messed up a point or two. One season, with Fort Wayne of the IHL, Burty had 30 goals and 64 assists, more points than anyone else on the team. He also played five years in Europe, where smaller, faster, not particularly physical players thrive. Ruddick is intererested in going there, and he knows Burty could help him out.

Burton also says that "a good-looking kid like that" is going to have a harder time winning over his teammates. It's an interesting observation. Sure, pretty people foster resentment and can seem more arrogant than they are, but for Burton even to mention this is evocative. You can just picture him in 1981, a few years removed from palling around with Gretzky, blond, handsome, confident, 20 years old. Think his Fort Wayne teammates welcomed him with open arms the minute he got to camp?

In the locker room after practice, Ross hobbles around on one foot, shaking off the impact of a Kyle Haviland slash. Havs knows it isn't cool to take out one of your team's top forwards in an intra-squad game, but the defenseman's gearbox simply doesn't run at neutral. He also two-handed Rob Hartnell, though not hard.

"Can you go?" Burty says, feigning concern as Roscoe limps over to a stall and lowers himself. Ross says he isn't sure. He's bruised, but the exchange is mostly comedy, for no other reason than to irritate Haviland.

Defenseman Corey Fletcher is the morning's other casualty. He took a puck to the brow, then made a huge rookie mistake— looking benchward for an ice pack while play continued. Fletch's teammates mocked him mercilessly for this violation of hockey etiquette, which basically says that if you aren't showing bone or spurting blood, you don't need help. Keep playing.

"Can you believe that?" a genuinely surprised Ryan Anderson says. Obviously, what they'd always told him about Ontario college types (Fletcher is a product of Laurentian University in Sudbury) was true.

Practice ends, lunch is secured and, for the last time other than the trip home, it's back on the bus. Today's journey is a mere four hours, though the way things have been going, that might mean six.

The new bus driver is Ruben, a rotund, soft-spoken Latino who seems to be enjoying the hockey and also has a taste for country music. Each day before the VCR gets going, he cranks up the radio. This is appreciated by no one more than "Tex" Fairfield. "Me and Ruben get along pretty good," the goalie says.

Still, Ruben could stand to borrow one of Tim Findlay's Prodigy CDs, just to pound a faster beat into his head. He is a very careful driver, so much so that you wonder about his confidence. Or his record. In a state where highway speed limits rarely drop below 70 miles per hour, even on two-laners at night, Ruben errs on the wrong side of law-abiding. The 420-mile trip from El Paso to Amarillo took 10 hours, which was great for the handful of people who wanted to watch *Donnie Brasco*, but disheartening to most.

Ruben guides the vehicle through the scrub, dirt and derricks of deep West Texas. The team is bound for Odessa–Midland, a mini-metropolis in the middle of nowhere, cradle of high school football, George W. Bush and a whole mess of oil money. "The armpit of the universe," writer Larry McMurtry once called it.

Burty looks out the window at the flat beige nothing all around him. "Every time I think I've seen the most desolate part of Texas," he sighs, "we go someplace else."

RICK GIRHINY was having a nice enough summer back home in Niagara Falls. His surgically repaired leg was healing on schedule, he was catching up with old friends, and things were getting pretty serious with his girlfriend, a stunning University of Texas student who worked in the Ice Bats' office. Then the phone rang.

It was Joe Clark, coach of the Odessa Jackalopes. He was just calling to let Girhiny know how pleased he was to get him in the WPHL expansion draft.

Clark proceeded to tell Girhiny what kind of coach he was. He said that because Odessa's ownership group also operated Midland's thriving AA baseball club, he could pretty much guarantee a stable organization that would keep the players happy and put people in the seats. Sure, Clark conceded, Odessa–Midland wasn't exactly a social playground like Austin, but there was plenty to do, and the natives were just as friendly. He hoped Rick would become a Jackalope.

It was a lot of information for Girhiny to absorb, considering he had no idea the Bats were going to expose him in the first place.

Now Girhiny sits in Zucchi's Sports Grill, which is right next to Zucchi's Ristorante Italiano, just a few miles from the Ector County Coliseum. Hockey players have been indigenous to Odessa for only a couple of months, but anyone who cares to already knows the location of their off-ice habitat.

On this particular evening, Girhiny is the only Jack in the room. This is probably just as well, lest his teammates spot him giving aid and comfort to the enemy. Hanging with your opponent on the night before a game may not be normal procedure, but this is the only chance he has. These are his friends. It's bigger than hockey.

In 1996 Girhiny, Kyle Haviland and Bobby Wallwork were roommates in Muskegon, where they played for the Fury of the Colonial League (now the United Hockey League). It was February—"Twenty below, snow up the yin-yang," Girhiny says—when Blaine Stoughton phoned Wallwork to pitch him on the new operation starting up in Texas.

"Bob was like, I dunno . . ." Girhiny continues. "I opened up the blinds and said, 'Bob, take a look. Open the window. There's no question. I'm there.'"

Wallwork took his friend's advice and became the player/assistant. Girhiny, Haviland and Brett Seguin followed suit, along with Wallwork and Haviland's former Memphis teammates Andy Ross, Chris Morque and Mike Jackson. Tonight that nucleus is reconvened, with Ryan Anderson filling in for Jake. Jokes are swapped, grievances are aired, six-month-old memories are rehashed and retold. The power of friendship can make even the very recent past seem nostalgic. A bar tab that flirts brazenly with $200 (at three bucks a beer) doesn't hurt, either.

Unlike many working adults, hockey players don't have trouble making new friends. Real friends, not just the kind you have a drink with every month or two. With the right group of guys on the right team, the closeness and intensity of a 70-game season forges everlasting connections. Rick Girhiny and Kyle Haviland have known each other for only two years, but their bond is such that you'd think they grew up in the same town or belonged to the same fraternity.

The hockey truism is "If they can't get along off the ice, they won't get along on it." It's part of the military mind-set: in battle, men put their lives on the line not so much for God and Country as for their closest brothers-in-arms. When Haviland lays down a beating on behalf of Seguin, when Anderson blocks a shot, when Ross drags himself to the corner at the end of a 90-second shift . . . they do it for the fans, the franchise and the coach, but mostly they do it because their teammates expect nothing less. They do it for each other.

Then one day your friend isn't around anymore. At this level of hockey, the players are nomadic mercenaries, and general managers trade or waive guys quicker than an Al MacInnis slap shot. A team with 50 percent turnover during the course of the season is not uncommon. "It's one of the things that sucks about this game," Haviland says.

On the surface, exposing Girhiny was a practical move. The Bats had to make eight players out of 20 available to the six-team expansion, and since Austin had five retirees (including Burton and Paul Lawless) on its list, losing two or three useful bodies was inevitable. Girhiny is a worker bee, a glue guy, a third-line center with more heart than talent. You don't win championships without those kind of players, but the reality is, compared with a Troy Binnie or Brett Seguin, a Rick Girhiny is expendable. It's just business. It's just hockey.

Haviland and the rest of the guys are bitter because in their hearts they don't believe the decision to dump Girhiny was entirely about hockey. Even the most casual Austin fan can look at last year's roster and spot the player who would have made a better write-off. Martin Duval was a moderately skilled, decidedly one-way player who couldn't crack the postseason roster, didn't re-up with the team and wasn't traded within the league. What's more, Jim Burton didn't know Girhiny wasn't on the team until the draft took place. It was entirely Blaine Stoughton's call.

Because Stoughton coached the Bats last year, and because his squad frequently floundered, there's a good deal of recrimination floating between the general manager/owner and the returning players. That tension only thickened when Stoughton spent the off-season demanding pay cuts. With Girhiny, he simply took negotiations to a more definitive level. He'd already lost a pissing match with Bobby Wallwork and was paying the likes of Ross, Erickson and Seguin more than he wanted. He wasn't going to let a short, slow, goals-challenged forward waste his time with salary demands.

Even if you spin it as a clash of ego and emotion, Stoughton can be defended as a pragmatist. A cold-hearted, inflexible pragmatist, certainly, but a pragmatist nonetheless. As a third-year veteran, Girhiny deserved to make a bit more than the minimum salary, but that didn't matter to Stoughton if he could get a rookie to do the same job just as well. As it turns out, the current occupant of Girhiny's old position is Rob Hartnell, so from an offensive standpoint the Bats came out of things with a major upgrade. At the same time, Joe Clark put a higher premium on intangibles: an alternate captain for the Bats, Girhiny now wears the "C" in Odessa.

So that's the way it is. Tomorrow the old pals will line up across the ice from each other and slash away like strangers, though they're certainly used to that from fooling around in practice the last few years. "I'm sure we'll bump into each other and have a little chuckle about it," Girhiny says.

The table moves on to other topics, beginning with yet another blunt dissection of a certain offensive defenseman's various shortcomings. "Softest guy I ever played with," Haviland says. Ross practically gives Girhiny a scouting report: "If you go into the corner with him, he won't do anything," he says.

Roscoe just wants to see the guy grow some guts. Ruddick has to realize that if anybody runs him, his teammates will right the balance. Nothing about pro hockey has ever come automatically to Ross, so he's both genuinely angry and genuinely disappointed to see a natural like Ruddick fail to go the extra mile. "He's got NHL speed, AHL skills and peewee heart."

Tonight, Roscoe's got at least one opinion for each empty. He's irked about yielding right wing to Binnie. He knows it's the best thing for the team, but it's still a struggle. On the left side, Ross's defensive responsibilities force him to stay high, but his offensive strength is down low, where he feasts on rebounds and makes things happen from between the circles and behind the net. The team joke is that Roscoe's entire game, especially on power plays, is to grab a patch of real estate in front and let his giant ass do all the work. All that beer has gotta be good for something!

Ross expresses sympathy for Fairfield, saying the kid is out of his league—literally. "He's working hard, but he should still be in juniors." And he's impressed with Findlay's and Pawluk's attitude. With the success they're having, it would be easy for them to act like they've got nothing to learn from anybody. But Roscoe has noticed the way they scope out Brett Seguin from the bench, awestruck by his skill and vision, wondering out loud why he isn't playing at a higher level.

Ross concludes his soliloquy with a Gunner Garrett testimonial, saying that, for all his bluster, the equipment manager is a sweetheart whose first priority is always taking care of his players, whether that means ordering gear or schlepping bags in the middle of the night. Roscoe sent him a thank-you note at the end of the first season, and brings him cookies or a muffin nearly every day. (Gunner is obviously grateful—once, I actually heard him skip an opportunity to throw a wisecrack Roscoe's way. "No, Andy's my guy," he said.)

The conversation is interrupted. A couple of buxom Latina girls—complete strangers—approach the table.

"We're going country dancing," one of them cheerfully explains.

"Come along with us," the other one commands.

No one's interested. They've got a game in the morning. Going out dancing would be irresponsible. No can do . . .

And anyone who believes *that* can pick up the next round.

Ross, who has been forbidden by the team from sharing an apartment with either a rookie (bad example) or an old mate (two troublemakers being worse than one), laughingly recalls a night last year when he stayed out in Juarez until 5 A.M. A little more than 12 hours later, he scored two goals in the final seven minutes (including the winner with four seconds left), leading the Bats to a 6–5 victory over El Paso. Some people can just hold their liquor.

"I've never played with a hangover," Rick Girhiny joked in an interview last year. "Still drunk, maybe."

It is getting to be that time, however. Both teams have game-day skates at 10 A.M. or so. Brett Seguin moseys over to the bar and requests a ride—an impressive undertaking, considering he has more or less lost the power of speech.

Ryan Anderson leans over and plants a kiss on Girhiny's left cheek. Kyle Haviland takes care of the right one. The cab arrives.

THE NEXT MORNING, Burton and a couple of players stand near the glass, sizing up Odessa's arsenal. "We can't take 'em lightly," Burty says. "They're hockey players."

The coach is eager to erase the memory of Amarillo. He knew he couldn't go undefeated forever, but that didn't make his first career coaching loss any easier to take. "It was really hard," he says. "I don't like losing." He half-kiddingly adds, "If it doesn't work out, I'm a golf pro. At least I can spend my winters in Florida."

As Girhiny puts one on net, Burton and Ross both notice what their equipment manager had already picked up: "Goddamn," Gunner had marveled a few minutes earlier. "Girhiny finally learned how to lift the puck!"

The Bats do their work, running through a new power play scheme, skating half-circles and shooting just enough to prep the goalies. Ryan Anderson, laboring with every stride, knows he isn't fooling anyone.

"Was that the worst fucking practice you've ever seen?" he says.

five

WAY UP AND DOWN
THE SWAN RIVER

THE BAT CAVE is crawling with bugs. Mudbugs, that is. Several hundred supporters of Shreveport's brand-new hockey team—the name a slang term for that bottom-feeding Cajun delicacy, crawfish—have converged on the Travis County Expo Center for the biggest battle of the still-young season. It's unusual for hockey fans to get worked up about a November game, let alone in Austin, on a Saturday, with the weather still sunny and the Longhorns playing football on the University of Texas campus. But the Bats, 3–2 since Halloween, are 10–3 overall. Shreveport, at 12–3, is a nose ahead. The brimming Bat Cave is primed for the inauguration of a first-rate rivalry. Official attendance is 7,921: a team record, as well as a fire-code violation. "If you want anything out of the owners, tonight would be the night to ask," one employee jokes.

In truth, not all the Shreveport fans are so fervent that they made the six-hour trip across East Texas. Many have come from 90 minutes down the road in San Antonio, where they used to cheer on the CHL's Iguanas. The "Iggies" have been chased out of business by an IHL team, but just because San Antonio is an NBA town doesn't mean its hockey fans want higher ticket prices, or games that feature older players, tighter defensive systems and fewer fights. Though the home of the Alamo is one of the 10 largest cities in America, and the second-largest market (after Houston) in the league, the Dragons have the worst attendance in the IHL.

The disenfranchised Iggie-lovers prefer life in exile. Some come to Austin regularly for Bats games, but there's a reason they've shown up en masse tonight: nearly all the major Mudbugs players are Iguana alumni.

In the game's first 10 minutes, the visiting fans are the only ones who feel like making noise. Shreveport, with their red and purple, Fruit Stripe gum–evoking sweaters, jump out to a 3–0 lead. Towering Mudbugs keeper Kevin St. Pierre is the difference. On one point-blank chance, he lowers himself onto a Findlay five-hole missile so easily, it's like his crotch has a vacuum attachment.

In the second, Austin converts a 21–9 shots advantage into actual goals, the crowd moving from relief (*loud*) to hope (*louder*) to joyous disbelief (*loudest*) with each successive score. By the end of the period the game is tied, and the fans are fit to be so.

Regulation ends at 4–4. But in the WPHL, that doesn't mean overtime. The league uses an Olympics-style shootout to settle matters. Both teams get a point for the tie, and the team that prevails in the shootout gets an additional point for "winning."

The hockey purists don't care for it, and it's definitely strange to end a physical game, your 18 versus theirs, with the equivalent of a home run derby (though the other team's goaltender does present more of a challenge than a batting practice pitcher). But no one likes a tie—or so the fledgling league believes. Unencumbered by tradition, the fans certainly get into it, whooping and staying on their feet for the entire spectacle.

Jim Burton thinks it makes the game better. "When you have that five-minute overtime period to break a tie, you're probably looking at one or two shots per team," he says. "Because nobody wants to give it up—they want the tie. With the shootout you're already guaranteed a point, so everybody's trying to break one at the end." Indeed, the NHL would soon embrace this logic, giving both teams a guaranteed point when it introduced four-on-four OT. The shootout format calls for five rounds of action. If it's not settled by then, it goes to sudden death. Tonight, it's tied after nine shooters, a large enough number that the coaches are finally forced to choose between their more skill-oriented defensemen and their third-line forwards. After Shreveport scores, Burty opts for one of the latter, Chris Haskett. The big rookie is unable to take it to the 10th.

In the locker room, guys are glum. "It was our best game of the year," Burton assures them. He feels the team would have doubled its scoring if not for St. Pierre. "Now get ready for tomorrow."

Meaning, get on the bus, pass out the Tylenol PMs and rest up for Lake Charles. The 5 P.M. Sunday contest is just 12 hours away by the time the bus exits Interstate 10 by the refineries, U-turns underneath the highway and pulls into a dark, sprawling compound. The Chateau Charles is a large, borderline-seedy motel–truck stop. You can order room service, or you can pull up and buy diesel just a few yards from your door.

Happily, the rooms, which run about $40 a night, are nicer than the exterior. And the food's not bad at all. By 10 A.M., guys are loading up on made-to-order omelets and pancakes in the buffet area. The only tough part is getting back to your quarters for naptime—with 15 buildings laid out over the equivalent of five or six city blocks, the place is hard to navigate. As the Bats pass through the lobby, a man with a black instrument case and a Koho equipment bag is complaining at the front desk. Claude the Agitated Trumpeter has been walking the property for 15 minutes, and he still can't find room 503.

The Ice Pirates team is just as lost. Bobby Wallwork boasts to his former comrades that he was out until 7 A.M. last night. He claims the coach, former NHLer Dennis Maruk, lacks the authority to make his team behave, mainly because he needs his Tylenol and coffee in the morning just as badly as the players.

The Bats stomped Lake Charles 9–1 in Austin a week ago. Afterward, Paul Lawless ran into Wallwork and gave him a mock double take. "Did you play tonight?" Lawless asked.

Before warm-ups, Wallwork takes Burty aside and asks if there'd be a slot for him in Austin. There isn't, and that's the coach's call, not Blaine Stoughton's. "He's a great player, but he's not great to have on a team," Burton says. "This game stops for nobody."

But it will wait a few minutes for just about anything, assuming "anything" is the sort of pregame distractions that hockey team promotions staffers dream up to entertain children and keep casual fans half-interested. Lake Charles has two mascots—Blade the Pirate and Puck the Parrot—and two more guys—"Jacques and Pierre, your high-flying bayou blasters!"—who rappel from the top of the building onto a ship-on-ice, from which they deluge the crowd with air gun–fired T-shirts.

It's a little too "Pirates of the Caribbean" for some Lake Charles fans. They're after another kind of action. "C'mon, fight," one whines, after four and a half minutes of perfectly straightforward hockey. "C'mon, fuck 'em up!" There is also a birthday party at the rink, 16 eight-year-old boys pressed against the glass, banging nonstop, screeching for penalties on every hit while yelling "Fight, fight, *fight!*" Neither constituency is mollified by the appearance of Claude in a red-lipsticked, black-bewigged, pink-dressed ensemble that's topped off with giant falsies, a conical Madonna-bra and dangling pasties. That man gives a team its money's worth.

Chad Erickson also earns his salary. With the goalie at the top of his game, the Bats overcome their post-Mudbugs, post–bus-ride malaise and play some pretty decent hockey. "Good teams don't take nights off," Burton preached beforehand. Andy Ross, Troy Binnie and Brett Seguin each get a goal—in recent weeks, that line has overshadowed the Findlay–Pawluk pairing, combining for 18 goals and 27 assists in 10 games.

But they are also on the ice when, with 1:24 left, a Pirate sneaks through the middle and comes in on Erickson alone with a hard shot from the top of the circle. It finds the net, and having coughed up a sure win, the Bats get beat in a shootout for the second straight night. It has become the season's theme: as good as the team plays at times, every game has a moment when they let the other club have its way—sometimes after jumping out to a big enough lead that it doesn't matter, other times when it does.

"We don't seem to be able to bury it," Burton allows, putting a happy face on the evening with a bit of coach-speak. "I like it when they learn how to play the ugly ones. It's a character builder, and it's the way you gotta play in the playoffs."

When the Bat Bus departs the civic center parking lot, the team is one man short. Kenny Ruddick, who lived in nearby Lafayette as a member of the ECHL Ice Gators last season, is staying behind. Earlier today, Ruddick almost missed the bus from the Chateau Charles to the rink. He strutted away from the passenger door of a pretty girl's Corvette just in the nick of time, boarding with a stuffed dog beneath his arm. His teammates figure he showed up late on purpose, just to stage the scene.

However, Ruddick's girlfriend is not his main reason for taking off. He needs to figure out what to do with his life. The defenseman wants a six-week sabbatical so he can study for and take the GREs, the U.S. graduate school entrance exam. Ruddick is unusual in that he chose major juniors over college, but after playing in the OHL from 1989 to 1992, he decided to get his degree at a Canadian university. That's why he was a 24-year-old rookie last year.

Burton is not going to deny the kid his education. The coach wished Ruddick well, and while he couldn't guarantee it, said there'd probably be a place for him if he was ready to return at Christmas. "Razor" (which has replaced "Hollywood" as Ruddick's more commonly used and less judgmental nickname among his teammates) has improved some since October. His attempts to play a more physical game often translate into penalties, but at least his teammates have grown to tolerate him.

Ruddick is not the only guy on the outs. The curtain is going down on Brian Fairfield's run as goalie understudy. The rookie appeared in one game, a 6–0 blowout by Fort Worth in which he relieved Erickson for 14 minutes, giving up one goal on five shots.

His fate was sealed when a wayward puck collided with Christian Soucy's hand at a Houston Aeros practice, shattering bone and putting Soucy out indefinitely. Now the Bats need a second goalie they are actually willing to play every couple of weeks. The youngster hopes to go back to juniors. Burton has arranged a tryout for him with Rouyn–Noranda of the Quebec league. "I'd like to play hockey as long as I can, and not just at this level," Fairfield says.

The goalie is just about the only Bat who doesn't relish tonight's postgame plan. The team adjourns to the Player's Island casino, one of two permanently docked gambling boats that are just about walking distance from the rink. While Lake Charles has more than 200 churches, six professional dance companies and the oil business, it's the miniature palaces of pink neon and free alcohol that give the city a good deal of its identity, at least to tourists and hockey players.

"I've worked for every dollar I've ever had in my life," Fairfield says, explaining his disinterest. He probably wouldn't make it past the doorman anyway—fellow 20-year-old Chris Haskett is turned away for not having ID.

Normally, postgame gambling trips only happen after wins. But it's early, just 9 P.M., and having played three games in three nights, the team won't practice tomorrow. Besides, they have to eat somewhere.

As Burton works on a sandwich, he contemplates the roster. The coach brought in an extra defenseman a few days ago, but even with Ruddick leaving, the player isn't showing enough to win the job, mostly in the attitude department. "First guy off the ice at practice, first guy at the bar," Burty says.

"But I like that Keith Moran kid," he adds. Moran hasn't played a game since his debut in El Paso, but he approaches practice the same way Fairfield did—since it's all you got, you may as well give your all.

By midnight, Chad Erickson has pocketed 200 bucks at the blackjack table and Rob Hartnell has earned a week's salary spinning the roulette wheel. The team stops for supplies at a Triple J truck stop, and it's back on the pressure cooker. "Could you take the heat off 'cremate'?" Ryan Pawluk yells, minutes after the bus gets rolling.

Chad Erickson and Brett Seguin return to their ongoing game of "Schnarples," a member of the hearts/cribbage family that gets its name, in rather mangled fashion, from the moniker of its presumed inventor, former Vancouver Canucks defenseman Harold Snepsts.

The goalie and the center are steady partners in cards, golf and not visiting the gym. "Peas in a pod," Brian Fairfield says of them. "Two out-of-shape hockey players who are somehow great." It's said that Chad never makes an effort in practice unless Seguin is shooting, and the goalie does not deny it. Tonight Erickson, though recently married himself, teases Seguin because he plans to spend Thanksgiving with his new girlfriend's family, instead of with the boys.

Two rows over, Kyle Haviland and Ryan Anderson begrudgingly knock back American beers. A lengthy, complicated debate on the topic of "Canadian versus Blue, which is better?" soon follows.

Andy Ross sleeps through it. "The old gray mare just ain't what she used to be," he says, before flopping on the floor.

The rest of the team settles in to watch *Species*. Jeremy Thompson proudly notes that star Natasha Henstridge is a native Alberta girl. "And she takes her clothes off the whole show!" Corey Fletcher adds.

Thompson, a.k.a. "J.T.," has a huge list of favorite shows, preferring Westerns and gory, anti-authoritarian fare like *Braveheart*. In the Ice Bats game program, his stated life ambition is to appear in a Robert Rodriguez movie. Rodriguez, the director of such shoot-'em-up action/horror fare as *Desperado* and *From Dusk 'Til Dawn*, is one of Austin's favorite sons.

Thompson is a "role player," meaning that when he gets praised for his hands, it's usually because they're doing something to another guy's face. He's the bruising, brawling hockey equivalent of a character actor, one of those tarnished anti-heroes who show up just long enough for whiskey, wisecracks and the bloodiest possible death.

J.T. embraces the part wholeheartedly, with long, disinterested hair, the occasional Fu Manchu mustache and an amusingly hoary flair for drama—he once responded to a potential fight overture with a line from the movie *Tombstone*: "I'm coming, and I'm bringing hell with me!" He also sells his own T-shirt (the profits going to the Ice Bats booster club) bearing the legend "WANTED: #21 JEREMY THOMPSON. FIGHTING, ROUGHING, ELBOWING, TRIPPING, CHARGING & INSTIGATING."

A Canadian Metis of Okanagan, Cree, Mohawk, French and Scottish genealogy, Thompson is the first guy to crack wise with the Native stereotypes, be it sexual potency, love of alcohol or tribal fashion sense. Last night at a Chevron outside Austin he forked over six bucks for a pair of blue-tinted, gold-framed aviator sunglasses. "If you're willing to wear 'em, you can have 'em," the guy behind the counter told him.

"If I was on the rez, 20 guys would be wearing these," Thompson said, putting them on right there in the store.

J.T. was born in British Columbia but grew up in Alberta, most recently Whitecourt, where his father, Walter, manages a pulp mill and his mother, Wendy, is a teacher's assistant. He is the oldest of three boys, all players. During this particular season the youngest son, Cody, was still in juniors, while the middle son, Rocky, was the Calgary Flames' enforcer-in-waiting with St. John's of the AHL. Rocky would go on to replace Sandy McCarthy on the big club's roster, commencing a brash but brief love affair with the Calgary fans and media. With Jeremy in Texas, Rocky in New Brunswick and Cody 11 hours from home in Tier II, Wendy and Walter had accrued a phone bill of something like $500 a month.

J.T. was nicknamed "Thumper" by his Moose Jaw junior teammates because, he says, "when I fought a guy in Regina I hit him so many times and so fast they said my left hand was like Thumper's leg in *Bambi*." It also describes the way he finishes his checks.

"Everybody's gotta play their role," Thompson shrugs. "Sometimes I have to go out there and take the law in my own hands," he says. "If the ref lets something go I'll say, 'Hey, if you don't take care of it, I'm gonna have to take control.' Ninety percent of the time it's emotional. You get to pushing and shoving, someone whacks you and then you just go at it. You get upset out there." After one game against New Mexico, the Austin penalty-box attendants were still buzzing about Thompson's overheated chatter. "I'll slit your fuckin' throat," he told his rival.

Another night, in the stands, I heard an Ice Bats fan come up with a perfect summation of why J.T. is an inspirational presence even though he's not, by enforcer standards, the biggest or most technically adept guy out there. "He might get beat up," the fan explained to his friend in a thick Texas twang, "but he'll fight 'til he does!"

Thompson's importance is more psychological than physical. Whether he's taking the body or forcing the other team to chase the puck in its defensive zone, he is the Bats' designated alarm clock. He goes out there and scatters kindling, revving up the crowd with a big hit, making the opposition's best players wish he'd go away, embarrassing his more gifted teammates because they don't sweat, struggle or sacrifice as much as he does.

"He knows when the team is flat," Jim Burton says. "He's a rough customer, he sparks us up and he doesn't need to be told how to do it. He's a smart player."

Like most players of his ilk, Thompson does what he has to do to play. But, again like most players of his ilk, he feels that, given the chance, he could do more. He scored 11 goals in 48 games in the West Coast Hockey League last year. He lacks speed but is enough of an athlete that he was nationally ranked as a high school wrestler. He also did pretty well in school, thanks to prodding from his parents—all the Thompson boys knew that if they didn't maintain averages of 70 or above, Walter and Wendy would pull them out of hockey.

J.T. wants to play for as long as he can, but he pines for the Canadian West—calving season, branding season, hunting season, Stampede week and "watching the canola turn yellow in northern Saskatchewan." The one thing that might get him home in a jiffy is if his wife, Jennifer, whom he met while playing for the WHL Tri-City (Washington) Americans, were to get pregnant.

"I don't want my kid to be born a Texan," he cracks.

IF THOMPSON had been a Bat from Day One, he might have been the number-one fan favorite. The title pretty much correlates with one's willingness to scrap.

Ryan Anderson has a headlock on the role. It only *seems* like the 22-year-old winger fought in every game his rookie season. He was second in the league with 20 majors, accompanied by a decent share of game misconducts. The first time I ever accompanied the team on the road, early in that first year, Anderson was tossed for starting something before a puck drop. It was his first shift of the game.

It's actually quite apt that Anderson is the best-loved public face of Austin's franchise. In a sense, he became an Ice Bat on the first day of his life.

It was February 1975. Dale Anderson, a minister's son who'd moved to Bowsman, Manitoba, at the age of 15, had a few months to go in his final season with the Brandon Wheat Kings. An offensive defenseman, he was skilled enough to be drafted by the San Diego Gulls of the World Hockey Association, at a time when the WHA was giving the NHL its last gasp of competition.

The pro game was not in the cards for Dale. His 17-year-old wife Molly was already pregnant with Ryan. "I had to make a choice," Dale says. "I started looking after my family."

"He got drafted and didn't go: he's a fool," Ryan teases. "No, if I was in the same situation, I'd do the same. It was probably a big decision for the both of them just to keep me."

Not really, Molly Anderson says. "At the time it just seemed natural. I never, ever regretted it."

No regrets, but on the day Ryan was born, lots of nerves. Initially, Dale was too jittery to pick up the baby. An hour later, his buddy and Wheat Kings teammate Gerald Stoughton walked into the room. "Ger" gathered up the little bundle without giving it a second thought, thus becoming the first man to hold Ryan in his arms. Twenty-one years later, they'd be roommates when Gerald's brother started his hockey team. Ryan was in a (relatively) big city for the first time, while Gerald was recently divorced. Opinions vary as to which of them had more curfew violations.

Anderson's hometown of Bowsman is a hamlet of about 500 people in the Swan River Valley, a wide-ranging, northwestern Manitoba community where kids travel as much as an hour to get to high school. For some residents, the grocery store is almost as far. But Bowsman does have its own enclosed outdoor rink, though the original structure burned down the year Ryan was born. He settled for his grandfather's backyard patch. "He was on skates when he was one—but by no means was he skating," Dale says.

Ryan started playing hockey at four. His mother remembers

him as a talkative peewee. If she was late to the game, or out working concessions, he would skate over to the boards and give her updates. "He aways liked to fill me in. He'd say 'Mom, Mom! So-and-so did this, or so-and-so did that,'" she says. "I'd tell him, 'Ryan, you gotta get back in the play.'"

His nickname was "Skinny," because he was the smallest kid on the team all the way to adolescence. But at 16 he sprouted up to six-foot-two, which improved his position on the Tier II Neepawa Natives. He knew what kind of player he had to be. "I couldn't score a goddamn goal," Ryan says. "Hands of stone."

At just 180 pounds, the old handle still fit, but Anderson made up for his slight frame with attitude. He also had some pugilistic skill. Dale sent him for boxing lessons with Rocky Addison, a former Canadian Golden Gloves champion who'd also coached the Wheat Kings. Addison had nurtured one of Dale and Gerald's young Brandon teammates, a tough customer named Dave Semenko, who went on to fame as Wayne Gretzky's personal on-ice escort—to the tune of nine seasons and two Stanley Cups—with the Edmonton Oilers.

Ryan racked up 222 penalty minutes his last year in Neepawa. The El Paso Buzzards invited him for a try-out, but Gerald invoked the personal connection. Ryan didn't expect to have a single shot at the pro level, let alone a pair. After Neepawa blew a 3–1 lead in the league finals, he figured that was his last hurrah. "I was like, man, I never want to play hockey again." He went so far as to memorialize his junior playing days by having his jersey number, 8, tattooed onto his right thigh in a mock-sweater design. Then fate intervened. Since rookies don't get any say in such matters—especially with Gunner in control—he wears 11 for the Ice Bats.

Now he's a pro player 26 hours from home, though it's a straight shot down Interstate 35 once you cross the U.S. border. Molly, who works part-time for the phone company and is deputy mayor of Bowsman, visited once last season. Dale made the trip three times, catching a total of 17 games. He has owned a roofing business since he was 20, so he gets the winters off. "That's the perk," he says. "When the kids were younger, it gave me the opportunity to coach."

Dale coached his boys for almost two decades, switching off

between Ryan and his younger brother, Dallas. "That way they never got sick of me. Then Ryan left to play junior, and my youngest had to put up with me for three years in a row." He still gets a kick out of working with the little ones. "It's the best," he says. "To see kids happy and smiling and working their tails off, it's so rewarding. Especially if you start them when they're little. You can't do a thing. They're just too godawful terrible. And then slowly, month by month they're moving."

Ryan shares his father's fondness for the youngsters. He's always signing autographs, patting kids on the back and affectionately calling them "little guy."

Dale thinks the isolation of Manitoba—and parts of other western provinces, certainly—is the reason the region produces so many gritty, snarly, blue-collar-type players. "You've got to travel so far to play hockey. You've really gotta want to do it," he says. "You get out there and it's 40 below and it's four in the morning and the vehicle might start, it might not, or it might die on the road. I've taken teams out the back door while they're still dressed because the fans were ready to beat on us. I had a midget team in Hudson Bay where we had to fight our way out of some rinks."

The fans in Texas are not quite so bad, but in certain barns, after the inevitable game misconduct, Ryan has run a gauntlet of screaming, jeering, frothing attendees. The worst thing he's been hit with is a cup of ice. This being Texas, most people appreciate the way he plays. "A lot of people, all they want to see is you smacking someone into the wall," he says. "I still get a kick out of it when people ask if the fights are real."

An old-time hockey acolyte, Ryan's dad scoffs at the notion that fighting has hindered hockey's chances in America. The commercial success of the WPHL certainly bears that out. "When there's a fight, how many people do you see turned around in the stands, covering their eyes?" Dale asks. "Come on. This is America. Hockey will be bigger because of the fighting."

And yet he won't take credit for his son's ability in that department. "I gave him the talent end," he says with a twinkle in his eye. "His mother is where he gets the fire from." (Jeremy Thompson's and Kyle Haviland's fathers make the same claim.)

One of hockey's inviolate truisms is that the dazzling, graceful superstar players are likely to be the less appealing human beings, whereas the major on-ice creeps are the guys you want to take home to Mom. That's what Karla Corbett did. She's a Swan River girl who is best friends with Ryan's little sister, meaning that, in the tradition of all great romantic comedies, they initially hated each other.

"He's only a big macho man on the ice," Karla says. "He's a sweetheart. He's outgoing and funny and he'll talk to anybody. He gets along with everyone."

As a player, Anderson made big strides last season. He began the year as a forward, the 10th man off the bench on a team that rolls three lines of three. But by the end of the year, he'd moved to defense and was learning the position up-close from Burton. Says Karla, "He told me last year, 'I thought I had it all down, but I'm learning so much. I knew that I didn't know everything, but I didn't realize how much I had to learn.'"

He always calls home whenever something good happens. Mostly, he revels in the culture shock. "I see more in a week than I could in a year at home," Ryan says. He flew on a plane for the first time in his life and stays in lots of "fancy" hotels, most of which aren't all that fancy. Even his wardrobe has changed, thanks to the team dress code. "I've got all these coats I can never wear back home," he says. "Back home, they'd think I was a pimp or something."

With his half-year, $350-a-week salary, Ryan has been able to buy a small house in Bowsman. But Dale doesn't expect his son to rush back onto rooftops any time soon. "You only get one life, and he enjoys his," the elder Anderson says. "Nobody ever says you go to *work* hockey—you go to *play* hockey."

six

THANKSGIVING

TROY BINNIE walks the hundred yards from his car to the locker room without acknowledging anybody. It's the day before Thanksgiving, and the Bats are spending it with a dull but pesky last-place team in a three-quarters-empty barn. Because it's America's worst travel day of the year, the bus to Waco, a mere 90 miles north of Austin, will leave at 2 P.M. for the 7 P.M. contest. But Binnie's pique is not about the trip. It's because he isn't going on it.

The veteran center is coming off his best week of the season. He got his 10th goal over the weekend, and last night he was at the heart of every key moment in a dramatic win against El Paso. Binnie scored twice as the Bats took an early 3–0 lead, watched the team blow it, shed blood on the receiving end of a high-sticking double-minor and later took a penalty shot, which he missed. He made up for that by scoring the winner in the shootout. By WPHL rules (only the decisive overtime goal is counted on the stat sheet), that's a hat trick.

"It's been a long time coming," he said afterward. "Hopefully I'll get another one soon."

His performance meant the team's two-line offensive depth was finally in full effect. "Brett and Roscoe and I are hot right now. We're working well, touch wood. Some nights Findlay and Pawluk and Jake are gonna win the game. Some nights we're gonna win the game. And the nights we're both going, there's not gonna be anybody around to compete with us."

But there will be no more of those nights. At least, not with Binnie in the picture. As the Bats players load up their equipment bags, Binnie yells above the din to get everyone's attention. All eyes go to his stall.

"I was going to retire Saturday," he says. "My family was coming to watch me this weekend. But now I can't play 'cause I've been traded."

Binnie's voice begins to choke. "The other team knows I'm retiring, but they want me anyway." As tears well up he flees to the isolation of Gunner's equipment room.

The remaining Bats, even those who'd heard whispers of Troy's plans, are shell-shocked. But they also have a bus to catch. Before pulling out, Burty kicks me off so he can address the team in private. That he does this, and that he allowed Binnie to make his own announcement, suggests he has strong, close-to-the-vest feelings about the situation.

Binnie had been agonizing over his long-distance husband/father role all season. It's almost like he had to break out of his slump to remind himself he still had it. Only then could he leave the game behind. He decided his wife and son would come down to see him play his final games, and then the three of them would head back to Toronto together.

Troy did not have many confidants on the team, but anyone who knew him, especially Burty, knew what he was going through. "On the other hand," the coach points out, "he said he'd play hockey for us all year."

That's about how Blaine Stoughton felt, times 100. Stoughton tried to squeeze Binnie's agent over contract stuff all summer long. Now the general manager felt squeezed himself. But he wasn't going to lose the final negotiation. Did he care whether Binnie's two-year-old got to see him play pro hockey, for the only time in the little boy's life? Did he care that the team could benefit from having Binnie for three more games?

Nope. The GM was pissed, and on a more practical level, had a chance to get a potentially useful player in return for one who wasn't going to be around. He could have waited until Monday to do it, but he worked a deal with the Central Texas Stampede in a matter of hours, swapping Binnie's rights for a tough-guy forward named Brad Wingfield. The offense-impoverished Stampede were willing to part with Wingfield on the off-chance that Binnie might change his mind later in the season.

That's the scenario Stoughton was blind to, which bothered Burton more than the deal's emotional fallout. Burty himself was only six months removed from playing. He'd seen guys "unretire" at least once a season for 20 years. Binnie could easily spend Christmas with the family, then have a change of heart. Or he could shovel snow to his heart's content in January and February, then come back to Texas for the playoffs, an easy four- or five-week curtain call.

Binnie is all too aware of that possibility. "I just hope Austin isn't playing Central Texas in the playoffs," he said the next day. Meaning, I hope they are.

"I've been wrestling with this for a year and a half," he continued. "My wife can't raise our son alone. It's made me feel guilty, and bad about being here. There's never been a question of whether I want to play. But my family is more important to me than playing."

When the Bats finally get to Waco, Burton forgets that Binnie's gone. He already had Keith Moran in the lineup for just the third time this season so that Mike Jackson could rest his shoulder. That's no longer an option.

"Go get Jake," he tells one of the Bats' front office guys, "before he loads up on too many hamburgers. Tell him he's playing."

Somewhat lost in the hubbub is new player Todd Harris, who's taking over Kenny Ruddick's spot. Harris is a big, skilled kid who doesn't like the dirty work any more than Ruddick did. But the Bats are desperate for offense from the point.

"Harry," who won a championship with Oklahoma City and is thus familiar to the former Central Leaguers, began the season with San Angelo. When the Bats visited there in October, Andy Ross's scouting report on the Outlaws' D was "One defenseman is gutless but okay. The others can't even skate backward." Harris can skate backward. His brother Ross is the Outlaws' best winger, but the blood tie didn't keep Todd from clashing with San Angelo's own family unit—owner Dick Moore and prodigal son/player/assistant coach Skeeter. Todd was briefly suspended, then traded for future considerations, which, depending on what those considerations turn out to be, is one small step above the waiver wire.

Burty sizes him up. Literally—the first time any coach gets a look at a six-foot-four, 220-pound defenseman, especially at this level, you can see him drool, no matter what the guy is really made of. He asks the new rearguard how he shoots.

"Left." Harris says.

Burty looks troubled.

"But I can play right. I played right for three years."

Burty grins. "You're playing right."

THE BATS DISPOSE of Waco in Waco, and then again two days later in Austin, though both games are a bit too close for Burty's taste, and too sluggish for anyone else's. Waco's 7,000-seat Heart of Texas Coliseum has different-colored seats across its sections, and with crowds that rarely top 2,000, every color shines bright and true on most nights.

High above center ice, a single codger with a bushy mustache spends the game shouting "HIT HIM! HIT HIM! HIT HIM!" It feels like he's yelling in church—though, given this is Waco, a Baptist enclave, and Texas, where mega-sized houses of worship are quite common, church is probably more crowded. And a tougher ticket.

Somehow, the Wizards feed off their building's anti-energy. "Their style is to bring the other team down just a little bit," observes goalie Jim Mullin, who won the first game in his Bats debut. "They did a good job of doing that."

The only point of redemption is that the Austin players get a twisted kick out of facing Chris O'Rourke, an ex-Bat who's another member of the Big-Not-Mean defenseman's club.

"He's scared of his own shadow," Andy Ross said before the game, then went after him all night long. Much to Ross's surprise, O'Rourke stood up to him.

"Why are you spearing me?" Roscoe asked his former teammate at one point.

"We've got a chance to win this game," O'Rourke answered earnestly. "I've got to try my hardest."

It wasn't enough. But at least O'Rourke, who Blaine Stoughton, general manager, traded for late last season, only to see Blaine Stoughton, coach, scratch him in the playoffs, still has a job. After being sent to Waco in the Hartnell trade, Jay Hutton, erstwhile star of the season opener, spent exactly 60 game minutes in a Wizards uniform before the team dumped him, ending his professional career.

For Austin, the game that matters most comes as the long weekend ends. The Fort Worth Brahmas are owners of a 14-game unbeaten streak, allowing them to surge into first in the division. The last time Austin faced them, in Fort Worth, the Bats were embarrassed 6–0. That was the game in which Brian Fairfield got his 14 minutes of fame.

This may be why Jim Mullin is back between the pipes. It is not customary for the number-two goalie to play two games of a three-game weekend. But then, it's also not customary for the starter to play 17 in a row, as Erickson did when Fairfield was around.

Mullin is a midwestern kid who grew up in Peoria, Illinois, and St. Louis, Missouri. Like his father, who played for the Rensselaer Polytechnic Institute in upstate New York, Mullin used hockey as his ticket to college, spending four years at the University of Denver. He earned regional MVP honors at last season's National Collegiate Athletic Association (NCAA) tournament and has landed in Austin after a brief audition in the IHL and a roster crunch in the ECHL. He has not been 100 percent because of a separated shoulder, which he got doing pull-ups.

Mullin played well in Waco, surpassing Burton's expectations from what he'd seen in practice. "Though if I had to start Chad

Erickson off of the way he performs in practice, he would never play a game," Burty jokes.

As for Fort Worth, "I just want to see if Mullin can handle a big game," Burty says. Pressed further, he admits the shelling Erickson took 14 days ago was a factor. "Yeah, they scored quite a few goals. It wasn't anything to do with him, but that was the reason I wanted a different look. Don't print that, okay?" Burton is not the sort of coach who communicates with his players through the media.

Mullin is sharp again tonight, but the game belongs to numbers 8 and 9. If, through the helmets and visors, you can identify the former as Tim Findlay and the latter as Ryan Pawluk, you're doing better than the coach.

"It always seems to me that their numbers should be reversed," Burton says. It doesn't help that the Bats sweaters have curving red numerals with little star shapes around the white space, making it tough for the official scorers, 30 rows up, to figure out ho's who.

Tonight the Windsor Kids are performing in front of the Findlay family. Father Bill is an older, stouter, bearded version of Tim. He works for Ford, just across the river in Detroit, while his wife Patty is employed by the Windsor Housing Authority. Their older son, Shawn, is not along, but a set of grandparents are here, and Tim's girlfriend Jenn Theriault, a nurse, has also made the trip.

They've noticed it's a very small world. "At this level, the hockey players are like a secret society," Bill Findlay says. Fort Worth's Todd St. Louis played with Tim and Ryan on the Spitfires. Jenn went to high school with Ryan McDonald, who's with the Wizards. "Even though we're 2,000 miles away, we still know somebody," she says.

Bill and Patty are out by the concession stand between periods when Jenn rushes out. "You've got to see what they're doing," she says. On the ice, a few lucky fans are participating in a relay race, sponsored by the Einstein's bagel chain, in which they get down on their knees and push a bagel from blueline to blueline.

At last night's game, Bill overheard two guys yakking. "One of them said, 'I think I could play this game, but I can't skate backward,' " he recalls. And the other one said, "Well, that's okay, you don't need to."

The Findlays cheerfully digest these little quirks. Hockey

naiveté aside, those crowds of 6,000-plus speak for themselves—literally. "This is one of the most entertaining, different, wild, crazy arenas I've ever been to," Patty says.

In a way, it's a nice change from Windsor, where 2,000 fans equals 1,000 armchair coaches and 1,000 Don Cherry–wannabes, all eagerly trashing a team of teenagers. Bill could not believe how the Austin fans reacted when the Bats blew that 3–0 lead against the Buzzards. "They're going, 'Okay, get the next goal,' " he says. "Back home it would be 'YOU BUMS!' "

Thanks to Tim and Ryan, the Ice Bats won't be blowing any leads tonight. It's 1–1, and the Austin penalty killers are staring at 80 seconds of five-on-three when Fort Worth is whistled with a makeup call. Seconds later, a Brahmas point man falls down and Findlay is off to the races.

"Skate, Timmy, skate!" Jenn yells. He pops in the shorthanded breakaway, and the whole family slaps five. It's "Timmy" 's 20th goal in 22 games.

Jim Burton says that when he picked up the phone to check in with Patty Findlay the first week of the season, her immediate motherly response was "What's wrong?"

Not to worry, Burty told her. He was absolutely thrilled with both the boys. But don't tell them that. He didn't want their heads to swell. By then, Burton and Patty were old friends. The coach figures he made at least 20 phone calls to both Findlay's and Pawluk's parents in the process of recruiting them. It wasn't just playing salesman, either—he was the one doing the buying.

"I knew they could play hockey, obviously," Burton says. "But the number one thing I look for when I pick up a new kid is what kind of character he is. You kind of get a feel for that when you talk to somebody's parents. I got the feeling they were good kids, and it all went smooth from there."

"I think Patty and I both taught him hard work and perseverance," Bill Findlay says. "Timmy's turned out to be not just a good player, but a good person. He always had a good work ethic."

Work ethic is clearly what sets the boys apart. Like most great athletes, Tim and Ryan do not want to be praised for their God-given talent. The ultimate hockey compliment is "He works hard."

"That's what you want to hear about yourself," Pawluk says. "When you work hard, things start going your way," Findlay says. "You've gotta want to get to the puck. You can't just skate around all day like you're carting eggs."

That's why they both love the corner. They're fast and slippery and reasonably strong, so they come out of it with the rubber most times. As for the other times . . . well, a little bone-crunching never hurt anybody. "I like it," Pawluk says. "I find I get into the game a little more if I get hit real hard or if I run someone real hard."

Working hard also means hours of practice and preparation. Last year in Windsor, Pawluk, then 19, went on a first date with Carol Kennedy, a childhood friend who's five years older than he is. She was rather nonplussed when their evening ended at the stroke of midnight. "He had curfew," she remembers. "He was always really responsible and disciplined. He would never miss curfew for anything."

They still became a couple. This past summer, she played second fiddle to the twice-daily workouts Tim and Ryan did with D. J. Smith, a Windsor teammate and Maple Leafs second-round pick. "In August, he was the hardest person to live with," Carol says. "He ate chicken three times a day."

"It's hard for the girlfriends sometimes because they haven't been in it as long," Patty Findlay says. "They don't understand the concept of having to step aside all the time. The career comes first."

"You have to have confidence in them, and you have to have a lot of support for them, and you have to be willing to stay by their side," Jenn Theriault says. "He might not tell his parents some things that he tells me. Like, if he had a crappy game and was ready to burst into tears."

As Ice Bats, Findlay and Pawluk are often the last guys to leave the ice at morning skates. "Save some for the game," Burty has told them on one or two occasions. It's not a matter of "practice makes perfect" so much as "practice makes you unconscious." They are trying to get to the point where the joints and muscles do things on their own, without the extra microsecond it takes if thinking is involved.

"It's repetition that makes the moves look so easy," Pawluk says.

"You want to get things down to a science so you don't even have to look at the net. NHL players take stuff that we have to think about and turn it into instinct."

One thing they don't have to work on is the awareness of each other. The years of comradeship on and off the ice have formed a near-clairvoyant bond. "I know exactly the way he plays," Findlay says. "Just by looking at him, by how he's skating or whatever, I can tell when he's going to pass the puck and when he's going to shoot, if he's gonna go or if he's gonna pull up."

Findlay was just 10 days old when he saw his first hockey game, one of Dad's senior league matches. Bill says that the first time Tim put on skates as a toddler, he glided right across the ice. "He didn't even realize what he'd done. Then he fell down."

At the age of nine, little Timmy scored 126 goals. That's when the Findlays realized their boy might be one of the lucky few, someone who gets to chase the dream—so long as the family was willing to make it their whole life. "The commitment is staggering," Patty says. "Absolutely staggering. Economically, socially, psychologically. It takes up a lot of your time." Even the player's siblings can't escape it—if they're not on a team themselves, they spend much of their childhood at the rink, feeding quarters into video games and gorging on French fries with the other brothers and sisters.

While Pawluk entered the OHL at an early age, Findlay considered higher education. He was offered a full scholarship to the University of Illinois–Chicago but decided the hockey at UIC was not as good as the OHL (a correct assessment, and also a fortuitous one, as UIC's hockey program folded two years later). Having expressed his collegiate intentions, Findlay had only been an 18th-round pick in the junior draft, but the hometown team took a flyer on him and he worked his way to star status. The next fall, he spent training camp with the Avalanche.

"We talked to him the next day, and he said, 'I couldn't believe it, they had the team meeting and I was in the same room with Forsberg and Wendell Clark!' " Bill remembers.

This is one difference between a young minor league player and a veteran one. Findlay and Pawluk still tell stories about their old teammate Ed Jovanovski. Chris Haskett says that playing against Joe Thornton was the highlight of his hockey career—and that's not likely to change. But you rarely hear Brett Seguin reminisce about taking face-offs against Eric Lindros seven years ago.

"When they first start out, every young boy dreams about being in the National Hockey League," Bill Findlay says. "Timmy still has that dream right now, and things are going exceptionally well. But I think you have to be realistic. This is a tremendous league, but if you're still playing in it when you're 29 years old, then you've kind of missed the bus somewhere." Or ridden it a few too many times.

Tim and Ryan's hunger to get to the next level is their competitive advantage. It fuels their fire on the ice, and hones their dedication off it. Burton has a personal stake in their success, as well as a professional interest in making the Ice Bats–Aeros partnership work. "I stay on them all the time," Burty says. "When they go up I want them to be ready. I can't let them pick up any bad habits."

Above everything else, they have to learn to get the puck deep in the offensive zone, usually by dumping it. If they try to carry the puck all the way through the neutral zone, they'd better not give it up. It's something they can get away with in the WPHL, but not at the next level. "If you do it once, Dave Tippett is gonna reprimand you," Burton tells them, referring to the Houston coach. "You do it twice, you're gonna be in the stands learning how the other guys do it. Then, if you are lucky enough to get back on the ice and you do it a third time, you're in the WPHL again."

"Burty told us he might give it to us every now and again for not doing the little things," Pawluk says. "I was impressed by that."

Even as he teaches, lectures and cajoles, when it comes to crunch time, Burton also makes them feel like heroes.

"He looks me and Finner in the eyes and says, 'Guys, I really need a goal here,'" Pawluk says. "And most times, we've gotten them for him. He shows confidence in us in all situations. That's why I don't want to let him down."

seven

THE IVORY TOWER LINE

The "Cafetorium" at Boone Elementary School is a dozen rows deep with Indian-style seated second graders. Five minutes ago, they were loud and fidgety. Now they hang on Darrin MacKay's every word.

"If we're good listeners today, maybe we'll get a poster," the left winger, in his number 12 practice jersey, says. "Who wants an Ice Bats poster?"

Fifty hands shoot up.

"And if you're not good listeners, well, I just talked to some of the older kids in the hallway. They probably want your poster."

MacKay is the Ice Bats' solo community outreach program. Once a week after practice, he grabs a teammate and conducts assemblies at schools all over Austin, putting on a presentation known as "score."

What's it stand for? The youngsters know. MacKay points to a chalkboard, and the students shout out the acronym in unison.

S! Start by thinking smart.

C! Choose teamwork.

O! Only you can make the right decisions.
R! Respect your body.
E! Every day counts.

MacKay talks to the kids about everything from the importance of a proper breakfast to when you should wear your bicycle helmet (always). Today, Jeremy Thompson is with him, and they put on a skit with the help of a classroom volunteer.

Her name is Lindsay. She wears the goalie mask.

"She's a good goalie," MacKay says, getting a laugh from the room. "I've already seen her play."

MacKay has a little "puck" he made out of used tape at the rink. He and J.T. grab their sticks and go to "net" on a two-on-none. MacKay is carrying the puck.

"I could pass," Darrin says. "But I think I can score. Should I?"

The kids have already sussed out the moral of this story. "PASS!"

"But I think I can score!"

"PASS!"

MacKay shoots anyway. He bungles it.

"Now my coach says to me, 'Darrin, why didn't you pass?' Well, I wanted everyone to cheer for me! But when your teammate is open, you've got to pass."

They go again.

"I think I can score."

PASS!

"But I want you guys to love me!"

PASS!

He takes a flimsy shot, and Lindsay stops the ball of tape with ease.

"Now the fans are saying, 'What's wrong with Darrin tonight?' "

The room titters. One of the kids is also named Darrin.

"Now," MacKay continues, "my coach says, 'You're sitting on the bench. You're not helping the team.' So I sit for a period.

"Then he puts me back in."

This time MacKay slides the puck over to Thompson, who buries the shot.

"Yeah, we scored! And the fans still love me, because the team scored."

MacKay's zeal for education is easy to understand. The youngest of four sons born to Neil, an electrician, and Fern, a nurse, he's the first member of his family to earn a college degree. And not just any degree—he attended Brown University, making him the first Ivy Leaguer in the history of Saltcoats, Saskatchewan, a town of 500 or so near Yorkton, not far from the Manitoba border.

"I didn't even know what the Ivy League was, growing up," MacKay says.

But he knew hockey. The MacKay homestead was just a block from the rink. Sitting at his bedroom window, Darrin could see whether or not the lights were on, a signal to go out and skate on dark winter evenings. Like most eventual pros from similarly tiny towns, he was better than the rest at a very early age. He could just flat-out skate.

"I was so much faster than the other kids that I scored at will," MacKay says. At age six, he was playing with nine-year-olds. Returning to his own age group a few years later, he averaged 10 goals a game. The angry parents of other players suggested he be exiled to a bigger city, a rather impractical demand to make of a 10-year-old.

"And then you have people saying, 'If this kid grows, he's gonna make it to the NHL,' " MacKay says. "I wasn't a small kid, but I was average-sized. So now I'm laying in bed at night praying, 'Oh God, just let me grow.' It was a lot of pressure."

By his early teens, it was time to move on. "The other kids were trying to kill me. It was literally, take a stick and try and knock a leg off if you could. I knew I had to leave home. I also knew that schooling was something I wanted to continue."

MacKay's nickname, "Wiz," referred not just to his wheels, but also to his classroom savvy. "I was doing other kids' homework, stuff like that. For me it was easy." He credits his book-smarts to a childhood watching his brothers study with Fern. As the family squirt, he'd beat the older boys to the answers as a way of getting Mom's attention.

A scholarship became the goal, and staying in Canada was not an option. "Canadian universities don't give full scholarships," MacKay says. "I thought, 'This is no good, I don't have enough money to pay to go to school.' So I told my parents, if I don't get a scholarship, I'm not going to college. Which seems pretty funny to me now."

A coach in Yorkton suggested he get on track for an NCAA program by attending Notre Dame, the second-most-famous sporting institution of that name. The Catholic preparatory school in Wilcox, about an hour south of Regina, provides both rigorous academics and a highly regarded Junior A hockey squad, the Hounds.

He was 15. If he already had some idea the NHL wasn't in his future, that first visit to the Notre Dame dressing room drove the point straight home. He weighed 155 pounds. Most of the other kids were at least 180, 190. And the "other kids" had names like Rod Brind'Amour, Curtis Joseph, Scott Pellerin and Mitch Messier (a cousin of Mark who starred for Michigan State and in the IHL).

"I was lucky enough to be there with all that talent," MacKay remembers. "We had the best team in Canada for three years. Nineteen guys got U.S. scholarships."

His feelings were not so magnanimous back then. "It was tough. Not only was it tough to leave my family, but all of a sudden, I wasn't the star anymore. It was pretty hard on my confidence. I didn't know how to play on a team. Before, I just took the puck and scored all the time."

He adjusted. "Everybody was saying to me, 'Where did you learn to skate like this? You're lightning,'" MacKay says. "I realized, okay, there are a lot of great players, and I'm not gonna make it to the NHL, but we all have our assets. Mine was skating." He put his speed to use as a penalty-killer and checking-line forward, earning his way onto the school's top squad for three straight years.

His Notre Dame experience got him to Brown. Ironically, Ivy League universities don't offer full athletic scholarships either. But they provide need-based assistance, and if the team wants you, that eases the process considerably. MacKay got the financial aid he required and double-majored in business economics and organizational behavior management. He graduated in four years.

Only thing is, his hockey experience wasn't great. He did well in his freshman and sophomore seasons, then fell out of favor with the coach, ending his college career on a sour note. To get the taste out, he joined a minor pro team in Moorhead, Minnesota. But that team's league went out of business two months into its first season.

MacKay migrated to Chicago, entering the real world with a position at a bank. In the course of playing pick-up games and men's league, he became friendly with one of the area's most famous rink rat families, the Granatos. MacKay dated U.S. women's Olympic hockey star Cammi for a year or so. He also landed a job as head coach of the varsity hockey team at suburban Barrington High, where the rink had chicken wire topping off the boards and players got dropped off for practice in Lexus coupes and BMW roadsters.

The other high school bench bosses, in their late 30s or early 40s, viewed him with suspicion. Chicago is a hockey town, a blue-collar city with an Original Six franchise. But those coaches couldn't possibly realize how much of the game had embedded itself in this particular 23-year-old's brain and blood.

"It was fun," MacKay says. "Our team didn't have a lot of talent, but we had a lot of heart. I stressed that. Our first year, we were 11th out of 12 teams in the league. Our second year we were fifth." The highlight was an upset victory over the defending state champions, a rival Barrington hadn't beaten in more than 15 years.

An opportunity arose to play in Norway, so MacKay went over as an import. Each day before practice, the guys had jobs at Taberna Ramme, a local picture-frame factory where the full-time workers blasted techno music at seven in the morning. MacKay got to be the player he'd been at 15 again, thriving on the wide-open European rinks, tearing up the league with offense.

It was a good way to go out. At the end of the season he went to Calgary, taking a job in commercial real estate. It was time to put that degree to use. "As I got on with my hockey career, the fact that I did go to a good school was gaining more significance," he says.

Fate intervened. In August 1996, Mitch Messier, his brother Joby and another former Notre Dame player named Jeff Batters were in a car wreck. Batters died, and Mitch Messier suffered career-ending injuries. The accident happened while the Canadian

World Cup squad was in Calgary, preparing for the September tournament with an exhibition against the Russian squad. Many of MacKay's Notre Dame comrades were there, grieving together. "It was the first time I ever had to deal with something like that," MacKay remembers. "I was in shock. And I thought, life's too short. I wasn't really happy with my job, and I knew I could still play. I had some buddies who were going to play in Waco. I thought, when am I ever gonna get a chance to live in Texas? When will I ever again have the ability to just pick up and go play?"

He had a good year for the Wizards, scoring 21 goals, 11 of them against the Bats. He also lit the lamp twice in the WPHL All-Star game. "I'm not so naive as to think I would have made All-Star if our coach hadn't been the coach for our division," he says. "But it was nice to go out and score a couple—to really feel that I could play in the game."

"My whole experience has been a lot of finding out about myself," MacKay continues. "You might not always fulfill the ultimate dream, but you can still be pretty happy with what you've done. I'll never play a game in the NHL. But there's a million kids that would kill to be in my skates on any given night at the Bat Cave. I'm totally genuine when I say to people, 'I'm the luckiest guy in the world.' "

Back at Boone Elementary, MacKay has asked for another volunteer to demonstrate hockey pads, which he'll use to draw parallels with bike helmets and seat belts. The kids are pretty worked up by now, buzzing loudly, hands waving in the air.

"I thought we had to be quiet to pick somebody," MacKay says.

The room goes still. "I do all the policing," MacKay had told the teachers at the beginning of the hour. They probably wish he'd come in and handle their classrooms on a regular basis. Or maybe just handle them—a few of the single teachers have sent him e-mails after the assemblies.

Now Darrin is remembering his own second-grade days, like the time he told his mother he was sick and stayed home from school. "I watched cartoons all day, my mom made my favorite food, I had the greatest time. Then the next day I get to class. Guess what we had that day?"

"A TEST!"

"And guess who didn't know what was on the test."

"YOU DIDN'T!"

"I knew what was on TV the day before, but I didn't know what was on the test. And you know what? I used to love getting A's on tests. I always tried to get a hundred percent. But I failed that test, because I made a bad decision to stay home and watch TV.

"Could you imagine if someone stayed home today when they weren't really sick? They wouldn't get a poster, they wouldn't meet some Ice Bats. So next time, when we're not really sick, are we gonna stay home or are we gonna go to class?"

"GO TO CLASS!"

Rob Hartnell says that when it was his turn to do a visit, Darrin's rap got him so riled up that he was unconsciously screaming along with the kids, and putting his hand up during calls for volunteers.

The presentation is almost finished. "There's about 180 school days in every year, right?" MacKay says. "And we work hard every day to accomplish our goal, which is to pass the class, right?

"Well, some days aren't good. On the Ice Bats, sometimes we lose our game. And we're disappointed, just like you're disappointed if you don't do well on a test. But do we give up?"

"NO!"

"No. We go back the next day and we say, 'Okay, I'm disappointed that we lost that game last night, but I'm gonna work hard today and we're gonna do better on the next one.' So when I say that every day counts, we have to realize that some days, we're gonna have setbacks. We're not gonna be happy about everything. But we can't give up. We've always got to do our best, try our hardest, and at the end of the year, we'll pass. We'll accomplish our goals.

"One last thing. I've been going to a lot of schools this year. And one of the best questions I've been asked is, 'What is your favorite part of hockey?' So I thought for a second, and I thought, well, it sure is fun to score a goal, right? You get all excited, and people cheer for you.

"But you know what my favorite part is? My favorite part is the friends I make. With all the teams I've played on, it's the friends I've made that make me the happiest."

MacKay is one of the players who hopes to take advantage of Binnie's absence. He has yet to put one in the net this season. There have been close calls, and he's taken the odd shift on a scoring line with Findlay and Pawluk, but mostly he's settled into the defensive role he mastered at Notre Dame. Hidden behind a half-visor, MacKay is a grim presence on the penalty kill, a square-jawed grunt with a long, poke-checking blade, scurrying between the point man and the half-boards to cut off passes, squatting down and springing up to discourage shots without leaving his feet.

The guy who really needs to send a thank-you note Binnie's way is Keith Moran. He sheepishly admits that while Troy was shedding tears and everyone else moped around in confusion, his first thought was, "I'm in the lineup."

The night before Binnie retired, Moran appeared in just his second game of the season. He made the most of it, beating El Paso goalie Chris Gordon to a loose puck after a blueline face-off. With Gordon far in front of the crease, Moran scythed the rubber into a half-empty net. Celebrating, he slid into the corner on his knees, crashing jubilantly into the boards, then bouncing up the glass to "hug" the fans.

"My 'Lambeau Leap,'" Moran says, paying homage to the Green Bay Packers' practice of jumping into the end-zone stands. "I've been dying to play a home game. It's a lot easier to play when the fans are cheering for you."

Like MacKay, Moran's a college boy. But their backgrounds and experiences diverge wildly from there. Moran is from Reading, Massachusetts, a suburb 15 miles north of Boston. The area is a hockey hotbed, with organized high school leagues serving the same function as juniors for such NHL stars as Mike Grier, Tony Amonte and Jeremy Roenick. When Moran was a freshman, an older player named Keith Tkachuck worked part-time at the Dunkin' Donuts near his house.

There was never any doubt Moran would go to college. Now that he's graduated, the only question in the minds of his traditional Irish Catholic New England family is, 'Why aren't you in law school yet?' Or, at the very least, getting work experience before applying for his MBA. Moran's father, Jim, is a financial analyst, and his older siblings, one brother and one sister, are also in the business world.

"I'm sure if you talk to a lot of guys on the team, their parents are encouraging them," Moran says. "They're wondering how they're doing, how's hockey going? My dad was my biggest supporter in college. But now he's kind of standoffish. He's not sure why I'm down here."

After all those nights as a healthy scratch, Moran might ask the same question. But he already knows the answer. He is on a quest, and it's about the journey, not the destination. His liberal arts education has served him well.

"It's encouraged me to explore things," Moran says. "Life isn't all about getting good grades so you can get a good job. Hockey is kind of a life experience for me right now. I have no misconceptions in terms of my ability, or how high I could actually get. I just want to see what it can bring me."

Really, Moran is having the same postcollege "lost year" that many students take advantage of. But instead of joining the Peace Corps or backpacking through Thailand, he's lugging a CCM bag around Texas and Louisiana. When the season ends, he plans to spend six months in Europe. "Then I'll get back into the corporate world and join the rat race. I'm 23 years old right now. When I'm 25, I'll still have 40 years to work."

Moran's college was Holy Cross, a small Catholic university that plays in the same hockey conference as the Ivy League schools. He spent his first two seasons as an offensive defenseman, then moved to forward. "I dislike defense now," he says. His last two seasons, he averaged more than a point per game at center.

When Moran decided to go pro, friends and teammates suggested he get an agent. "So I asked them, 'Well, what do they do?' " he says. "And they said, 'Well, they put a résumé together for you, and they contact all these teams, and they cost about four or five hundred dollars.' I said, 'I can do that myself.' "

He worked the fax machine, sending his info to every team in the East Coast and Central leagues. A few had seen him at the East Coast Athletic Conference All-Star game, which he played in his senior year. Ultimately, he attended training camp in Birmingham,

Alabama, home of the ECHL Bulls, where the player/assistant coach was a friend.

Moran appeared in three exhibition games, hanging on to a spot while nearly every other rookie was released. Then, on the first day of the season, he went to morning skate and discovered Cincinnati, the Bulls' IHL parent, had sent down a passel of players. He was done.

"So it's a Tuesday, and I'm at the team hotel in Birmingham and I have no place to go," Moran remembers. "Every team I called had finalized their roster. I was going to drive home, but I thought, what's the point of that? I knew I was good enough, and there were plenty of leagues. I figured I'd be able to hook on with another team."

At this point, an agent might have come in handy: 72 hours passed without a nibble.

"Now it's Friday morning, and the hotel, where I'm also getting three meals a day, tells me I have to check out at noon. I have an hour to decide what to do with my life."

Moran forestalled that crossroads for at least a weekend, driving to New Orleans to hang out in the French Quarter with friends from home. Then he decided to swing through Austin, where his uncle, John Powers, is a vice-president at Dell Computer. When Moran had called the Bats earlier in the week, Burty had told him he liked his team the way it was.

Moran called again anyway. "I said, listen, I'm in New Orleans and I'm going to drive to my aunt and uncle's. If I come, will you give me an opportunity to skate? I figured originally he said no because he thought he was going to have to fly me down. But I knew that if I came and he saw me play, he'd have to make a decision. Over the phone he didn't have to.

"I had a great weekend with my friends in New Orleans, I got to Austin on Tuesday, skated Wednesday and Burty's like, 'Great, we're going on the road for eight days tomorrow.' Before I knew it, I was on the bus."

Having relatives in town has made it easier for Moran to endure the uncertainty of his last two months. "They only moved out here four years ago, so it's not like, 'distant aunt and uncle in Texas,' " he says. "They'd been in Boston my entire life, a few miles

down the road. So it's real family. That offers a lot of support." Instead of living at the Quality Inn until the team gets him perma-
nent digs, Moran is staying at Uncle John and Aunt Eleanor's, a
definite upgrade—over the team apartments, too.

Whether he's in the stands or on the ice, being a Bat is everything Moran had hoped. "I grew up around all middle- to upper-
class white Catholic kids," he says. "And college was even more of
that. It's kind of sad. You get isolated in that world and you don't
get to see how the other half lives. So just playing with kids that
haven't grown up with 'Okay, you'll go to high school, then you'll go
to college' is different. There are kids on our team that haven't
finished high school, kids where hockey has dominated their lives.
It's been an eye-opening experience."

Of course, hockey itself also has its charms. "You put so much
into it," Moran says. "In no other sport is there such a drain, where
you're out for one minute and you can't go any more, your legs just
burn and you go, 'Okay, I gotta stop.'

"I don't know why I'm so in love with this game . . . why my
children will play it, and I'll encourage them," he adds. "I guess it's
because I've gotten so much out of it. It's such a passionate game."

BY THE TIME SHREVEPORT returns to town in early December,
Moran doesn't have to worry about whether there's a job for him.
There are four.

Jeremy Thompson has a broken thumb. Mike Jackson's got an
achy hip. Ryan Pawluk has been called up to Houston. And Brad
Wingfield never made it to Austin. The Bats were able to nix the
Binnie deal before the WPHL finalized it.

"We felt that if there was a chance Troy could come back at the
end of the year, we'd be willing to take it," Jim Burton tells the
press. Unofficially, Burty knows the club has alienated Binnie to
the point that he's unlikely to return. The important thing is,
Binnie won't be able to embarrass Austin in a Central Texas uniform. Word has also leaked out that Stoughton tried to get Central
Texas to do the deal without informing them of Binnie's plans,
though it's doubtful such a transaction would have survived league
scrutiny.

The atmosphere for the Mudbugs' second visit is not quite as taut. The crowd is sparser, with the San Antonio delegation in single digits. But the game is no less crucial. The Bats are in the thick of a four-game, four-night gauntlet, a schedule that cuts down on travel costs, maximizes weekend home dates and absolutely kills the players. Tonight the team will overnight it eight hours to Monroe for a Saturday evening game. Then the Moccasins will join the Bats in retracing the route to Austin for a 3 p.m. Sunday game.

The Bats got one point at home last night—another shootout loss—and anything could happen Sunday, so this is the home game Burton and his players really need, especially since the Mudbugs have a three-point hold on first.

A little big-time flavor is provided by Asleep at the Wheel, probably the most famous national anthem performers ever to grace the Bat Cave. However, Ray Benson and Co.'s dandy four-part harmonies don't exactly provide Kate Smith–level inspiration. As with the first game, Shreveport flies around the ice early, taking a 2–0 lead after one.

"Been here before, been here before," Rob Hartnell says in the locker room during the first break.

Burty is not so even-keeled.

"Does anybody think we can't win this game?" he says.

It could be the start of a rousing pep talk. It's not. Well, not exactly.

"If you don't, I'll play two lines and three D," the coach continues. "Because some people in this room are playing like they don't think we can win.

"This is our fucking rink. Play our game. Be aggressive. Get your chances and bury them."

Tonight, Moran and MacKay are joined on the checking line by Keith O'Brien. A defensive specialist who plays bigger than his five-foot-nine size, O'Brien works full-time for a local software company. He joined the team in training camp, setting himself up as an on-call reinforcement, someone Burty can move on and off the roster whenever he needs an extra body.

O'Brien delivers a nice crunch early, going head-to-head with Jim Sprott, one of the WPHL's bigger, more experienced defensemen. "I'm too old for knee-to-knee contact," Sprott grunts after the collision.

"O.B." takes off his boots between periods to give his feet a rest. He can't really practice with the team or do as much skating as he'd like on his own, so he's at a disadvantage conditioning-wise. It's also a mental challenge, getting focused and in a hockey frame of mind with little advance notice. Sometimes O'Brien will hear from Burton the day before a game; other times he only has five or six hours' warning.

Fortunately, his job is simple. "Just hit your guy and make it four on four," Andy Ross tells him.

One thing is certain: the MacKay/Moran/O'Brien trio is the best-educated line in the minors. O'Brien grew up in Belmont, Massachusetts, coming of age in the same hockey universe as the other Keith. Then he went to Princeton, where he played hockey for the Tigers and wrote his senior thesis on gambling:

"I talk about how it's changed from something that was looked upon as immoral 40 years ago into something that's a leisure activity," O'Brien says. "Now people set aside money for the entertainment aspects of it." If he ever gets to go on a Louisiana road trip, O'Brien can write a sequel about his teammates.

Keith was preceded at Princeton by his older brother, Sean, who was a senior when he was a freshman. That meant they got to play together for one season, and having two boys at the same school improved the family's overall financial-aid scenario. To cover the rest of his expenses, O'Brien opened up an on-campus video store. He knew most of his classmates were either too rich, too busy or too lazy to worry about late charges. "They rent a movie, then they don't return it for three weeks." The business also came in handy on those 10-hour road trips to Plattsburgh.

Sean, four inches taller, 30 pounds heavier and just a little more ornery than Keith, carved out a niche for himself at the AAA level, first with the Utah Grizzlies of the IHL and then with the Philadelphia Phantoms of the AHL. Keith was tempted to follow in his brother's footsteps, but after making a list of the various pros and cons of hockey, he decided against it. He knew he wouldn't have the same opportunities Sean did, a reality that had not only athletic ramifications, but also financial ones. AHL stalwarts might seem like paupers compared with Chris Pronger, or even Jody Hull, but they make a nice living by most white-collar standards. AA salaries are dicier. O'Brien chose to be a pragmatist.

"If I was going to devote my time just to hockey, I'd want the opportunity to improve, to get a call-up to the next level," he says. "With my size and a couple of other factors I didn't think it would happen. And I knew going to the workforce from minor league hockey, you really have to know the right people. They have to have the right attitude about athletes in order for you to get in the door at major companies."

Whereas PC Order, a start-up at the vanguard of Austin's dot.com boom, had no qualms about a freshly minted Princeton grad. O'Brien interviewed with the company on campus, and after accepting the job, Bill Underwood, a scout in the Philadelphia area, suggested he check in with the Bats. When teams at this level get hit with injuries or suspensions, it's not easy to get new players. It costs money to fly them in and house them, and you don't always want to keep them under contract. A guy like O'Brien, Underwood reasoned, could come in handy.

That's exactly how it's turned out. O.B. made his mark in training camp by fighting in the second exhibition game. The players accept him, and don't even ride him much about only practicing on weekends, when the sessions are usually low-impact game-day skates. "It's not like I don't want to be there," O'Brien says.

Burty is glad to have him. When O.B. is in the stands, the coach uses him as an extra set of eyes, bringing him into the locker room between periods. "He's always asking me what's going on," O'Brien says. "What do you see? What can we do differently? Just little hockey things."

"He's an intelligent player," Burton says. "He got great coaching at Princeton, and he's a fireball out there."

The only person who really rides Keith is Gunner, which just means he's truly part of the team. "What are you doing here, stickboy?" the equipment manager says any time he shows up for a game.

O'Brien's PC Order colleagues give him a harder time. When the Bats lose, he has to hear about it all day long. Some co-workers bodycheck him. "Seriously," O'Brien says. "I'll just be walking down the hall, and someone will come from around the corner and knock me into the wall." They—and the drywall—are lucky O.B. doesn't hit back.

People are always asking O'Brien how he manages to balance work and hockey. The way he sees it, he's got it easy compared with what his parents went through, balancing *their* work with hockey.

"I don't know how they did it," he says. "They went to every game. They'd drive down to Princeton, which is about a four-hour trip. They'd drive to Colgate or Clarkson or wherever we were playing. They drove unbelievable amounts of miles, and that's just when I was in college, never mind when I was growing up and getting up at five in the morning every day. And then all the money—unbelievable."

His one hope for his current hockey "career" is that he might get into a game with enough advance notice that his parents can fly down to see it.

Too bad they aren't here tonight. Burton's motivational tactics are on target, as Findlay makes it 2–1 early in the second and Andy Ross slaps one home on a 5-on-3 to make it 2–2 10 minutes later. Meanwhile, Erickson shuts the door, turning aside an uncontested breakaway and everything else the Mudbugs hit him with.

It's still 2–2 early in the third period when O'Brien skates up left wing and jumbles with defenseman Cory Keenan in the neutral zone. He poke-checks the puck toward center, and it ends up as a blueline entry pass for MacKay. With one D-man still occupied, Mac has Moran all alone in the slot. Moran waits at the doorstep for a beat, gets St. Pierre to commit and pops the puck in high off the right post. It'll take another 12 minutes (plus a full-on brawl at the buzzer), but the guys with the sheepskins have given the Bats their biggest win of the season.

"That was the most fun in a game I've had in a couple of years," O'Brien says in the locker room. "I was just trying to play the body, 'cause the fans love hits. I ended up knocking the puck away, and I was still wrestling with the guy when Keith scored."

Paul Lawless ducks his head in. "Best fucking game you guys played all year," he says.

The players are on a cloud. They're pleased to have pulled out the win despite the early hole and the crucial absences. Pumped and cheering for themselves, they crank up the boombox and re-live every big hit and bigger play as if the game hadn't just ended five minutes ago.

This particular victory was meaningful, passionate and greatly needed. The season-opening winning streak was fun, but those early games were fluffy and unreal. Now the team has been through some stuff. It's the heart of the schedule.

What's gone unnoticed amidst the various distractions and per-sonnel changes is that the team is doing even better now than it did in October. Because of the shootout losses, it hasn't always felt like it, but the Bats have strung together a fairly remarkable 12-game unbeaten streak. The team is 8–0–4 since that 6–0 thumping by Fort Worth.

"That's right," Burty says. "Nobody says anything about it, but we haven't lost in a month. We're playing well. I'm real happy with everything."

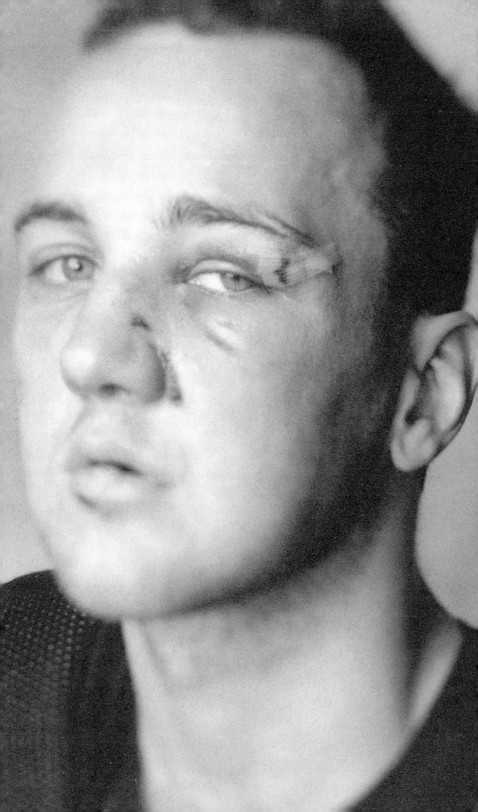

eight

FORECHECK. BACKCHECK. PAYCHECK.

MIKE JACKSON has never been so happy to be hurt. He's perched comfortably in the stands, a cast on one arm, watching his healthy teammates play party to an incredible hockey atrocity.

If the Bats were struggling to keep a guy in front on the power play, Jake would feel guilty about his absence. If Waco's defensemen were running Tim Findlay, he'd fume from a distance. But the horror that's before him has nothing to do with the game itself.

It's the sweaters.

Minor league hockey was churning out gimmick jerseys long before the NHL allowed its teams to create a third one. It's another way to kick up revenue, though in most cases the game-worn shirts are auctioned off for charity after one-time use, generally on a holiday. One February 14, the Indianapolis Ice, then of the IHL, wore pink, with red hearts.

Those Indy players must have looked a cross between Bobby Baun and Marty McSorley compared with the Bats, who are apparently moonlighting as chorus boys in Radio City Music Hall's annual Christmas Spectacular. The solid red–bodied jersey is festooned around the middle with a wide, gold-buckled "belt" that bears the words "Happy Holidays." The red socks, secured with several wraps of white tape, look like misshapen candy canes. On the back, the players' names are spelled out in fuzzy, slanted, wreathy-green letters.

Best of all is the long, white, V-shaped blob that starts at the collar and continues down the belly. This particular design innovation is meant to be Santa Claus's beard. (Little-known fact: Santa's beard began life as a hockey playoff goatee. He'll shave it off when the Leafs win the Stanley Cup.)

Between periods, Jackson is asked to join a couple of Ice Bats significant-others at the auction table, where they are modeling the garment.

"I'm not wearing those things," he grunts. "It looks better on the girls."

The Bats win 6–4 despite a night of embarrassing trash talk. Truth is, the Wizards don't have a leg to stand on when it comes to sartorial slams—every road game they wear turquoise, purple and pink unis with a cartoon character on the chest.

Afterward, Kyle Haviland makes his way past the usual crush of young admirers at the dressing room door. "I like those jerseys," one 10-year-old says.

"I don't know about that," Havs replies, trying to be polite.

Others are less diplomatic. "I'm never fucking wearing that again," one player offers.

He won't have to. The sweaters sell quickly. Findlay's and Pawluk's rake in the most cash—one thousand dollars each from Maggie's Heart of Texas, a local Dodge dealer that's one of the team's major corporate sponsors.

As December wears on, style points are not the only thing the Bats could use a little more of. Suddenly, points in the standings are hard to come by, too. The Monroe home-and-home ended the unbeaten streak. The Bats held on for one more night, dropping yet another shootout in Louisiana, but the next afternoon in Austin, it looked like only one team had a grueling bus ride. While the Bats were bumping along backroads for a 7 A.M.

arrival, the Moccasins left town at four in the morning on a sleeper coach, each player relaxing like a rock star in his individual bunk.

The search for bodies continues. Reinforcements, including a highly touted former Windsor teammate of Findlay and Pawluk, aren't expected until New Year's. On the night of the Christmas sweaters, owner Paul Lawless tries to be a finger in the dike. "Lawly," who could still be the team's best player if health and conditioning were not a factor, rifles a goal from the slot early in the game. Later, he goes after former Bat Chris O'Rourke, resulting in an attempted-spearing double-minor. Lawless protests the call, but his teammates figure taking the penalty was just his way of taking the final minutes off—"pulling the 'chute," as the saying goes. He never plays another game.

Thus the Bats travel to Shreveport with five defensemen and eight forwards. Thompson and Jackson are out. Haviland is suspended. O'Brien isn't available. Binnie's roster spot is still vacant. And the owners aren't interested in picking up a veteran salary to spell the injured reservists.

What's more, two of the so-called healthy Bats are in less than tip-top shape. Already bothered by an elbow that's chased him from the face-off circle, Brett Seguin is also playing with a brutally bruised-up backside. He was going hard in practice the other day, flying around on a brand-new pair of Tacks, when he ran into an open bench door.

"He shouldn't even skate," Andy Ross says.

Minor league teams used to dress 20 guys, just like the NHL. But that made it easy for coaches to send out unrepentantly goonish fourth lines, so rosters were trimmed. Ross has been around these low-budget cowboy leagues long enough that a game with 13 skaters is nothing new for him. "We'll play two lines, go into a defensive shell, barely even forecheck," he says.

Ryan Pawluk is the other addition to the corps of walking wounded. He's recovering from a crowd-surfing accident. At a recent Our Lady Peace concert, a charged-up Pawluk was floating high above the moshers when someone in the pit failed to pull his weight. The dreaded chasm opened, and Pawluk crash-landed on the club floor, which, being a club floor, was strewn with broken beer bottles. By the time they got him safely back to the apartment, Findlay, Andy Ross and Todd Harris all had blood on their clothes.

Pawluk will survive a couple of off-ice gashes no problem. But on the hockey front, his wrists are banged to hell. Kelly Cunningham, the team doctor, thinks he developed tendinitis in Windsor. This year, with everyone hacking him, it's worse.

"He doesn't complain about it," Burton says.

"He's 20," the Doc replies.

Pawluk sits down with trainer Eric Seeber to get taped up extra-tight. He will ice his wrists between periods, and maybe even between shifts.

Watching Eric work, Gunner Garrett marvels at his patience. "In my day I'd just tell 'em, 'Go whine to your agent,' " Gunner says. The equipment manager walks the walk—one night, he slashed his finger on the skate sharpener and stood there quietly with a towel in his hand while Seeber finished up what he was doing at the time.

Burton and the abbreviated Bats squad know they've got a long night ahead. "Get all the whistles you can," the coach says in the locker room. "Let's play within ourselves, play an old-fashioned road game. Short shifts. Don't waste too much energy."

"Give it all we've got, boys," Chad Erickson bellows. "If it ain't enough, it ain't enough. But let's give it."

It ain't enough. Though a 1–0 lead should energize Austin, it only seems to make Shreveport faster and meaner. By the end of the first period the Mudbugs lead 3–1, with a 20–9 shots-on-goal advantage. The Bats go into the locker room on a power play, but no one's feeling good about it.

"That was godawful," Gunner says. "They left their balls in the dressing room."

There are two ways to respond to the situation—gut it out, or let the hopelessness feed upon itself. Burty stands in the arena hallway, smoking and brooding while the players stew. He comes into the room when the break is almost over.

"I have a plan," he says, grinning sheepishly. "Four-on-four hockey."

He wants the team to play a left-wing lock. But instead of the winger simply cutting off a portion of the ice, he will shadow a single player. It's the same role Keith O'Brien played against the Mudbugs in Austin.

"I don't care where he goes—if he gets a shot, it's your fault," Burty says. "He doesn't go beyond the dots. Lock onto him and take him out of the play."

Seguin is in genuine agony, so Burton will roll Hartnell/Ross and Pawluk/Findlay as two lines, rotating three different left wings for the dirty work.

"Get this power play goal and we're right back in it," Burton says.

Phase One accomplished. Ross skates to the heart of the slot and slaps one in with just six seconds left in the advantage. Then the designated hookers/holders go to work. The idea is to take Shreveport's best player on any given line out of the game, while limiting the other forwards to low-quality chances. The strategy also invites the Mudbugs blueliners to join the rush.

Cue Phase Two. Cory Fletcher blocks a shot and Tim Findlay is able to get it past a pinching defenseman to Pawluk. Pawlzy goes in two-on-one with Chris Haskett, who draws the remaining defender. Pawluk cradles the puck a good six or seven seconds before picking a spot past St. Pierre. The crowd goes mute.

"I was looking to pass the whole time because I can't even grip the stick," Pawluk tells reporters later. "I couldn't even tie my fucking shoes—oh sorry, my shoes—this morning. But the defenseman decided to go to Hasky."

At the break, the Mudbugs have 41 shots to Austin's 14. But it's 3–3. The visitors' locker room brims with confidence.

"If we win this one, we might even get an hour at the casino," Darrin MacKay says, punning the word, pronouncing it "ca-sin-o."

MacKay and Haskett commiserate about how tough it is keeping up with Brandy Semchuk, a veteran Bug who was once a second-round NHL pick, selected by the L.A. Kings just before the Rangers took Doug Weight.

"He's got wheels, eh?" MacKay says. "I took three goals away from that guy."

The customary yell goes up: "Twenty miles to go!"

"We're gonna get this done," Rob Hartnell says. "Let's go out and get another three or four shots!"

Burty makes his entrance. "Okay, guys . . ."

"Got another plan, coach?" Erickson teases.

He does, sort of. He wants the left wing to push off his man down low and help out on offense. The Bugs will be taking chances for the lead, so Austin will too.

Shreveport cracks first. Chris Morque and Rob Hartnell break an odd-man rush. Hartnell's slap shot caroms off St. Pierre and right to Ross trailing in the slot. It's 4–3 Austin.

When the Bats go on a power play minutes later, life is truly grand. But seconds after the face-off, referee Scott Hughes whistles Tim Findlay, of all people, for hooking Jim Sprott, who tumbles to the ice convincingly. It's Findlay's second penalty—of the year.

"I mean, c'mon," Findlay says later. "I just wouldn't do that in that situation."

During the game, Gunner pleads Finner's case. The equipment manager is in touch with his emotions and has no trouble expressing them. "I called Hughes every name in the book," he admits.

For Gunner's troubles, the Shreveport PA man gets to make the following announcement: "The Austin team trainer has been given a game misconduct."

Gunner watches the rest of the action from the stands. The Bats survive the four-on-four. But Shreveport is biding time. Eventually, its greater numbers and fresher legs pay off. Erickson's been spectacular, but he can only do so much. Finally, he stops a slap shot, sprawls successfully for the second attempt and is helpless when the weary Bats allow a third one.

For the fourth time tonight, ceremonial mudbugs litter the ice. It's a beautiful scheme—the fans buy little red plastic ones for a dollar, then indirectly return them to the merchandise stand to be sold again, ad infinitum. Perhaps that—rather than the mess and the stink—is the reason Shreveport officials are trying to stop folks from tossing real crawfish as well.

"Score enough goals and we'll have a boil before too long," the locker room security guard drawls.

Regulation ends at 4–4. Needless to say, the Bats lose the shootout, their seventh overtime defeat of the season. But it's a point in the standings and, all things considered, a huge moral victory. The final shots on goal are Mudbugs 60, Ice Bats 17.

THE NEXT STOP is Monroe. A good plan, as the home of the Moccasins is just 70 miles east of Shreveport. Yet this is the only time all season the Bats will visit both cities on the same trip.

Monroe's Guest House Inn has a 24-hour greasy spoon that's right up there with Denny's or Waffle House, except it's not a chain, so you can't be sure what you're gonna get. "It'll be good to see Flo and Alice and the girls at the diner," Andy Ross deadpans.

The motel, located 500 yards from the civic center, just under a freeway overpass, is everything you'd expect from minor league hockey accommodations . . . in 1975. The lights in the rooms are controlled by a metal panel in the wall, three switches lined up under a tiny white bulb, long since burned out, with a "call front desk" notation. Several players share quarters with unwelcome insects. The lodging charge is 28 bucks, the breakfast buffet $3.95.

Tonight, Rob Hartnell can't afford it. After an incredible $1,200 blackjack performance in Lake Charles two weeks ago (on the heels of a hat trick in the game, no less), Hartsy leaves the Bossier City–Shreveport Harrah's $300 poorer.

Yes, as Darrin MacKay predicted, the effort against the Mudbugs was enough to get the team a little playtime. Even with a game tomorrow, the trip to Monroe is short, and as usual, Burton wants to try his luck as much as anyone. In fact, he's the reason why—as Gunner is quick to gripe—the midnight bus doesn't leave until 12:30.

"Coach got hot," one player explains.

"How hot?" another asks.

Burty enters the vehicle.

"Ten hundies," he reports. "Enough to pay Gunner's fine."

The coach is kidding about the amount, but not the punishment—players who get misconducts have to contribute to a locker room kitty, and Gunner is no exception.

"The whole bench just deflated when he got tossed," Burty cracks. "That was the turning point of the game." For the next 24 hours, Garrett cannot say a word without someone yelling: "Shut up and pay your fine, Gunner."

The next day at the civic center, it's another busy pregame session for Eric Seeber. Tonight, Brett Seguin will rest. "If he's out there, I'll be tempted to play him," Burton says. The center lies on a wooden trainer's table, two bags of ice tucked into his sweatpants. His rear is completely purple, like two miniature versions of *Charlie and the Chocolate Factory*'s Violet Beauregarde—big old blueberries.

"It feels like I'm laying on a water balloon," Seguin says.

"How do you take a shit?" one teammate wants to know.

"I can almost sit on my left cheek," is the response.

"We're keeping him loaded with Immodium so he doesn't have to," Seeber offers.

Chad Erickson stops by to check on his buddy. "What's wrong with this picture?" the goalie says. He suggests that if Brett is going to spend the night lying around buckets of ice, he may as well have a few beers.

"He'll probably end up in the stands," Chad says. "Someone will come down and say, 'Hey, there's this incoherent fat bald guy passed out up here. Is he one of yours?'"

Andy Ross also visits. Like everyone else, he's exhausted from the previous two nights. Seguin is the lucky one. "I don't want to play tonight," Ross says.

"Just put it on net, even from the redline," Seguin suggests.

"But what about my shooting percentage?" Ross retorts. He's kidding. Ross may not be pumped for this evening's muckfest, but he's never been on a team this high in the standings this late in the season—and it isn't that late. Roscoe thinks they'll have a championship club when a few guys get healthy and the new ones come in.

The game plan for tonight is the same as at Shreveport. "Just know which guy the winger has so you don't have to worry about him," Burty says.

"Give 'em a little bit of their own medicine," he adds. Burton considers the Mocs to be the worst clutch-and-grabbers in the league. He had already planned to use this system here, regardless of what happened in Shreveport.

"Hey Eric, got any gum?" Burty says as they approach the rink door. He knows that Seeber does—but it's his nightly ritual to ask. It's also Eric's job to catch Burton if he slips on the ice while walking to the bench. Tonight, the lights are already down for the pregame, so everyone stays close to the boards.

Not counting the goalies, there are seven guys on the bench and five on the ice. That's it. The Monroe players must be thinking, "Where's the rest of the team?"

I, on the other hand, view the team's trimmed-down ranks as an opportunity. I've been waiting for a chance to spend an evening on the bench, taking in an ice-level, player's-eye view of the sights, sounds and (ugh!) smells of hockey. Suddenly, there is space available.

Despite the aforementioned stench—a putrid, dirty-sock-infused cocktail of sweat and body oil, gestating in a vacuum of lousy ventilation and hot/cold/hot/cold temperature—I know I have to take advantage of this opportunity. After all, that is what you do in hockey—take advantage of your opportunities. (You also avoid mistakes, capitalize on your chances and "finish" things—checks, plays, drinks).

I knew the Shreveport game was too important to allow for my scribbling distraction. But another yawner against Monroe? No problem. All Burty requires is that I dress the part. Unfortunately, I've not thought to bring along a suit and tie, so I can't play pretend assistant coach. Instead, I borrow Mark Martello's warm-ups and blend in with Eric and Gunner. Eric even lets me throw a couple of towels the boys' way.

I haven't filled up more than a few lines of my notebook when the linesman and several players deliver an urgent "Heads-up!" By the time their warning registers, the wayward puck has already whizzed past my head and over the glass. Like ESPN's Steve Levy says about a goaltender facing his first shot, I was "in the hockey game."

The players talk to themselves and yell at guys on the ice just like fans, except with less profanity (okay, that part's a lie). There's lots of *C'mon boys!* and *Here we go, here we go.* Whenever an odd-man rush unfolds, everyone yells out how many attackers the team has up in the play—*Three, three!* if it's a three-on-two.

Line changes on the fly are carefully delineated. Tonight, it's not very important, as Burty can merely specify which of the two available left wings will go out with the only center and right wing sitting on the bench. For example, "Keith, you're up next with these two." Still, to avoid confusion, the forwards always state their intentions for the next shift. "I've got Pawluk," one will say, identifying the player on the ice he'll replace. "I've got Findlay," the other guy will confirm.

Monroe is the smallest of the WPHL's three Louisiana cities, a college town that skirts the edge of the league's market requirements. The Mocs cannot fill their building, which holds more than 4,000, but the folks that do show up are rowdy. This is Louisiana—they sell hard liquor at the concession stand. During every stoppage of play, a spotlight circles around, focusing on whoever's shaking the most tail to "YMCA" or "Cotton Eyed Joe." When the good guys score, black plastic snakes (technically, the team's name is short for "water moccasins") go flying. At one game, someone threw an actual moccasin—a shoe, that is, not a reptile.

One on-the-glass blueline fan pounds away all night, yelling at the official in front of him each time a penalty is or isn't called, unaware that the linesman has nothing to do with those decisions. Last time the Bats were here, a fan next to the visitors' bench was ejected at the end of the third period.

"He just kept yelling 'Fuck you, fuck you,' " Burty says. "So I said, 'Fuck you, you don't get to see the shootout.' "

The Bats loathe being here, but the fans are not the reason. "The ice makes a hollow sound when you tap it," Andy Ross says.

"They make ice here like I fuck," Gunner, ever the *bon mot* specialist, says. "All over and not very well."

As the game wears on, the corners become little rivers, with cracks and chips and bare spots everywhere. "I just got soaked," Keith Moran complains after falling near the boards.

The Bats and Mocs have been automatic rivals since the first meeting, an Austin laugher that ended in a five-on-five brawl. It started when a spectator dumped his soda on a Moccasin, who moved to retaliate.

"The guy took a swing at one of our fans, and we definitely can't have that," Kyle Haviland said at the time. "We're trying to get these people to come back to the games."

Monroe's play has improved considerably since they picked up André Racicot. The goalie's presence is a glaring reminder of just how far these players are from the Show. The most maligned of Patrick Roy's many back-ups with *les Habs*, Racicot's annual sub-.900 save percentage earned him the brutal nickname "Red Light." He still turns up as a punch line in the Montreal media every year, most recently in unflattering articles about Jose Theodore. But against WPHL competition, "Red Light" finally looks as good as Roy.

A more accomplished NHL veteran lies at the core of Monroe's club. Brian Curran was the 22nd player taken in the 1982 draft. Back then, that was the first pick in the second round. The six-foot-five, 220-pound defenseman played five full seasons in the NHL, plus parts of four others, with five different clubs. In 1989–90 he appeared in 72 games for the Maple Leafs, racking up 301 PIMS. The past few years, Curran has maintained a steady IHL/AHL career, but last season an injury limited him to three games with the Philadelphia Phantoms. The WPHL will be his curtain call—he's Monroe's player/assistant, and will soon swap his sweater for the coat-and-tie. In the meantime, he's a big, strong, nasty physical presence.

"Our kids are terrified of him," Gunner notes, meaning Findlay and Pawluk. Neither rookie has backed down against Curran, and Pawluk has even taken a few swipes at him, but Gunner believes that's just proof the D-man gets them off their game.

Curran has an extra-special kinship with Rob Hartnell. Every time the Bats face Monroe, Hartsy piles up an assortment of roughing, fighting and game misconduct penalties. More often than not, "the Colonel" is the guy he mixes with.

Nearly a full foot shorter than his target, Hartsy can whack away without looking like he means to, and loves to start what he can't—or won't have to—finish.

"It's like me throwing myself up against a tree," Ice Bats fan Paul Trimble says of one Hartnell–Curran collision.

When Hartnell gets on Curran's case, the big man turns beet

red. You can just see him thinking, "I want to pummel you, but you're too small." If Curran actually gets close to throwing punches, Hartsy turtles, or lets the linesman step in. But he never interrupts the flow of invective.

"I tell him he looks like Michael Flatley, Lord of the Dance," Hartnell says.

"Fourteen hundred penalty minutes in the Show and Hartsy is spearing him," Keith Moran marvels.

Rob doesn't always come out on the right side of the referee's decisions, and his fuse can be a little short. But that's an occupational hazard. He's doing the job Burton wants him to do, getting under the other team's skin, giving everyone a charge. If he gets Curran in the box, even on coincidental calls, that frees up space for Austin's offense.

Tonight, the team is too depleted to play that way. Staying calm is an asset.

"Way to hold your tongue, guys," Hartnell says, after Curran accidentally slips near the Austin bench. "Let him sleep."

While Hartnell's been finding the net lately, especially with some of Binnie's ice time, he's made a fine transition from puck-carrying sniper to third-line superpest. His effort, humor and energy have made him one of the team's emotional leaders, and he moves easily between the various groups on the bus. He and MacKay are already friends from Waco, and they both get on with Thompson and Jeff Kungle because they're all from Alberta or Saskatchewan. "You don't have to really know a guy," Hartnell says. "If he's from the West, you already know each other."

Hartnell also has a friendly competition with Andy Ross— a $100 bet as to who will get 30 goals first. (Hartsy currently has 9 to Ross's 15.) Most of all, he has a tight bond with Findlay and Pawluk. It's part peer relationship, part veteran taking two rookies under his wing. The three of them pal around together as if Hartnell's known them both since Windsor.

Not quite, but he can relate to where they're coming from. As a Lethbridge Hurricane, Hartnell led the WHL in scoring for half a season. Then he got mono and missed the rest of the year. A few NHL teams expressed interest, but his illness-abbreviated season, combined with other nagging injuries, cost him any shot at being drafted. At five-foot-seven, he wasn't kidding himself about his prospects anyway.

"I always knew that, other than Theo Fleury, there's no small men who dominate the game," Hartnell says. "I knew I'd have to start at a lower level and work my way up."

He played his first two pro games for the Salt Lake City Golden Eagles of the IHL. "They said, 'Hey, we're going to send you down for a couple of weeks; we'll call you up,'" Hartnell says. "It's been five years. I don't wait by the phone much anymore."

He says the IHL is a "big boys' club," a place for bigger, stronger, older players who operate at a higher level both mentally and tactically. He thinks Findlay and Pawluk—"two of the best young players I've played with at this level"—have a good chance of getting there, but it could take four or five years of development.

Hartnell was born in Rocky Mountain House, Alberta, but his family has been in Wetaskiwin, which is closer to Edmonton, since he was three. Living there allowed him to see the Oilers in person at the height of the Gretzky years, while still coming of age in a small-town environment where ice was readily available.

"It almost seems surreal to look back on my childhood and think about how much of the day we spent on hockey," he says. "If we weren't in school we were playing, watching or thinking about it. It was the funnest time. You could play back then without pressure."

He ran a hockey school for several summers, so he's seen how pressure takes the fun away. On his left shoulder, Hartnell has a tattoo of a heart with a stick through it, underlined by two words: "The Game." But he knows the game doesn't equal life.

"When I grew up, my parents never said, 'Hey, you've got a game tomorrow, so don't go to the school dance.' They'd be like, 'Why aren't you going to the school dance?'" he says. "Nowadays kids are in hockey year-round. They get to be 12 to 13 years old and it's like, no girls, no soccer, no anything. That's why they're quitting."

For Hartnell, the decision was college versus juniors. Mom was in favor of education, but Dad was a WHL scout. When Rob had a big tournament coming up, his father would help him cut school so he could get in some extra skating. "My mom worked at the school as a secretary, so I would play sick, Mom would leave for school and Dad would pick me up and take me to the rink," Hartnell remembers. "I'd skate all morning, Dad would pick me up again and I'd be back in bed before Mom got home for lunch. Then I'd say I was feeling better and go to class in the afternoon."

But his mother plays a part in his hockey life as well. "I can talk to my mom differently than I can talk to my dad about a game, you know what I mean?" Hartnell says. "Mom wants to know how many people were at the game. Dad wants to know, 'How come you got 25 shots on net and no goals?'"

Hartnell loved juniors. "It was a lot of fun. I would have played junior all my life if I was allowed. We were the tightest group. We were picked to finish dead last one year, by *The Hockey News*, by everybody, and we ended up going to the finals. We had no stars, but we had a close group of guys that bought in together. We were like brothers. We did everything for each other. If one guy was going to sleep, we all went to sleep, that kind of deal.

"I've never played on a team since where everybody was like that."

Hartnell's junior career ended on a down note. He clashed with coach Bob Loucks and got shipped to the Tri-Cities. Loucks was a take-no-prisoners kind of guy—"a negative motivator," as Hartnell puts it—who was fired a month after the trade. Coincidentally, he resurfaced as Dennis Maruk's replacement in Lake Charles a few weeks ago, which might be why Hartnell had that hat trick against the Pirates.

Following juniors, after the Golden Eagles sent him down, Hartnell played three seasons in the ECHL. He played for the Huntington Blizzard one year after Todd Brost did. That indirect connection brought him to El Paso.

Casting his lot with a brand-new league was scary. "When I went to my first camp and the ice wasn't ready I thought, 'Oh my God, I've really shot myself in the foot,'" Hartnell says. "But as it turns out, the league has really taken off."

In the off-season, Hartnell works an oil rig in the Alberta bush. He's been doing it since 1995, when he realized that taking his winter hockey earnings and cruising through the summer on a favorable exchange rate wasn't doing him any good in the long run.

"A lot of my buddies worked on a rig," he says. "All of them came home with all of their fingers, so I thought, 'Heck, why don't you give it a try?'" It's grueling labor. The workers live in trailers for weeks at a time, with no phones and nothing to do but put in 12-hour days, lift weights, eat and sleep.

But is it harder than hockey? Sort of. On one level, the daily grind of the rig is more taxing than playing a game you love for money. But sometimes, especially with the WPHL's patented three-game-three-night weekends, hockey is worse.

"I don't think I can even explain how your body feels sometimes," Hartnell says. "I wake up and, honest to God, I can't even lift my head up. Or you get a deep bruise on your tailbone so bad that you can't sit down, and you still have to go out and play. If you get hurt on the rig, you can take a day off."

Hartnell makes more money working two months in the bush—with no living expenses while he's out there—than he does in six months of shooting pucks. "Hockey is my holiday," he says. "I work in the summer. If I worked steady on the rigs I could clear $60,000 a year." That won't happen—he's not interested in spending February outdoors in Alberta. He's been down South too long.

"Yeah, I like it that I get to winter in warm weather," he says. "Then I go home, see a bit of the springtime. You can still do some ice fishing, ski a little. Then it's summer."

Quality of life is a big issue in AA hockey. "At this level you play for fringe benefits," Hartnell says. "You want to make the most money you can, but also you want to go to a place where you can go out, and instead of paying $3.50 for a beer you pay a dollar. Or there's free golf. Or workout memberships. Things like that make the hugest difference, especially for a first-year guy that's making $300 a week."

Hartnell has found the right situation in the WPHL. "I'm enjoying the last two seasons the best out of all my pro seasons," he says. "The weather is great. And the people in the South are so friendly. If you're going to play at this level, you might as well make yourself as comfortable as you can."

BACK ON THE ICE, Hartnell and the Bats stay with the Moccasins at 1–1 for two periods. There are close calls on both sides.

"C'mon, Kid, you're smarter than that," Andy Ross says from the bench after Ryan Anderson takes his man at an improper angle and gives up a scoring chance.

"He missed that day in geometry class," Darrin MacKay says.

Anderson is having a tough time of late. His plus/minus rating has sunk into sub-zero double digits from December alone. "Let's get the Kid into January," someone said during one pregame pep talk.

A few shifts later, Ross goes in for a breakaway, the puck bouncing crazily in front of his stick. The Austin bench rises to its feet. "That's it," Burty yells. "There's a chance!"

Racicot turns away the shot, and Roscoe climbs over the boards, huffing and puffing.

"Good job, Andy," Gunner says.

"Didn't miss by much," Burty says.

A few minutes later, the Bats almost bounce one in the net off a long dump. "That's my kind of goal right there," Chris Haskett notes.

Both teams are obstructing in the neutral zone, and Burton is frustrated by the lack of power plays. "Fuck, Hughesy, what the fuck's going on?" he says to the ref, assigned to Austin for the second night in a row. "That's about three you let go."

As a teenager, Burty wore black-and-white stripes himself, so he knows firsthand how much flak officials take. Once, while jumping to avoid a puck, he toppled over the boards onto one of the benches. Instead of helping him up, the coach stubbed out a lit cigarette on Burty's hand.

"I yell at them during the game," Burty says of his present-day patter. "Then I talk to them afterward and it's all forgotten."

A few shifts later, one of the linesmen rules a promising Ice Bats rush offside.

"Aw, fuck you," Burty says evenly. The guy is standing five feet away. "The puck's over the line, a guy makes a good play and you get whistle-happy all of a sudden."

The zebra finally turns his head. Chris Haskett looks him in the eye. "The game is over there," Hasky says.

It's been a long night. "Shit, I'm a young buck and *I* don't feel good," Ryan Anderson says.

Monroe takes over with a pair of unanswered goals. But it's still early in the third. At 3–1 the Bats believe they can come back, because they've done it before—in this very rink, for that matter. Then Corey Fletcher accidentally kicks a puck past Erickson. Burty pounds the floor with his foot. That seals it.

Or so you'd think. "Timmy, give me a time-out," the coach tells Findlay when there's two minutes left. He beckons Chad over. "I've seen stranger things happen in this game," Burty says, explaining why he'd bother to go six-on-five in a three-goal game. "Just win the draw and get it deep."

Monroe gets the empty-netter.

Burton is pretty bummed about the game, mainly because he knows his team is better than its 1–2–1 record against the Mocs. More than that, he's worn down by the shorthanded stretch.

"I've got guys coming in," he says. "Soon, someone will be sitting in the stands."

The players are too relieved their week is over to beat themselves up about the loss. They've got an eight-hour bus ride to go, but at least they get to chill in Austin for a day. There won't be practice Monday.

"Sunday night: can you say 'shitfaced'?" Andy Ross exults. "A girl is driving me home, and I don't care if she weighs 800 pounds."

This is a slight exaggeration. But only slight. One recent evening at the Mobil station near the Bat Cave, Ross, Haviland, Mark Martello and I were all enthusiastically ogling a woman filling up her car at a distant pump. Martello even waved. Inside the store, the young lady turned out to be, as Darrin MacKay once said of an opposing team's cheerleaders, "good from far but far from good."

Roscoe was nonplussed by this news. "Shit, I don't care," he snorted. "Have you seen some of the women I've been with?"

Before heading home from Monroe, sandwiches are distributed, and the convenience store is fully raided—beers for everyone, plus the usual assortment of Powerbars, Gatorade, Evian, beef jerky and Moon Pies.

Corey Fletcher is one of the last guys to reboard.

"There ya go, Fletch," Burton says as the defenseman passes by. "It'll start going in for ya now."

It's been pissing rain since game time. The bus driver is concerned. "I've never driven in the rain before," he says.

He's kidding. Dave the Bus Driver is a decided change of pace from his immediate predecessor, Ruben, who specialized in slow, bumpy journeys. Two weeks ago the team made this same trip on East Texas two-lane highways. Every time there was a railroad crossing or stoplight, the bus would come to an uneasy halt, waking everybody up. In the town of Athens, there's a square that requires four full stops and four hard turns—more than enough to ruin anybody's nap for good. After one particularly screechy application of the brakes, all 20 heads jolted up, waiting to hear the sound of metal on metal.

"I was lying on the floor imagining which way the chairs would collapse on me," Ryan Anderson says.

Dave, on the other hand, has figured out that the Interstate 35 north to Interstate 30 east, while less direct on the map, is both faster and smoother. He knows how to sneak through every speed trap in Texas and has already bounced over curbs and cut through gas stations to keep the Bat Bus moving. Dave has logged 3.1 million miles in his career, taking out one Louisiana alligator and one 9' 4" bridge (a bus is 11' 1") in the process.

What Dave the Bus Driver can't do is fix the bus. Star Shuttle recently sent it to Dallas with a list of 15 problems that needed repair. In the shop, they discovered 14 more.

Those were addressed, but here comes problem number 30—there's a clogged drain in the innards of the vehicle, underneath the passenger compartment. Rainwater is pooling there, and it's starting to rise into the floor itself.

"My first year of pro hockey, and we get this bus," Ryan Pawluk complains.

Eric Seeber heads for the back with five ice packs and some tape. One of the most agile things any of these guys do is maneuver through the narrow aisle. Forget pylons on the ice at practice—straddling small plastic armrests while legs, arms, blankets and possessions block you at every interval is more difficult. But if you sit up front and want to go to the bathroom, avoiding the obstacle course is not an option. Chad Erickson says that, to his knowledge, front-row resident Gunner Garrett has only been there once. "And Seguin goes, 'Uh-oh, better get some guys to the front,' " Erickson remembers. " 'We might pop a wheelie.' "

Tonight's entertainment is *Sleepers*. When the young Brad Pitt character gets abused by Kevin Bacon, the peanut gallery pipes up.

"TURTLE," someone yells.

"GO DOWN!" someone else suggests.

Pitt's presence in the movie prompts a discussion of cinema's other current hearthrob, Leonardo DiCaprio. Tim Findlay concedes that he's a good-looking kid.

"He can get any girl he wants," Hartsy says.

Then they both marvel at the fact that Jim Carrey can as well.

Keith Moran is missing out on this bit of Hollywood analysis. He prefers books, be they on tape or between covers. Of late, he's read *The Perfect Storm* and *The 7 Habits of Highly Effective People*, as well as J.F.K. conspiracy theorist Jim Garrison's tome and Arianna Huffington's *Picasso: Creator and Destroyer*. "It's basically about how he was just a rock star who abused women," Moran says. He even tackled *Dianetics*, out of curiosity more than inspirational zeal. "It was interesting, but I don't understand how it sold so many books." When all else fails, he goes back to Socrates' *Apology*. "I've studied him so much. I like what Hegel thinks, I like what Hume thinks, but I like the logic behind the Socratic Method, and his interaction with Aristotle—the best."

"Hey Keith," Ryan Pawluk interrupts. He's wondering, perhaps because of his injured wrists, if Moran would be willing to break in a new pair of gloves for him. "I'll give you five bucks a day."

Moran is dumbfounded. Oh sure. He doesn't get nearly as much ice time as his fellow rookie. He makes about half as much money. He obviously has nothing better to do.

Yet there wasn't a trace of arrogance in Pawluk's voice. He is completely unaware that he's done something offensive. Blame it on the beer, perhaps.

Sleepers ends at 2 A.M. It's still raining. The bus floor is now completely soaked, along with any blankets, sleeping bags and foam pads that happened to be placed there. No one is getting any rest tonight.

"Unbelievable," someone says. "I bet 11 out of 12 players get clinical pneumonia on this trip."

In Tyler, an hour east of Dallas, the boys demand another convenience stop. But they don't sell beer in Texas after 1 A.M. They'll have to make do with what they already have on hand.

Ultimately, Findlay, Pawluk and Hartnell prove that you *don't* have to run the obstacle course to use the bathroom. Those empty, wide-mouthed Gatorade bottles come in handy. But the piss-bottle still has to be emptied periodically. The trio take turns ferrying it to the back.

Hartnell picks up the bottle for his shift. "Hey, feel how warm this is," he says to the other two. They oblige.

nine

JUST TRYING TO CAPTURE
THE SPIRIT OF THE THING

"THEY'RE GONNA RUN CHADLY," Andy Ross warns.

"Shoot, that's easy," comes the inevitable Gunner Garrett retort.

It's January. The holiday season is a memory. The Bats are back in Shreveport. And the Mudbugs are about to introduce a trio of imposing new additions.

Seven thousand puckheads (including 10 hardy Austinites) cheer lustily as the rink announcer's voice booms through the public address system, bearing news of a "major, late-breaking trade."

"Ladies and gentlemen," the announcer continues, "the Mudbugs have acquired the rights to . . . the terrors of the Federal League! . . . Now starting at right wing, left wing and center . . . the Hanson Brothers!"

Outfitted not in Shreveport unis, but in the same Charlestown Chiefs sweaters they first wore on-screen in 1976, Dave, Jeff and Steve Hanson triumphantly raise their sticks and line up for the opening face-off. On the other side of the circle, Brett Seguin's grin is so wide he could swallow the puck.

There are two referees, and the second one, with white sleeves sticking out from underneath his stripes and the hint of a beer gut, doesn't look like much of a skater. No sooner has the puck dropped than the newest Mudbugs give this guy the business. After a brief argument, the three brothers surround the ref, yank his pants down to his ankles and hit him with a cream pie.

"I recognize that guy," Darrin MacKay says of the foam-faced faux official. "Hasn't he done a couple of games in this league?"

Skating unimpeded down the middle of the ice, hockey's most notorious goons bump Chad Erickson, who topples like a bowling pin. The puck goes in the empty net, and the celebrating three-some parades over to the Austin bench, challenging all 14 giggling players with the universal "Wanna go?" gesture.

Reality intrudes.

"At 0:00 of the first period, penalties on the Shreveport Mud-bugs," the announcer intones. "The Hanson Brothers, game misconducts for fighting, pie throwing and dorky eyewear."

Steve Carlson, Jeff Carlson and their cousin Dave Hanson have made the most of their notoriety from appearing in the movie *Slap Shot*. The three of them, along with the eldest Carlson sibling, Jack, played for the Johnstown Jets of the old Eastern Hockey League when writer Nancy Dowd spent a few months on the bus, laying the groundwork for a screenplay about the minor leagues.

Dowd's script wound up as the basis for something bigger than hockey. "It's the best sports movie ever made, if you leave out boxing," *Semi-Tough* author and former *Sports Illustrated* scribe Dan Jenkins has said.

Slap Shot is not just a great sports movie, but a great movie, period. It's a scabrous artifact of post-Vietnam America, a society that was down on its luck but still full of itself, awash in violence, spectacle, sex and feminism. The film is one of the last relics of Hollywood's more cynical, less special-effects-oriented golden age of the 1970s.

In the hockey world, the movie is a bible. Just as every long-haired rocker who's ever turned his amp up to "11" can cite chapter and verse from *This Is Spinal Tap*, every rink rat in North America quotes *Slap Shot* so automatically that you sometimes forget the lines are from the movie in the first place.

"There's not one word of dialogue every guy doesn't know," Andy Ross says. Ross figures your average hockey team sees the movie at least twice a year—"You watch it once, and then there's always one trip where you forget to bring other videos. It's already on the bus, so you watch it again."

At the time the film was made, Jack Carlson was on his way to a lengthy WHA and NHL career, which is why Dave stepped in. (He was originally going to play the role of "Killer" Carlson.) As real-life players, the Hansons never actually gussied up their fists with Reynolds aluminum wrap—"putting the foil on"—but they did use golf gloves, soaked in water then dried to a crispy-hard texture, for similar effect. Most of *Slap Shot*'s other infamous, seemingly out-landish moments were taken straight from life, unfiltered and exactly as they happened.

"We did fight, we did jump a team in warm-ups, we did go in the stands to attack a heckler, we did get arrested," Steve Carlson says.

The game, and the minor league life, hasn't changed much. Most of those things have already happened in the WPHL.

Despite the cartoonish antics and voluminous penalty minutes, the real-life Brothers were normal, capable, hard-working hockey players. "We weren't just big idiots," Carlson, who put in time with the Edmonton Oilers and L.A. Kings organizations, says. "We also had some talent. I led the Jets in scoring that year, and we won the championship."

After the movie, they all played the game for another eight to 12 years. "We'd go into arenas and there'd be entire sections of fans with glasses and fake noses on," Dave Hanson recalls.

Taking their shtick on the road is the only reward the three men get. They were paid to be in the film, of course, but the "charac-ters" of the Hanson Brothers belong to Universal Studios. While the brothers sign and sell all kinds of merchandise, they don't get a cut of the actual product. Dreams of a sequel were routinely quashed by the studio for years. (One finally went into production in the spring of 2001, a low-budget, low-profile affair with the Han-sons joined by actors Daniel Baldwin and Gary Busey.)

Steve Carlson and Dave Hanson continue to work the hockey biz. Hanson, a former AHL general manager, now runs the massive

Pittsburgh rink complex where Mario Lemieux held his clandestine comeback workouts. Carlson conducts summer hockey camps and also does color commentary for Milwaukee of the AHL. Prior to that, he coached in Johnstown (now part of the ECHL) and Memphis. In the latter city, Andy Ross was one of his stars. Before the game, Carlson kidded his former player while looking over the Ice Bats stat sheet. "I bet you've never been minus-one before in your life," Carlson says. "And what about these 30 PIMs? Are they all misconducts?"

"No, we've got another guy who does that this year," Ross deadpans, referring to captain Chris Morque's special rapport with the officials. (Gunner calls him "Ten-Minute Dork-way.")

As you might expect, Carlson is the epitome of old-time hockey. He has nothing nice to say about today's NHL, a.k.a. the "No-Hit League." And he admits he isn't cut out to coach the modern player, even at the lower levels.

"You can't ask a kid making 300 or 400 dollars a week, a kid with a diploma in his back pocket, to sacrifice his body or possibly break a bone to save a goal to win a game," Carlson says. "They're going to look at you like, 'Are you nuts?' Nowadays, players feel that hockey owes them a career. When we played, our theory was it was a privilege to play the game. We would do anything we possibly could to play."

The Hanson Brothers' temporary presence in the Mudbugs lineup is remarkably intimidating. At least, that's the only conclusion that can be drawn from the 60 minutes that follow their routine, during which Austin gives a performance of its own—a poor imitation of a hockey team.

"New year, full roster . . . fuck, it doesn't get any better than this," Burty had said just last night, when his club, bolstered by fresh faces, snapped a five-game winless streak by beating the Odessa Jackalopes at home.

Burton spoke too soon. Right after the game, Houston called. When the Bat Bus left for Shreveport, Tim Findlay and Jeff Kungle were not aboard.

Findlay may be the star, but Kungle is the hardest guy to live without. The second-year player is as quiet off the ice as he is on it, and that's as it should be. There's a cliché about defensemen that if you don't notice them, they're doing a good job. Kungle fits that archetype beautifully.

A farm boy from Wakaw, Saskatchewan ("Don't spell it backwards," the townsfolk like to say), Kungle splits his off-season between his family's canola, wheat and barley fields and a straight job crunching numbers for the Caterpillar corporation in Illinois. (He'd previously played for the Peoria Rivermen, after attending St. Lawrence University in New York.)

"He's my rock back there," Jim Burton says. "He kind of calms the whole unit. They feed off him. He has that influence over the guys just by the way he plays."

Ryan Anderson is trying to overcome his struggles by partnering with the steady Aeros prospect. Last year, the Kid had Burton to show him the ropes. This year it's Kungle's turn.

"He plays exactly the way you're supposed to play," Anderson says. "He's not the biggest guy, but he never gets beat and he always takes the body. And he's way smarter than me. He uses such big words. I'm always telling him, use stuff I can understand, like 'puck', 'stick' or 'board.' "

Kungle adds offense, and he doesn't mind banging around in the slot, but his key contribution is what he doesn't do. Every time an opposing forward rushes in, Kungle weaves right with him, guiding the play to the side or the corner, eschewing the high-risk plays or bad decisions that lead to penalties, mistakes or goals-against.

Tonight, the Bats are real familiar with goals-against. It's 3–0 Mudbugs after one.

"Know why this team can't win?" Gunner says, eyeing the pyramid of hockey gloves drying out before his box fan in the visitors' dressing room between periods. " 'Cause they stack their gloves in front of the fan. Think the Russians do that?

" 'The gloves are wet, the skates are too small, the sticks are too short,' " he continues, mimicking the gripes he hears every day. "They can't get out of their own way."

Burty simply calls the period "a stinker." The Bugs hold the shots advantage, 16–7, and Austin has given up some uncharacteristic three-on-twos.

"Take care, kid," Gunner says, tapping Jim Mullin on the pads. "You're only going to see about 40 more shots."

Mullin started tonight, which is why Erickson got to do the opening honors with the Hansons. The second-string goalie has been on Gunner's case because he's playing in the same beat-up red pads he came to town with. Mullin is supposed to get blue ones, which go better with the Ice Bats uniform. He figures the team is too cheap to spring for new equipment.

"I'm color blind," is Gunner's explanation. Privately, the equipment manager tells me that he hasn't placed the order because he doesn't know if Mullin will be around long enough to justify it.

He's not around for long tonight. "Mullin, you've got more holes than my drawers," a Louisiana fan heckles after the Mudbugs make it 4–0 mere moments into the second.

That sends Erickson to the crease. "Hey Mullin, not going anywhere for a while?" the fan comes back with. "Have a Snickers!" This uninspired bit of Madison Avenue mimickry is made slightly funnier by the fact that Mullin has in fact sought out candy between periods—provided by yours truly during my between-periods visits—on hungry nights when he knew he'd never play.

The fan's derision also highlights his casual knowledge of the game. The Ice Bats have been conducting a series of inadvertent odd-man-rush drills all night long. Goaltending is the least of Austin's problems. When Erickson gives one up after several unchallenged rebound chances, the fan finally gets the picture. "It's not your fault, Mullin," he gleefully apologizes. "Y'all suck."

At the end of two periods, it's 7–0. "We weren't ready to play, myself included," Kyle Haviland says. Brett Seguin has been demoted to the third line for not playing defense. In the locker room, Burty doesn't say a word. Then, after all the players are on their feet and almost through the door, he tells them to hold up.

"This is rock bottom," the coach says. "Nowhere to go but up. When this happens, you've got to work it out among yourselves. I want to see lots of talk on the ice. Help each other out. Play for each other. Don't play for me."

The final score is 10–1. It's the worst loss in Ice Bats history.

"I've never been so humiliated in my life," Haviland says following a long, closed-door meeting. "That's the worst game I've seen a team play in six years. I would have liked to break a few sticks in there, but I'm not the captain."

Two hours into the bus ride, Burton fumes quietly. The only time he opens his mouth is to ask Nathan Jones, the team's webmaster and statistician, for a printout of all the WPHL rosters.

"WAIVER WIRE," reads the handwritten sign some anonymous prankster has taped up to the inside of Austin's dressing room door.

"Andy Ross—Age: Unavailable."

"Chris 'Ten Minute' Morque—Part time defenseman."

"Rob Hartnell—Shoes for the rig is his purchase price."

"Brett Seguin—DOB: 1940. Salary: $1,000/game."

At Ryan Pawluk's stall, a mini stuffed Bert from *Sesame Street* hangs from an equipment hook. The number 9 is scrawled on its back, and a sign taped to the front reads "Anybody have tweezers?"

For his part, Pawluk recently presented Corey Fletcher with a special plaque. *First goal, Monroe, December 20,* it says.

Sometimes, it's hard to tell the difference between a team that's wound too tight and a team that's wound too loose. The morning after the Shreveport fiasco, Burton made the team watch a video of every goal the Mudbugs scored. They responded that afternoon by handling the Fort Worth Brahmas.

Afterward, the dressing room TV is tuned to Fox Sports Southwest, which is carrying that day's Houston game. And there he is. Wearing number 15 instead of number 8, Tim Findlay is an Aero.

"What, he's not wearing a visor?" Todd Harris asks. "Thinks he's a tough guy all of a sudden?"

"He's been out there for two minutes," Andy Ross critiques. "Who does he think he is, Pig?"

But when the rookie gets sent out on a power play, earning a scoring chance to boot, the whole room cheers. The IHL may not be the big time, but it's the bigger time. And it's on TV. Findlay won't be there long—he's only there because of a short-term injury to another player—but this is still what he's been working toward all season.

The Bats head into the All-Star break with a road win over Lake

Charles—in a shootout, no less. Findlay, Kungle and Seguin remain in Lake Charles for the All-Star festivities, Findlay as a starter. The rest of the Bats enjoy a little January golf in Austin. Then it's back on the bus—and none of that single-weekend overnight nonsense, either. The team begins the second part of season as it did the first, by heading west for a week-long, four-city swing. The enforced camaraderie of the road will be much-needed medicine for a team that needs to refocus and reconnect, without the distractions of home.

There are also new players to accommodate. "It feels like training camp again," Andy Ross says.

The latest batch of Ice Bats whiz kids, OHLers all, have been trickling in since Christmas. Dean "D.J." Mando played with Findlay and Pawluk in Windsor. With the Spitfires in disarray, he has decided to go pro in the middle of his final year. Richard Uniacke was a two-time 100-point scorer for Sault St. Marie who followed his linemate Joe Thornton into the Boston Bruins organization. But Uniacke didn't quite cut it with the Bruins' AHL affiliate, and Burty scooped him up. The coach also made a nice acquisition in Joe Van Volsen, who was having a little trouble in the classroom at the University of Guelph. Before that, Van Volsen also played in the Soo, leading the 1995–96 Greyhounds with 82 points.

Mando, Uniacke and Van Volsen were all captains or alternate captains at some point in their career, which Burty considers crucial. "We need players who don't make excuses, who continue to take responsibility," he says. "When a player does something wrong, he has to understand that he's letting down his teammates. When you're 10 or 11 years old and you screw up for the first time, it breaks your heart. You know you let your team down. It's only later, as you grow up, that you learn to make excuses."

Any one of the rookies could pick up the scoring slack left by Binnie, and take away another guy's ice time, too. When Jackson and Thompson come off the IR, changes will be made. Trade rumors have attached themselves to everyone from Seguin (who approached Burty privately and promised to pick up his two-way play) to Kenny Ruddick (who asked to be dealt just two weeks after returning from his academic "holiday"). The irony is, if Burty were to trade a player as good as Seguin, it would almost certainly be for an offensive defenseman capable of more than Ruddick or Todd Harris.

The numbers crunch is so profound that Jim Andrews, a sportscaster for KXAN, Austin's NBC affiliate, is tagging along for a multipart story on Chris Haskett, Darrin MacKay and Keith Moran—the three players fighting hardest for their jobs.

Moran has become a more physical, defensively conscious player. His ice time is up. But his situation hasn't changed. "I realize that every day could be my last," he says. "It's definitely a numbers game. Injured reserve kind of holds my fate."

"It's difficult because I don't know where I stand," he continues. "It's such a different game from college. You have no stability. A lot of guys I've talked to from juniors, they say it's the same way there. Whereas in college, once the team is picked, you're not getting any new guys. They can't afford to give financial aid to anyone else. Admissions doesn't let a guy in halfway through the semester. Here, there's thousands of players floating around from team to team and league to league. You're very replaceable."

Darrin MacKay will be the first to go. He was almost waived a few weeks earlier but got a reprieve when Corey Fletcher pulled his groin. Mac still hasn't scored a goal and admits to "losing his edge." Yet his feeling for the game makes him an asset to the team, and his involvement in the SCORE program is invaluable.

"Okay guys, we got about five minutes here," Burty says in Amarillo. It's the same line he utters every night. It doesn't matter if there's four minutes or six minutes, there's just a certain comfort in saying it, same as "Eric, do you have any gum?"

After a pregame address that's mostly tactical, Burton makes the big announcement. "One last thing," the coach says. "Mac's going to be running the D. So don't tell him to fuck off."

Then Eric officially conveys assistant coach status on Darrin MacKay by handing him a stick of Wrigley's. As the players march onto the rubber mat outside the locker room, MacKay is transported back to his high school coaching days. "What do you say, Keith!" he says, tapping Moran on the shoulder with the enthusiasm of a cheerleader. "Chris!" he bellows when Haskett goes by.

Amarillo has a compact rink that was actually built for hockey in the late 1960s. The Amarillo Wranglers played two seasons (though not in a row) in the old Central Hockey League, then revived in 1975 as part of the Southwest Hockey League. Cal Farley Coliseum, which is part of a larger civic center complex, has just a single level of seats—and not a bad one in the house.

For the first 60 seconds of the game, the announcer keeps the whole crowd on its feet, yelling. This so-called "Mad Minute" will earn the loudest section a free pizza, and the din is so overwhelming that the players don't really bother getting into the game until the gimmick is over with.

Later, the PA salutes the alcohol-free section, prompting boos from all the other ones. They also give out a nine-pound Nestlé Crunch bar to the largest group in attendance. Giant foodstuffs are common in this corner of West Texas. It's possible that the second-most-famous landmark in Amarillo (after the "Cadillac Ranch" of Bruce Springsteen fame) is the Big Texan Motel and Steakhouse, home of the 72-ounce sirloin. If you can finish it, it's free.

The fresh start the Bats were looking for does not come in Amarillo. The Bats blow a 2–0 lead and lose in . . . that thing that happens after regulation . . . the overtime period that dare not speak its name. Funnily enough, Amarillo is the only team in the WPHL with more shootout losses than the Bats. The Rattlers have been in 16, losing eight out of the last 10 before tonight. Goalie Todd Laurin celebrates the victory like he just won a playoff series.

Afterward, Burton isn't down on himself or the players. It's still a point on the road. "We outchanced them 10 to 1," he says. "I thought we outplayed them." As for the shootout struggles, "Maybe I'll put four defensemen and a back-up goalie out there next time."

The only indelible moment came early in the game. After Uniacke goes hard to net and puts the tiniest of bumps on Laurin, Rattler tough guy Keith Bland retaliates. In his first fight in three years, Uni holds his own, earning the takedown.

"Anderson will get that guy," MacKay predicts between periods. But the Rattlers coach, conscious of that fact, doesn't give his enforcer another shift until the last minutes of the game. This time, Mando, Bland and Anderson end up in a minor scrum. The two

Bats each get roughing minors, and Bland gets four minutes for attempted spearing.

Just another bit of blood and brawling on an average night in the WPHL. Or so it would have been, if not for the arrival of the Amarillo newspaper at breakfast the next morning.

"I've got my hammers back when they come to Austin, so there'll be payback," Burton had said of Bland's activities. "Going after Uniacke . . . that kid's never fought in his life. Bland'll probably be hurt when he comes to Austin."

The Amarillo paper interprets the quote to mean that Burty wants his guys to injure Bland. "Burton said one Rattler will pay for his physical play when Amarillo visits Austin," the story says.

The coach is mortified to come off that way, especially with a news crew following him around. He even checks with me to see if he really said what the Amarillo writer says he did.

According to my trusty chicken scratch, he did. But when he said it, what I thought he meant, based on the way Bland was utilized so sparingly when Anderson wanted a piece of him, is that Amarillo would probably sit him out in Austin, knowing that he'd be a target. Cowardly or not, that's a hockey tradition, one that rose to particular prominence during my beloved Flyers' Stanley Cup years, when the Broad Street Bullies gave many an opposing player a sudden case of "Philly flu."

But having been embarrassed in print, Burton spins the interpretation to an even more palatable consistency. "The reporter took it out of context," he tells the TV people. "We try to conduct ourselves with class in this organization. What I was trying to say is the way that kid plays, he'd probably get hurt before they come to Austin. I was obviously a little upset about the loss. I certainly didn't mean we would hurt the kid. Even if you'd like to threaten a player, you never say that in the paper."

Spin or not, Burton backs up his words with action. Before traveling to San Angelo, the Bats return to Amarillo's barn to practice. The Rattlers are finishing their own session. Burton confers with Amarillo player/assistant Ken Karpuk, who calls Bland off the ice, saying that the Austin coach wants to talk, "which is very big of him." Burton privately explains himself to Bland, and he also tells his own players that, regardless of the circumstance, that kind of chatter is not his style, and it shouldn't be theirs either.

His lecture falls on deaf ears.

"Hey, Reg!" Chad Erickson shouts, using the name of Paul Newman's *Slap Shot* character. "Reg! Did you bring your leather jacket, Reg?"

"How much do we get for Bland?" another player cries. "Fifty dollars?"

Joking references aside, when the two teams do meet again, nothing will have changed. "We're still going to hurt him," Rob Hartnell acknowledges.

Unless they hurt each other first. Practice has barely begun before Kyle Haviland and Erickson are jawing at each other by the goal crease. "Third day of the road trip!" Andy Ross exults, using a tone similar to Robert Duvall's "I love the smell of napalm in the morning!" from *Apocalypse Now*.

Then Chris Morque takes out Jim Mullin, going for the goalie's jugular. Morque was trying to shoot five-hole and Mullin poke-checked. The goalie hit the ice, and Morque's shot smacked him in the neck, the one place where there's no padding or protection.

"Bet you can't do that twice," Rob Hartnell says, ignoring Mullin's pain.

"A little dissension in the ranks," Tim Findlay says. "That's good. It's been like a country club around here."

Mullin is still down, his neck pummeled purple and red. Eric Seeber is nowhere to be found. "I didn't know he was hurt," the trainer says, emerging with some ice a few minutes later. "I thought Burty wanted gum, or a fucking Rolo or something."

The forwards start a shooting drill, and Darrin MacKay, warming to his new role, tells Andy Ross that if he scores on both shots in the drill, he'll buy him a pack of cigarettes.

No sooner has Ross begun handling the puck than Rob Hartnell sneaks in to steal it. Ross is hugely pissed. He really, really wanted those cigarettes.

Next thing anyone knows, the six-foot-three, not particularly pugilistic Ross and the five-foot-seven, ill-tempered Hartnell are going at it, trading blows and trash talk like it's the second period of a 2–2 game.

"Okay, so you're not a chickenshit," Hartnell says after Roscoe lands a good one.

"You show up at home," Ross counters. "Or against Amarillo. But let's see you do it against Fort Worth."

Boys will be boys. The bout eventually cools, and later in the practice, Ross skates by Hartsy and nods toward the exit with a wink, like they're going to settle it for real outside. Then they hug.

"This team is tough against itself," Seeber says.

"See what happens when you put a bounty on a guy's head," Mark Martello admonishes.

"Yeah, they're tuning up for the big one," Burty says. "They want that hundred dollars.

"But that's a good sign," he continues. "It means they want to compete. They're frustrated. They want to kill somebody. They want to dominate."

"It's no biggy," Ross tells the TV guys, citing the pent-up frustration of recent games, combined with the grind of the bus ride. "I just bought him a juice in the locker room."

As the boys trickle in and out of the showers, Hartnell and Haviland adjourn to a nearby corridor for a push-up drill. They do ten, then nine, then eight, all the way down to zero. Findlay and Pawluk participate as well. On their way back to the dressing area, they hit the motherlode—a room down the hall laid out with a mid-morning feast of doughnuts, bagels, orange juice, cream cheese, fruit and coffee.

The Bats load up and snack away. They've pretty much laid waste to the entire spread when a man in a tuxedo appears, telling them to stop. It would seem the members of the local symphony, who have a morning rehearsal at the civic center, will not get their usual breakfast today.

ten

BIG STICK, LITTLE COJONES

UNLIKE THE HOCKEY TEAM, the Bat Bus is performing up to expectations—rather easy to do, as what's expected is failure.

Yesterday, during postpractice lunch, the vehicle was parked on an incline, draining the air out of the fuel tank. A couple of guys killed time by accompanying Findlay, who feels like there's something in his eye and thinks he may have astigmatism, to a strip-mall optician. While Findlay got checked out, his teammates scored phone numbers from the counter girls.

The bus got back to the hotel at 3 P.M. Wake-up calls were an hour later.

On the bright side, Dave is back behind the wheel. The last time Ruben had the gig, the team hit a rainstorm on the way out to Lake Charles. East Texas was a bayou, but Burty insisted on a stop for chocolate. Ruben sloshed the bus through five feet of water all the way down the exit ramp, giving the entire underside—including the cargo hold with all the gear—a thorough bathing. At game time the next day, the stuff was still damp.

Whenever Dave slows down or comes to a complete halt in mid-trip, the players refer to him as "Ruben." But that doesn't happen often. After a quick pit stop at an I-40 corner that includes a Burger King, a Taco Cabana and a mini-mart, the Bats have yet to cross a single county line when a state trooper blinks his lights. Apparently, the bus was going 85 miles per hour in a 70 zone.

"What, you were going uphill?" Burty says to Dave.

The driver climbs down the stairs and spends a few minutes in the front seat of the patrol car. When he returns, there's a piece of paper in his hand. It's good news.

"We got off with a warning," Dave reports. He asks Chad Erickson what that would be in hockey terms—"five minutes?"

"That would be a minor that should have been a major," Chad says.

Darrin MacKay gestures to the video machine. "Okay, boys, here's what we've got," he says. "Either *Fried Green Tomatoes* or *Steel Magnolias.*"

Actually, with Corey Fletcher sitting out this road trip, it's a shame Martello didn't bring some slasher flicks. Early in the season, Fletchy vetoed a showing of *The Relic* because, he confessed, "Horror films give me nightmares."

"Great," Burty joked at the time. "Last year we couldn't watch porn"—a rule instituted by born-again Christian John Blue—"this year we can't watch scary movies."

Actually, the team favorite since December has been videotapes of *South Park.* Guys walk around the dressing room singing the theme song. If a player needs Immodium, the condition is now described as "having a little brown baby boy."

"I can't believe they're allowed to show that crap on TV," Gunner says.

Another day means another climate-control battle. "Could you take it off 'cremate'?" Ryan Pawluk asks. When the guys in the back are cold, the heat they demand ends up roasting the rest of the bus. When the guys in the back are hot, the blaring A/C transforms the front into a meat locker. ("Could you turn the air off 'cryogenic'?" is what Pawluk says at those times.)

"Quit your bitchin'," Gunner says.

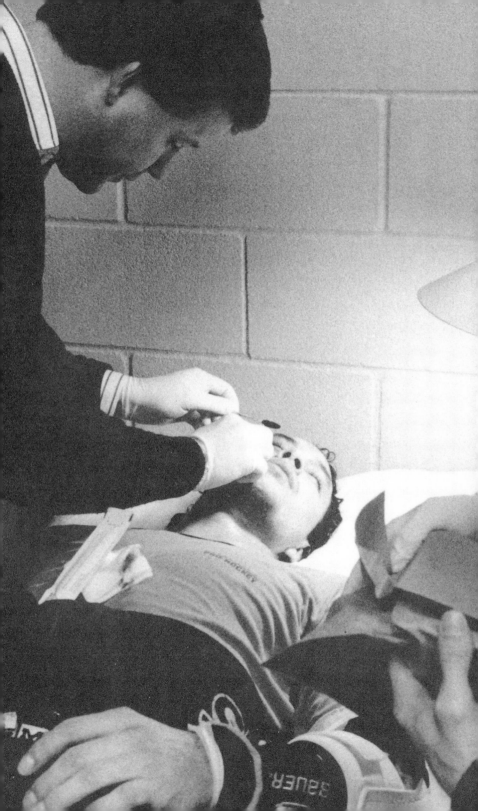

"C'mon, bring the heat down to 'inferno,'" Rob Hartnell implores. "Down to 'Canadian summer.'"

They get no sympathy from the back.

"Can you turn up the video?" Chad Erickson shouts, setting off a sarcastic litany of complaints.

"Fix the tracking!"

"Can we stop at the convenience store?"

"A/C please!"

"More beer!"

Back up front, D.J. Mando—a.k.a. "Teej," as Gunner mistakenly called him the first day and never bothered to correct, on purpose—is buried in a book. Chris Haskett says Mando reads more than anyone he's ever met. He's currently tackling Stephen King's *Four Past Midnight*, and the giant hardcover can't help but draw attention.

"Whatcha reading?" Hartnell begins.

"Is it in English?" Tim Findlay wonders.

"How much does it weigh?"

"Do you like it better than TV?"

Mando turns up the volume on his Discman.

"Whatcha listening to?"

Mando foolishly allows that he's enjoying a CD by Big Head Todd and the Monsters.

"Do you like him?"

"Where's he from?"

"If I had a band," Hartnell wonders, "would it be called Big Head Rob?"

At the back of the bus, the card game is well underway. Ryan Anderson decides he doesn't like his hand and opts out of the round.

"No cojones," the other players tease.

Thus challenged, Anderson pulls down his pants.

"Ohhhhhh . . . ." comes the retort. "*Little* cojones."

As the miles of West Texas nothingness go by, Burty expectorates Hawken chaw into an empty Gatorade bottle and reminisces about his own days as an up-and-coming bus leaguer. Burton played his juniors in Windsor and began his pro career in 1982.

The NHL had recently absorbed the World Hockey Association. Jobs were scarce, and pro players were getting bigger every year. Burty never made it to the Show, but he had the quickness and savvy to excel at every other level.

In 1982–83, he had 62 points as a rookie for the Fort Wayne Komets of the IHL. He was just 20 years old, at the tail end of his second pro campaign, when he went from the Komets to the Hershey Bears of the American League. Brian Curran and Central Texas Stampede coach Lee Norwood were both teammates for a spell. Burton lived in an apartment just 50 yards from the rink, and almost every night at 4 A.M.—closing time—one of the veterans would show up with a bottle of vodka and pass out on the younger player's couch. That way, no matter how bad his hangover was, the guy still made it to practice on time.

Another NHL-bound Hershey teammate was famous for the size of his stick, so to speak. The other Bears used to take turns telling dirty stories in the locker room, just to see if they could get the guy to fly at full mast. This is not unusual behavior. Jeremy Thompson tells of a juniors hazing ritual where a rookie would be banished to "the black box" (the shitter), forbidden to come out until he had a hard-on.

Burton spent the 1983–84 season in Hershey, then returned to Fort Wayne for four campaigns before taking his game to Europe. Indiana remains his full-time home; summers, he works there as a golf pro. Burton and his wife, Sandra, have two sons; by 1996, having completed the playing portion of his PGA certification, he was looking forward to a long, comfortable career teaching on the links.

But the hockey player in him wanted one more season. Burton turned down a chance to play in Germany—that was too much to put himself and his family through. He had a brief stint with the Phoenix Roadrunners of the IHL, but found he couldn't do at the age of 34 what he'd been able to a decade younger.

When Austin called, it seemed like the perfect opportunity—for both hockey and golf. The grass on some Texas courses may be brown, but you hit a lot more balls than you can in the Indiana winter. With his wife's blessing, Burton became an Ice Bat. "I told her, 'This is what I want to do, because I've put a lot of years into hockey. I went to some places that I really didn't want to go, and stuck it out and went to Europe for a long time because of the money. This year is for me.' She agreed wholeheartedly. She said I deserved it, and I should go out and have some fun.

"And that's exactly what I did," Burton continues. "Unfortunately, my knees didn't think I was having that much fun—or maybe knew I was having too much. But it was one of the best years I've ever had. We were having a good time, we were playing some good hockey, we were having beers afterwards. There wasn't a lot of pressure because it was a new town."

After all those years with teammates who didn't speak a lot of English, Burton enjoyed the role of veteran wise man. "They called me the Old Guy," he says. "There was a lot of respect there. They wanted to know how . . . you know, how to be the kind of player that I was."

When Kyle Haviland broke his arm in late November, Burton's leadership earned him the "C" for the rest of the season. By February, it was an open secret that Stoughton had anointed him as coach-in-waiting. In truth, he was already on the job. "I felt myself coaching every day," Burton says. "I was the blameless coach."

Now, he gets to take the blame. But for Burty, coaching is about more than hockey. Having an inexperienced team makes winning harder, but working with young players is his favorite part of the job. "I hope they remember this as a year that's had an impact on them," he says. "Not just as players, but as people."

THE BUS HITS SAN ANGELO at sundown, allowing the boys a few hours to roam around before an appropriate game-night bedtime. I join Tim Findlay, Ryan Pawluk, D.J. Mando and Rob Hartnell on a cross-town dinner journey. Although the WPHL circuit is a culinary carnival of regional specialties—Cajun and Creole and seafood in Louisiana, Mexican and chicken-fried steak and barbecue in Texas, green and red chiles in New Mexico—hockey players rarely venture outside their gastronomic comfort zone. Habit, lack of an adventurous culinary spirit and nutritional necessity keep them on a limited menu that's cheap, easy and familiar—sandwiches, salads and pasta, plus fast food and pizza when it's the only thing available. On the road, even on an off-day, guys just don't have the time, energy or interest to seek out the best enchilada in San Angelo, or Monroe's finest bowl of gumbo.

Tonight, it's remarkable enough that we're not headed to the Olive Garden for the millionth time. The clerk at the Inn of the Conchos has pointed us in the direction of a locally owned establishment called A Taste of Italy.

Our cabbie is from Alaska, and sure enough, he's got a connection to the game of hockey. He says he grew up skating with a guy, last name Ring (the first name he can't remember), who went on to be a Mighty Duck. Apparently the Bats, being mere WPHLers, are supposed to be impressed. But nobody has ever heard of this supposedly awesome player—nor could I find anyone who fit the bill on a subsequent Internet search. Maybe he was in the movie.

The driver is a satirical target for the remainder of the evening.

"Well, back when I was playing shinny with 'The Ringer,'" Hartnell mock-begins one conversation.

"Oh yeah, 'Ringsy'!" Ryan Pawluk joins in. "He had the quickest release you ever saw!"

A Taste of Italy is in a strip mall, but its Friday evening crowd is well turned-out, enough so that the players, who are in their off-day outfits of jeans and baseball caps, feel underdressed. Mando takes one look at the place and promptly tucks his shirt in, as if that alone will bring him up to code. Still, our little group gets seated, and after salad and a bit of cheap Chianti, Tim Findlay proclaims his fettucine Alfredo to be the best he's ever had.

There's a club next door, but when we get there it's still too early—11 P.M. Nothing's going on, and this group is planning to honor curfew. The team's struggles have gotten serious enough that everybody's honoring curfew: the other night in Amarillo, Kyle Haviland and Andy Ross resisted the urge to go out for a few beers because, Haviland said, "We don't want to set a bad example."

Rob Hartnell has faith that the hijinks of last season's team will not be repeated this year. "You give up that stuff for one month," he reasons, "and you win a championship."

SINCE THE BATS last visited San Angelo, the Outlaws have come around. They're not a great team, but they have one of the best—and best-marketed—scoring lines in the WPHL.

"The Three Amigos" are Jean Blouin, Carl Boudreau (leading the league with 85 points in 46 games) and Ross Harris (Todd's older brother). They have inspired the Outlaws faithful to sport sombreros and plaster the rink—dubbed The Hideout—with Spanish-themed signs.

The club also has a huge fan favorite in goalie Al Rooney. "Looney" Rooney—so named for both his all-over-the-place style and his fondness for pumping up the crowd during stoppages (his other nickname is "The Dancing Goalie")—has only been skating since the age of 17. One year later, the Long Island native went to what he believed to be a fantasy camp in Deerwood, Minnesota.

It was actually a try-out for junior-age U.S. players. The coach, unmoved by Rooney's mistake, told him to get his ass between the pipes. Thanks to sheer physical ability and lingering soccer instincts, Rooney stopped enough pucks to start a new career. He served a brief stint in the Marines and played two years at Division III Buffalo State University, then strung together opportunities with pro teams in Michigan, Alabama and Tennessee. He was working for a moving company in Nashville ("Two Guys and a Truck") when a Web-surfing cousin noticed San Angelo had lost a goaltender to injury. Rooney has delighted Outlaws fans ever since, as much for his personality as for his play, which can still be spotty.

"They're going to light this guy up," Darrin MacKay says.

"Lots of holes and a bit of a hot dog," is Jim Burton's assessment.

The Outlaws are coming off a surprise pasting of the Shreveport Mudbugs, so they're feeling good about themselves.

"They won't in eight hours," Haviland promises at morning skate.

"We have to win," Findlay says.

Everyone on the team knows they dodged a bullet in Amarillo—the Outlaws' victory over Shreveport, combined with a Waco upset of Fort Worth, means the Bats gained ground in the standings despite the shootout loss. "It was a good night in the WPHL," Burton says.

The Ice Bats take a 2–0 lead and it feels like another good

night. Then "Los Tres Amigos" make it 2–2 in a single shift, and it feels like every other night.

But MacKay's scouting report proves to be correct. The Bats score shorthanded late in the first, then add a couple of quick ones in the second, sending Rooney to the bench at 5–2.

Nine different Ice Bats—Seguin, Pawluk (2), Hartnell, Findlay, Van Volsen (2), Uniacke, Haviland, Haskett and Ruddick—get goals in what ends up an 11–2 thrashing. All 5,512 faithful San Angelo hockey nuts continue to cheer and clap until the bitter end, shouting "Let's Go Outlaws" and counting down the time of all the home team penalties. They do a pretty good wave, too, if you like that sort of thing.

At the buzzer, Jim Mullin and Keith Moran celebrate with a sarcastic hug. Despite the lopsidedness, Moran didn't take a shift. That was also the case in Amarillo. "I got about as much ice time as you," he says to me after the game.

With the addition of the high-skill rookies, Moran has slipped to number 10 on the depth chart. The job of extra forward usually goes to a fighter, and will again when Thompson and Jackson get back. Moran's U.S. citizenship may keep him on the roster, but he's losing ground to Haskett. Burton has taken a shine to the big rookie, who's dropping the gloves and taking shifts with some first-line forwards. Haskett, Ross and Mando have comprised a "Triple Tower" power scoring line. Moran isn't thrilled about his situation, but he's happy for Chris, who has a lot more at stake.

As for Mullin, he hasn't seen the net since Shreveport. Burton jokes that Erickson, with his calm, perfectly positioned stand-up style and minimal practice/workout habits, doesn't move around enough to need days off. Mullin hasn't earned his teammates' confidence, partly because he hasn't had a chance to. "I'm not a back-up goalie," he says. "I need to play game after game after game."

There is no time to enjoy the win. El Paso looms. Halfway there, near Fort Stockton, Dave makes another friend with his heavy foot.

"11–2?" the highway cop says. "That's not much of a game. What place are y'all in?"

The driver, who's learning fast, explains that while the team is in second, with 57 points to Fort Worth's 67, the Bats have seven games in hand. What he doesn't mention is that Austin's respectable 24–9–9 record includes a mark of 8–7–6 in December and January. Once again, Dave gets away with a warning. "Be careful," the officer says, telling him to stay at 65.

Finding fault with an 11–2 victory is easier than you'd think. Winning so handily allows the players to disregard the little things. The Shreveport disaster at the beginning of the month came about partly because the Bats forwards had convinced themselves they were the Gretzky-era Oilers in a flashy win the night before.

Something similar happens in El Paso. El Paso dominates play from end to end, taking every opportunity Austin gives them. It's 1–1 when Seguin forces an offensive rush and turns the puck over to the Buzzards' Jamie Thompson. The WPHL's most dangerous player—the one guy you'd like to account for at all times—zips in and buries a shot from the face-off circle to make it 2–1. Then, with just 13 ticks to go in the second period, the Bats lose a defensive-zone draw and Todd Harris leaves Thompson open at the back door. He makes it 3–1. Chad Erickson is still lecturing his defenseman as the teams line up at center ice.

It's a typical mental gaffe: a player starts thinking, "Oh, there's only 13 seconds left, we'll win this draw, ice it, period over."

"But you can't think like that," Burton says. "A team like that will shove it right up your ass, and that's just what happened. Harry's 220, Jamie's a buck-eighty . . . he can't hold that guy?"

On top of everything else, Tim Findlay is barely in the lineup. He's getting time on the power play, but his eye is really acting up.

"It's a little bit of a blind spot," Findlay says. "If I'm looking down, I can't see up. I want to play, but it's too fast-moving a game. You can get hurt so easily. It's not a good situation."

He could be talking about the game itself. In the dressing room, Burton is particularly cutting. "I don't care how you play against fucking San Angelo," he says. "I want to know how you play against this team."

Burty is not prone to tantrums. He says whenever he's about to throw one he thinks of Bobby Knight and takes it down a notch. Nobody says "fuck" in a more mild-mannered, gentle way. He is such a good-natured, Ward Cleaver sort of figure that when he does get pissed, the players feel it that much more.

"When I was a player, I played by one rule," Burton continues. "I let my conscience be my guide. I told myself before every game that if I bailed in the corner or didn't go to the net because I was afraid, I was going to get tubed. If I didn't hustle back as hard as I fucking could, it made me sick to my stomach. It would eat me up inside that I played like a chickenshit. That I let everybody down."

El Paso wins the game, but Burton is much happier with Austin's third-period effort. "If we play with that kind of determination all the time, there's not many games we'll lose," he says.

So the speech worked?

"I told them what I played my career by," he says. "It's a good way to play. You have to look yourself in the fucking mirror every day."

LAST STOP, Albuquerque. After a couple of days of downtime, the team makes its first visit to Tingley Coliseum in thinned-out form.

Ryan Pawluk is in Houston for his second call-up of the year. The first time, he returned after one night and giddily announced that he had five scoring chances.

"We know about warm-ups," Rob Hartnell retorted. "What about the game?"

Yesterday, Tim Findlay flew back to Austin to see an ophthalmologist. The preliminary diagnosis is a detached retina. Just when Burty thought he could stop working the phones . . . But secretly, the coach is addicted to recruiting. He already has hundreds of pages of notes on this year's crop of junior players, all potential building blocks for next year's team.

The Bats will also face the Scorpions without Jeff Kungle. The defenseman broke a skate blade in practice, and a replacement wasn't found. "That's why I always traveled with two pairs of skates on the road," Jim Burton says. But this is not the IHL. Thousands of dollars for back-up skates are not in Austin's budget. "Maybe not all of our players should have two pairs of skates," Darrin MacKay suggests, "but our best ones should."

The last time Austin lacked top-notch players, the response

was panic. Tonight, it's poise. Burton puts his fresh new players on the attack and the Bats deliver a near-perfect first, taking a 3–1 lead into the locker room. Both teams hang tight from there. Austin goes up 4–2 early in the third. The Scorps strike right back. Then Joe Van Volsen scores his second of the night to give the Bats a 5–3 edge. Austin goes into a defensive bubble.

POP! With 3:30 left, New Mexico makes it 5–4 on a hard shot from the blueline. The pass to the point went right through the legs of Keith Moran, playing defense because of Kungle's absence and a Ryan Anderson fighting major.

With about a minute remaining, D.J. Mando is drawn into a skirmish. The penalties offset, but that was sort of the point—with the goalie pulled, New Mexico can attack differently five-on-four than it would have six-on-five. Burton thinks the Scorpions played the official for a sucker, and his team will suffer because of it.

The Scorps get an open shot. Chad Erickson goes down as Chris Morque tries to block it out. The puck skips over Morque's stick through the unprotected crease, and New Mexico's Sly Naud dives in from behind to knock it in. In the press box, a New Mexico official blacks out the three stars of the game, which he'd selected with four minutes to go.

New Mexico wins the shootout it in the seventh round.

Outside the locker room, Burty kicks over an ice bucket. Morque seethes quietly. Kyle Haviland is apoplectic. "Nobody should be moving around in our zone like that at the end of a game," he says. "It doesn't matter if it's a lucky bounce. The bottom line is we're not going to win a championship if we play this way. We can't let guys park at our net in the last minute of the game. Even if we have to hit them in the hands."

The 14-hour bus ride home should be lots of fun.

eleven

THE CHANGING OF THE "C"

THE BATS LEAVE New Mexico on a Tuesday. The bus is back in Austin by noon on Wednesday. The team takes the ice again on Thursday against its favorite opponent, Shreveport.

Even though the club earned four out of eight possible points during the four-game trip, two shootout losses and one win against a so-so team is not much of an accomplishment. The week on the road has taken its toll, mentally and physically. Although Corey Fletcher, Mike Jackson and Jeremy Thompson are finally back in uniform, Richard Uniacke has joined Pawluk with the Aeros. That's because the center Houston would have wanted—Tim Findlay—is recuperating from eye surgery.

Management is greatly concerned—about the rookie all-star's medical bill, that is. Findlay says the owners are hemming and hawing over whether the injury counts as "work-related." While it's possible his detached retina began with some kind of degenerative condition, getting checked into the boards every night couldn't have helped much.

"Take a look around this room and see who's not in the lineup," Kyle Haviland says, minutes before the Ice Bats take on Shreveport. "We're not just playing for respect. We're playing for our jobs."

Alas, Tim Findlay might be the only spectator who enjoys the game—he can barely see. You know you're in trouble when the national anthem, provided by portly Austin yodeler Don Walser, is the best part of the night. Shreveport takes a quick 2–0 lead and ends up with a 4–1 win. Attending his first hockey game ever, Walser suggests Erickson has a five-hole problem. "We should get a goalie who isn't bowlegged," the country singer jokes.

Between periods, there's a crawfish race. Four fans run to center ice, scoop up as many live, squirmy crustaceans as they can, then go around some pylons at the blueline. When the competition is over, the little mudbugs are quickly taken off the ice, lest they sneak into Austin's zone and score at will.

"Ten o'clock tomorrow," is all Burty says afterward, tossing a piece of balled-up tape across the dressing room.

Meet the new low, same as the old low. Or lower. The next night, Waco comes to town and tops Austin for the first time all season. The Bats trail 3–2 when the game erupts into a penalty-filled disaster. Austin amasses 142 PiMs, mostly in the third period, allowing 11 power plays for the game. Somehow the score doesn't change, but the Bats spend too much time in the bin to get the equalizer. Jackson takes a retaliatory double-minor after Rob Schriner lays lumber on him. Morque cheapshots a guy. Finally, Anderson, Ross, Haviland, Thompson and Mando spark a line brawl.

Burty chalks the rough stuff up to frustration, both with the losing streak and with referee Jeff LaFave. LaFave is not known for his consistency, though it seems like he consistently jerks around the Bats. "When you don't get the calls and things aren't bouncing your way, somebody's gonna pay the price," Burton says. "You can't beat up the ref."

As a result, the coach will no longer have "his hammers back" when the Bats finish out the weekend against Amarillo Saturday. Thompson is suspended for seven games and Haviland for three, partly for the Waco melee, partly as an automatic result of past infractions and total game misconducts.

The next morning before practice, there's a closed-door meeting. When it's over, the letter on Chris Morque's sweater has changed from "C" to "A." Jeff Kungle is the new captain.

"I wasn't dissatisfied with Morqs at all," Burton says. "He's a good leader and a good captain, but where Chris is a little more emotional, Jeff is more level-headed. Together I think they make a good package. And Jake"—Mike Jackson, who wears the other "A"—"obviously he leads by example."

Burton adds that the decision came from him, not the owners.

Shaken and stirred, the Bats take care of business against the Rattlers, 5–3. The previous controversy with Keith Bland was, Burton says, "the furthest thing from my mind." The Rattlers' enforcer isn't "hurt" after all, but none of the Bats are going for the fabled bounty. They have bigger problems to contend with.

One win, after a dramatic change, doesn't automatically solve them. "It all stems from lackluster training," Burton says in his postgame interview. "We aren't prepared mentally or physically for the games. We aren't concentrating in practice, and you need that to be able to make plays successfully in the game. Tonight was more on heart and determination and effort. The rest will come with commitment and practice. We've all got to pick it up, the coach included."

Kungle and Morque are both low-key about the change in captaincy.

"We haven't been performing as well as we should have, so there's going to be some changes," Kungle says. "There's no reason to press the panic button. It's a long season. But if we want to win a playoff, we've got to play better than we have been."

"It was a team thing," Morque says. "We had a good run there for a while, and then we got in a bit of a rut. Injuries and call-ups didn't help. We just had to shake something up."

THE CAPTAIN SWITCHEROO wasn't the only wrinkle. Against the Rattlers, Burton also made Brett Seguin a healthy scratch.

"He wasn't playing that well," the coach said. "He played through that injury for me, which was really admirable because he could hardly walk, let alone skate. But the defensive part of his game is not solid. I wanted to give Brett a game upstairs because you get a different perspective. He's a great hockey player offensively, but that's only half the package. If he played the other part as well, he'd be the best player in the league."

"It sends a message to anyone and everyone that no one's job is safe," Morque notes.

"We've all gotta look in the mirror," Ryan Pawluk, who's back from his Aeros stint, says. "Some guys maybe think the squad is etched in stone. I want to make sure that I don't put Burty in a position to sit me out."

Seguin acknowledges that the night might clear his head. But he isn't happy. "It's a pretty unique experience for me," he says. "If they want a 30-goal scorer that never misses his man backchecking, they probably need to go up a level at least, you know? I mean, we're all here for a reason. We all admit it."

In addition to his injury, Seguin has not been helped by the Binnie factor. The former juniors teammates were not the perfect couple, but no other suitor has stepped up. All the latest candidates are rookies. "That makes it tough on me because I'm known as a passer," Seguin says. "If I don't have a guy scoring a lot of goals, that reflects on my input to the team."

Seguin comes from itinerant hockey stock. A dual citizen, he was born in Rochester, New York, where his father Danny played in the AHL. The elder Seguin also laced up his skates in Rhode Island, Germany, Seattle, Iowa, Tulsa and Memphis. Brett learned much of the game from his father's friend and juniors teammate Walter Tkaczuk, a former New York Rangers great. In addition to operating a hockey school, Tkaczuk and Danny Seguin owned 75 acres of land in St. Mary's, Ontario, including a pig farm. Eventually, they turned the place into the nine-hole River Valley Golf and Country Club, famous for its llamas. The beasts of burden, which take the place of golf carts, have been the subject of newspaper articles and TV reports all across Canada.

Seguin's stint with the Ottawa 67s included three 100-point seasons, most notably a 100-assist, 34-goal campaign in 1991–92. One of his sticks is in the Hockey Hall of Fame, commemorating his then OHL-record 303 career helpers. (Seguin and current record holder Bill Bowler are the only players in league history to crack 300.) Drafted in the sixth round by the Los Angeles Kings, Seguin still relishes the memory of training camp with Gretzky. His vision, timing and sheer clairvoyance are similar to the Great One's, albeit against a lower level of competition.

"Give the puck to Pig, get open"—that's all anyone on a line with him needs to know. "Brett controls the flow of the game," Jim Burton says. "If he's got open ice and he's got the puck, he slows it down, draws people to him, and if you just keep skating you'll end up getting it. He's a special hockey player."

Seguin's hands enabled him to win the rapid-fire shooting contest at the WPHL All-Star game. Once, at practice, he stood in goal and stopped five shots out of eight with the blade of a regular stick. He loves to shower pucks on unsuspecting teammates, doing it with so much touch that he never misses and no one is hurt.

"You'll get hit in the head by a puck, you turn around and Seguin just feathered it over six guys," Keith Moran says.

Seguin's defensive struggles have opened him up to the obligatory ribbing. "It must have bumped into ya," Chad Erickson says after one game, during which Seguin claims he blocked a shot.

Another time, on the road, Gunner watched the stocky five-foot-nine center gingerly work his way across a busy intersection. "That's about as fast as you backcheck," Garrett said when Seguin finally made the bus.

Trying to keep the banter light, Seguin responded that his favorite defensive hockey player was another guy named Brett . . . Hull, who, prior to joining the congregation of Ken Hitchcock's Church of Defensive Hockey on the Dallas Stars, was roundly criticized as a one-way player even when he was scoring 80 goals a year.

Like so many players at this level, Seguin began his career with an annual cup of coffee in the IHL. He saw time with four different teams in three seasons, a total of 27 games, while playing for Muskegon. He was with that Colonial League franchise for four years, the last one with Haviland, Bobby Wallwork and Rick Girhiny. Seguin can definitely relate to Findlay and Pawluk's ambitions and is more realistic than bitter about his own hockey destiny.

"There's always guys, and I was probably one of them when I was 20 years old, where the other guys are saying, 'This kid should have a shot at playing in the IHL,'" Seguin says. "I say that about Pawluk and Findlay, and I hope they do move up. Coming into this level at their age, you look at the older guys, the ones who are 26 or 27 and have been here for five years, and say, 'I'm never gonna do that. If I don't make it to the I, then that's it.'"

Indeed. "I'd be bummed if I played here next year," Tim Findlay said recently.

"But you just keep playing," Seguin says. "That's what we know. That's what we grew up with. We're still having fun. If you're not gonna make the I, what do you say? 'Ah, that's it. I'm done. I'm gonna go work at the plant back home?' You just keep playing and let it last as long as it can. If guys like Pawluk and Findlay don't make it, they'll be the ones that are 26, looking down at some young rookie that's scoring a lot of goals and saying, 'I hope he makes it.'"

For some veterans, this existential attitude carries over into training habits. NHLers make so much money, and are under so much competitive pressure, that every second of every player's life is on-the-job, from diet to bed rest to exercise to leisure time. WPHLers have it better than factory workers, but it's easy to understand why, especially at 300 or 400 dollars a week, some guys prefer golf to four-hour lifting sessions, or beer and burgers to salad and protein powder. Findlay and Pawluk say they've never seen Seguin in the gym at the apartments. Rob Hartnell says he's there, but only for 15 minutes a day of bike riding. Since it doesn't stop him from being a brilliant player, how can he be any more motivated?

"You gotta make the most of where you are," Seguin says. "Things happen at every level, but you gotta just bear with what comes at you. If your bus is broke down halfway to El Paso, what are you gonna do? You just gotta chalk it up. There's some fun experiences and some crazy times. You'll laugh about it when you're 35. You'll laugh about it next summer. So you might as well laugh about it now. I know a hundred kids back home that would kill to be doing what I'm doing. So I'm just gonna have fun. If they don't like the way I play, maybe I'll get traded. So what? I love Austin. But if I gotta go somewhere else for two months . . ."

Seguin also takes a big-picture view of the Ice Bats' current struggle. "Every team I've ever been on you start off winning," he says. "Everyone's happy, everyone likes each other. You start losing, guys on the team are fighting with each other. Guys and the coach are fighting. The coach and the owners are fighting. And then you start winning again and everybody's buddy-buddy. The best teams are the ones who can say, in the down parts, 'Look, guys, we're still buddies, and we're gonna be buddies in a week when we win the next two.'"

BURTY IS TAKING things more personally. "I'm not used to losing," he says. "I've never been on a losing team." Question is, is it good that Burton has never lost—that he just can't tolerate losing and expects his players to be the same way? Or could this be a crucial learning experience for the rookie coach? Does a taste of defeat make it easier to spit it out next time?

Either way, the change-of-captain bump lasts all of 60 minutes. Three days after beating Amarillo, New Mexico comes to town and delivers a top-to-bottom humiliation, hammering the Bats 7–3.

In the locker room afterward, it's meeting time again. Except that nobody really has anything to say.

"I just don't know what it is," Burton offers. He wants the discussion to come from the players, not from him.

"I wasn't ready to play tonight, I'll be the first to say that," Chad Erickson offers.

"Guys aren't showing up," Ryan Pawluk says.

Burton is so frustrated he chooses to be more specific. "How can you play so great on Saturday but not Sunday?" the coach asks Rob Hartnell, who had the winner against Amarillo.

And "Look, we all know Roscoe's been having his struggles. He's not putting the puck in the net. But he's still the first one in the corner.

"Think back to when you were a kid," Burton continues. "You always wanted the puck. Suddenly the guys are bigger, you don't want the puck anymore. If you don't want to play at this level, well, you can't really go down. I don't call guys up from the whatever league."

In his postgame interview, Burton remains flummoxed. "They're not actually playing hockey," he says. "They don't want to pay the price to make the play to get the goal. We have enough good hockey players on the ice. They should be able to play the game, or at least compete. But there's a few guys trying to hide out there, and it's quite obvious that they can't. They're just in the way. They're embarrassing themselves."

"It's mental lapses," Darrin MacKay opines. "And really, at the professional level, I don't think that's a coach's responsibility. I think Burty does a great job of motivating the guys. But he also gives them their space. Some guys need a kick in the butt, some guys need a pat on the back, some guys just need to be left alone. If they make a mistake, he puts them back out there to redeem themselves. I think every individual has got to look in the mirror and motivate themselves, do whatever it takes to get themselves ready for these games."

"I understand how sometimes there can be mistakes, but we're 20 games away from the real season, and we're coming up with nights where we don't even belong in this league," Burton says. "So what do I do? I really don't know."

Blaine Stoughton has a few ideas. Or at least one. When the team reconvenes against Lake Charles three days later, their former captain is a former Ice Bat. Chris Morque and Corey Fletcher have been traded to El Paso, even-up, for second-year defensemen Derek Riley and Jason Rose.

"It's tough," Stoughton says. "Morqs is one of the original guys I had. He committed to me two summers ago. I really didn't want to make the move, but we've been pretty flat the last 10 or 12 games. I just felt we needed a shake-up in the locker room. These other two kids, they're young, they were rookies last year, but they won a championship, so they must bring something to the table."

Rose's and Riley's youth is exactly why Todd Brost gave up on them. Mark Hilton, the defenseman El Paso had picked up in exchange for Hartnell last season, got called up to the IHL and isn't coming back. Brost needed an experienced hand on the blue-line and was thrilled to get his old ECHL teammate. Stoughton made the move without Burton's input. He notified Morque about the trade via answering machine. Burton isn't exactly ecstatic. Sure, the overhaul was needed. And yes, Morque had been struggling—and will probably benefit from the change of scenery. But the actual deal is a lateral move at best, one that doesn't truly improve the team or address a pressing need.

Morque's friends think this is another manifestation of Stoughton's grudge against the veterans. But other players think it isn't such a bad thing. Everybody understands something had to be done.

"I think we've had some complacency here," Rob Hartnell says. "The guys know we have it good here in Austin. Maybe they took it for granted."

Everybody is also thinking, "Thank God it wasn't me."

MORQUE'S TRADE makes a statement about the Ice Bats' social structure. The team is no longer ruled by the back of the bus. When two rookies are your most productive players, the traditional balance of power skews.

"You're not really a rookie after Christmas," Andy Ross says, especially given that most of the Bats' youngsters have already been through the crucible of the highly competitive OHL. Still, no matter how great he is on the ice, no matter how much he may think of himself, a player like Ryan Pawluk feels he's in the seen-not-heard phase of his career.

"I speak up as much as I can, but a rookie only has so much say," Pawluk says. "I just try to lead by example and let Burty and the guys with the letters say what has to be said."

Which isn't to say that Pawluk doesn't have opinions. "If we want to win this year, we're going to have to go with the new guys," he says. "The young guys have been pulling a lot of the weight."

He pauses, realizing the comment sounds like finger-pointing.

"I shouldn't say that," he revises. "It's more like, we've been helping on a consistent basis. Burty just wants some of the older guys to contribute as much they should be. And the young guys who aren't contributing as much, they have to pick up their game a step as well."

As captain, Jeff Kungle is the consensus-builder. He's a second-year pro but comports himself like an older player. On the ice, he's Austin's most reliable performer, which is all the credibility he needs. His status with the Aeros conveys additional gravitas. Most of all, the defenseman is not especially close with either the veteran clique or the rookie faction. He gets along with both groups without being part of either. He and his fiancée Lisa spend most of their time with Jeremy and Jennifer Thompson.

Ironically, through all the rigmarole, the Morque trade isn't even the biggest news of the Ice Bats' day. After hobbling through practice earlier in the week, Brett Seguin went for an X-ray. The result means he'll now have plenty of time to get that "different perspective." A broken foot will put him on injured reserve for at least a month. As the great poet and hockey scholar William Butler Yeats once wrote, "Things fall apart/the center cannot hold." With Findlay still wearing sunglasses at night, the turmoil-ridden Ice Bats are without both their All-Star pivots.

THE NIGHT OF THE TRADE, the Bats beat Lake Charles handily. Rob Hartnell gets another game-winner. Derek Riley arrives from El Paso in the middle of the firsst period. With a sweater waiting and his name already on the lineup card, Riley works in a quick ride on the exercise bike before taking the ice in the second.

The Bats then endure another up-and-back Monroe trip, squeezing in a 4–1 triumph between two eight-hour bus rides.

Back home for another 3 P.M. Sunday contest, the Bats are ravenous for a "W" over Central Texas. Since beating the Stampede on opening night, Austin has lost three straight shootouts to its nearest rival.

They've all been doozies. Way back in December, the Bats lost a last-minute five-on-three advantage in a deadlocked game when Jeff Kungle was caught with an illegal stick. In the extra frame,

CenTex forward Mike Dick taunted Erickson after scoring, earning him a game misconduct. But the Bats were unable to get one past Stampede goalie Larry Dyck.

Yes, the fans took full notice of those names. Most popular cheers: "Dyck, you're a pussy!" and "You suck, Dyck." For their part, the Belton fans make signs saying things like "Austin Wishes It Had a Dyck" and "The Bats Can't Touch Our Dyck." To my knowledge, no one from the sheriff's department has ever confiscated them.

As the teams left the ice, through a shared exit, a Central Texas fan came over and started yelling "Choke, choke!" Chris Morque almost speared him, while another player claimed the fan, a used-car salesman named Howard Kinsell who would go on to self-styled infamy as the Internet columnist and radio host named "the Warrior," also did a little spitting. Burton had to be restrained from jumping into the stands. Kinsell was led away by an Austin cop, though he was not arrested.

Meanwhile, Stampede pest Peter Zurba was in Gunner Garrett's face, yelling "Two points, two points!" Jim Mullin interfered, telling Zurba that he's bush. "I'll fucking kill you," Zurba responded.

The next game, 24 days later, finished up the same way. This time, Dick missed his shootout attempt and Erickson taunted *him*, with no penalty. But the Stampede won again. "It's okay, Chad. Maybe you'll be a star of the game one of these days," CenTex player/assistant Jason Taylor said. Zurba got into it again, and Kyle Haviland, in street clothes from an earlier suspension, almost jumped him right in front of the preteen autograph seekers.

Haviland is known for his super-short fuse. He's the epitome of the hockey cop, a low-rent Scott Stevens who plays every shift on a slippery emotional edge. He's also as tough as anyone in the league. As an underpaid rookie in Memphis, the defenseman put his body and bare hands on the line so often and so aggressively that the coach used to give him an extra 20 bucks a game out of his own pocket.

Haviland is different from the other Ice Bats thugs. Sure, there's real violence and real rancor in both Ryan Anderson and Jeremy Thompson, but they also bring an element of showmanship to the ice, while cultivating a friendly just-doing-my-job air off it. Haviland couldn't be a sweeter guy—loyal, sincere, great with kids—but during games he's like Bruce Banner. You don't want to make him angry.

Yet opposing players do it all the time. When it happens, you can actually see Haviland's nervous system boil, the adrenaline shooting from the anger in his brain to the motion of his body. He bounces in place, like a jogger waiting at a traffic light, anticipating the bout with a little dance of readiness, skates tensing, gloves dropping, sleeves pulled up, the linesmen circling cautiously at a distance. Then, BAM!—he's the Incredible Hockey Hulk.

Haviland's father, Bruce, says that Kyle literally sees red when fighting, like a bull. The blazing color in his head blots out everything but the brawl, which is why he doesn't always make the best decisions in the wake of one.

Jim Burton thinks that Haviland has to lose it every once in a while—it's part of his game, the thing that makes him so effective. Rick Girhiny recalls that in his two seasons playing with Kyle, he knew he could barrel into opposing goalies with no retribution, because anyone attempting it would face the same from Havs. That's also why Brett Seguin can recklessly wield his stick to break free of defenders. And Ryan Pawluk certainly knows how much he has benefited from Kyle's services. One night at a convenience store, the rookie was mock-attacked by Andy Ross. He stood up to his aggressor for a moment, then jokingly yelled out for a bodyguard: "Havy!"

But Havs' volcanic streak has also had its costs. In December, he was on the receiving end of a one-punch knockdown from Lake Charles' Darcy Verot, a mere six-foot 190-pounder (Haviland is six-foot and 220). Getting clocked was bad enough, but Verot, who would later stick with the AHL Scranton–Wilkes Barre Penguins, also gloated.

Red red red red red. Haviland smacked his stick into the glass, whirled away from the rink door and skated to the Ice Pirates bench, challenging every player. This was in a game Austin was winning, with less than five minutes remaining in the third. Several Ice Bats intervened, but not before Haviland's free-swinging tantrum took down a linesman, earning him another half-dozen games in street clothes.

Serving suspensions is part of Haviland's job. But the incident, combined with the team's overall defensive struggles, has eaten at his confidence. Having been absent so frequently, including the last three games after the Waco fracas, Havs is particularly juiced for Central Texas on this night. "Don't forget what these guys fucking did last time," he says in the locker room before warm-ups.

Just to add a little extra spice to what is already an ill-tempered rivalry, the Stampede have picked up a player named Gary Coupal. In his hockey career, Coupal has been suspended for life by the OHL, the ECHL and the UHL (the former Colonial League) for various stick infractions, including tossing his lumber into the stands.

But there is a place for him in Central Texas. Austin fans show up with signs proclaiming "Ban the Goon." (Later, the team's operations manager, Jim Bond, admits to making them, then passing them along to ticketholders.)

After all that, tonight's game is not about the rough stuff. The Bats build on the previous two efforts and play well, leading 3–1 after two periods. Yet somehow, Central Texas has a 4–3 lead with 9:05 remaining in the game.

Rob Hartnell saves the day. He gets an unassisted rebound-scrum goal, squirming and squiggling off his own initial wraparound. Then he pops the winner in the shootout. It's the first time the Bats have won three games in a row since Thanksgiving weekend.

"It was a slump, but we were .500 the whole slump," a relieved Jim Burton says. "With a lot of inconsistencies in the lineup."

Through it all, Hartnell has been one of the guys who has turned it on. His practice fight with Andy Ross has turned out to be some kind of catalyst—much to Roscoe's regret, considering their $100 wager. With tonight's hat trick Hartsy now has 21 goals to Roscoe's 23.

Like Kungle, Hartnell is in a good position to lead the team. He's a fiery, talkative guy. He has the trust and friendship of the rookies, but as a five-year veteran, he has the authority to butt heads with the rest of the players.

"You can tell there's no complacency anymore," Hartsy says. "Everybody's working hard and wants to be a part of this team. That's the way it's got to be from now on for the rest of the regular season and right through the playoffs. Everybody's pulling in the same direction now. It's good to see, and it's a good time of the year to do it."

FEBRUARY 3 . . . *New Mexico 4, Austin 3.*

If everybody's pulling in the same direction, it must be backward. In Albuquerque, for a game the team travels to via Southwest Airlines, Burton benches half the team in the middle of the second period, including several defensemen.

"I don't know what to do," he says. "I put Keith Moran back there, and he looks as good as anybody else I got. Doesn't say much for the defense, does it? They do what they can, I guess, but they're not good enough to play."

The biggest problem is not giving up goals or beating guys along the boards, but simply breaking out the puck. "Our D can play D, but they can't get the puck and move it out," Burton says. "They can't make a stick-to-stick pass. No team at this level has got an overabundance of those players, but it seems like every team has got six more than I've got. Even Jeff Kungle. He's my best defenseman, but he's a defensive defenseman. He needs to play with a guy who can move the puck."

What about Todd Harris, who's supposed to be that guy? "Mistake after mistake. He skates around out there like he has eggs in his pockets."

Kyle Haviland sits out the entire third. In the heat of postgame anger, he talks about retirement. "I'm tired of the mind games. All I ever wanted to do was play hockey, and now it's no fun."

February 5 . . . *Monroe 3, Austin 1.*

Christian Soucy returns. André Racicot outduels him.

February 7 . . . *San Angelo 5, Austin 2.*

Before the game, Burton scoffs at the notion that San Angelo and Al Rooney might bounce back from that 11–2 beating. During it, the coach has to be revived with smelling salts after catching a stick to the face in the middle of a skirmish at the Austin bench.

February 8 . . . *Fort Worth 5, Austin 1.*

The first-place Brahmas now have 81 points. The third-place Ice Bats have 66. Austin's games-in-hand have shrunk from 10 to 5.

At the booster club table in the Bat Cave, two fans wear bags over their heads. The comments from the peanut gallery are similarly inclined.

"Hey Anderson, your defense is really coming around!"

"Hey Thompson, if you score a goal I'll shave my head."

"Give Binnie a call!"

"That's it, Hartnell. You're the only one who tries!"

"Hit someone, Harris!"

Ryan Anderson is in the penalty box when he hears that remark. "Better chance of winning the lottery than Harry hitting somebody," he mutters.

I spend this game in the box, hoping for a bloody, inspired evening of book-worthy material. But the players are too downtrodden to be colorful, let alone chatty.

"We're struggling, Cozy," Anderson says, in the middle of another fighting major. "It makes me sick to my stomach."

(No, I was not called "Cozy" with any regularity. The two Ryans were the only guys who favored the nickname. Personally, I think it's a darn shame the practice of adding "-er," "-y" or "-s" to some permutation of a player's last name has replaced colorful tags like "Boom-Boom" and "Pocket Rocket.")

When Jeff LaFave sends Hartnell away with a minor, Hartsy doesn't look to curry favor for next time. "You bald dipshit," he rants. "What an asshole you are. You must have gotten cut from a lot of teams, you fuckin' loser."

Fort Worth scores while Rob is in the box.

Mike Jackson also gets sent away at one point. He is fuming so quietly that I don't try to engage him in chat. Then he scares the hell out of both me and the attendant by springing up after another misplayed Ice Bats chance. "FUCK! CAN WE BUY A FUCKING GOAL!" he bellows, slamming his hand against the glass.

Between the second and third periods, Anderson, Haviland and Ross sit on the stairs outside the locker room, openly bemoaning how low everyone's confidence is. They are bitter, resentful and resigned. "There's lots of places to play at this level," Ross says.

"There's a lot of pressure on the veterans because we're the first ones that'll be traded out of here," he says after the game.

That pressure isn't really fair. The team needs to produce, no question. But December was riddled with bumps and bruises. Management didn't replace Binnie. The injuries to Findlay and Seguin are devastating.

In the meantime, Ross says, "They're throwing a bunch of $300 kids in here and expecting to win." Those kids—and he is not referring to Findlay and Pawluk (who make $500 and $600, respectively) or any specific player, just the fact that the team is 50 percent rookies—are good players, but experience counts. As tough as the OHL is, most of them have never before endured the long, highly compressed, travel-heavy schedule that is a fact of life in the professional game.

Even Burty acknowledges that he feels hamstrung by the owners. The brass talk about needing a young team that doesn't run out of energy and health, which is what happened to last year's squad of oldsters. But the minimum salaries and lower insurance premiums are also attractive. Those decisions are not necessarily made by Stoughton or Lawless, but by Ed Novess and Daniel Hart, the two owners with the fatter wallets and thinner hockey backgrounds. Dr. Hart is nothing more than a good-natured guy with money who enjoys his proximity to the athletes. But Novess, the only owner with real business experience, is Mr. Bottom Line. Even Stoughton feels heat from him occasionally.

Burton knows that the difference between winning three and losing three is often a couple of bounces. Games turn on a single mistake, on one timely power play goal, on a crucial save. He needs his centers back. And he's got his eye on a couple of players, currently with European teams, who might join the Bats in March.

But for the most part, with just five wins in the last 15 games, the coach has run out of postgame rhetoric. "You need to work things out among yourselves," he says, banishing everyone—doctors, trainers, journalists, owners and coaches—from the locker room for yet another group therapy session.

"And if you decide the problem is me, I'm willing to hear that too."

twelve

LAYING DOWN THE LAW

IN AN ATTEMPT to put the latest lousy weekend behind them, the Bats still get their usual Monday off-day. I drop by Andy Ross's apartment to see how he and Kyle Haviland feel about the current gloomy vibe. Since the Morque trade, the team has been so wound up that no one's speaking freely—except among themselves.

The way Ross and Haviland see it, problem number one is, there is no problem. The team overachieved in December, when it didn't have the bodies to ice three lines. By January, that caught up to everyone, mentally as well as physically. No sooner had fresh troops arrived than Findlay and Seguin were hobbled. "When they get back in the lineup, we're a number one contending team all over again," Haviland says.

"I didn't think we were going to finish in first," Roscoe reasons. "Besides, we're not going to get home ice anyway."

That's because the Austin Rodeo and Livestock Show takes over the Expo Center until a week after the playoffs start. It would be fruitless for the team to expend its health and energy trying to take over the division. But there could still be home ice in later rounds. Either way, the players shouldn't think consciously about the situation, lest they use it as an excuse for slacking.

"We're working hard," Ross contends. "We just gotta pull together. You don't want to make excuses, but we can't let this get us too crazy either, 'cause then you're just going to have another meeting."

Which brings us to problem number two: ownership. Their impatience is the reason things are tense. Stoughton and Co. are putting a lot of pressure on Jim Burton, but it doesn't end there. The general manager treats the players with disdain, further eroding what is already a dysfunctional relationship.

Haviland says that in yesterday's loss, he tried to play a simple game. He knows he hasn't been performing well and was hoping to get back on track. "So I go out and have a good physical period," he recaps. "I'm just getting my confidence back up. Then Blaine comes in the locker room and throws a shit-ass remark at me. He knows I put enough pressure on myself already."

While they are hardly impartial observers, Haviland and Ross believe that Stoughton traded Morque mostly out of spite. "He has it out for us," Havs says, meaning all the second-year Bats. "It's personal to him. When he walks by, he doesn't even say hi to us. He puts his head down. What's that about?"

In their mind, it goes back to last year's playoff flop. Stoughton feels personally affronted that the team didn't win for him. He and the other owners lost money because there weren't more profit-making playoff home games.

"Blaine says to us, he can bring in 18 rookies and pay them all 300 bucks if we're gonna lose," Ross says.

Frugality is also the reason every team in the WPHL has sweat-suits except for Austin. This may seem like a minor issue, but when you're not making much money and half your working life is a dreary bus ride, little things matter. Especially since those bus rides would be a lot more comfy in sweatsuits than in the current khakis-and-collared-shirt travel outfit.

Now, whether you're talking George Steinbrenner, Harold Ballard or Blaine Stoughton, owners are owners. It's their team.

They can do what they want with it, and that's exactly the message Stoughton sends. Instead of basing himself in the business office, he occupies the same rear corner of the dressing room that he did as head coach. Meanwhile, Jim Burton works out of a smaller enclave—the assistant's office, most people would call it. All four owners use the place as a clubhouse, meeting in Stoughton's office and cracking beers together after games.

"They come in our locker room every day," Ross complains. "They're around us all the time."

Losing is bad enough. The added scrutiny is chipping away at the players' sense of joy. "We were sitting there yesterday during the third period and Jake turns to me and goes, 'When's the last time you remember having fun?'" Ross recalls.

"It's not a game anymore," Haviland adds. "It almost feels like work."

Whatever else is going wrong, neither player believes Burton is to blame. "I think he's doing an unbelievable job," Ross says.

"I don't think we have anything to worry about," Haviland reiterates. "When we get those guys back for the last 10 games we'll get a good run going. It's the perfect time to peak—right before the playoffs."

TUESDAY BRINGS the toughest practice of the year. I get there almost an hour late and it hasn't even started. *Austin American-Statesman* reporter Amy Hettenhausen and freelance photographer Shelly Kanter are already there. Team meeting, they inform me.

But of course. A team meeting to talk about the results of Sunday's team meeting.

Finally, the players march down the rubber mat, a noticeable jump in every step. Kyle Haviland is the last man out. He trails the rest of the guys by several minutes.

Uh-oh, I think. But Havy's not too addled—no more than usual, at least. I figure that's a good sign, since Kyle's no good at hiding his emotions.

I couldn't be more wrong. I grab a seat, and soon the Bats are huffing through a high-intensity workout. Darrin MacKay and Gerald Stoughton are both in jumpsuits, putting players through their paces. They're joined by a similarly attired Paul Lawless. Two assistants and an owner, cracking the whip. With Stoughton looking on from behind the goal. Serious stuff. But where's Burty?

It just doesn't register. I'm thinking he must be on the phone, working out a trade or reeling in one of those European free agents. Obviously, it's something so big that he had to handle it immediately, leaving the other guys to supervise the mundane drills.

Ryan Anderson's father makes me see the obvious. Dale, visiting Austin for the second time this season, goes to practice nearly every day. Since Gerald Stoughton is his oldest friend, he's more clued in to the workings of the team than your average player parent.

I ask him if it isn't odd that Burty's missing.

"I think you'd better go talk to the GM," Dale advises.

Now I get it. I still can't believe it, but I get it. Burty's history.

My sense of embarrassment is tempered somewhat by Amy and Shelly, who are watching practice in a similar state of naive bliss. I give Amy the heads-up and she goes to call her editors.

The team meeting began with Burty and the owners making the announcement together. Then the owners and the players "cleared the air"—or so it was said. The reality is, while both sides did plenty of bitching, there wasn't much catharsis.

"No, things got a little more cluttered, probably," Chad Erickson says later. "Blaine basically challenged some guys. He criticized the team for breaking into cliques, and he criticized the team for griping about ownership. He stepped up and said if we didn't have the guts to come to them and say what we wanted to say, then don't say it at all."

Stoughton's points have merit. But directness is a two-way street. Coming from him, the players considered such talk to be laughable hypocrisy. This is the guy who agreed with Erickson last summer on a specific salary, then mailed out a contract for several hundred dollars a month lower, without warning or explanation. This is the guy who tried to deal Binnie to Central Texas without telling the Stampede GM that Binnie was retiring. This is the guy who, as Brett Seguin discovered when he was a healthy scratch, sits there in the press box giving his own players about as much respect as Don Cherry gives to visor-wearing Swedes.

If honesty is the best policy, when is the s going to tell all the veterans about the "available for trade" fax their names have been on since the beginning of the season? Sure, such faxes are standard operating procedure in the hockey business—but not when your team is 10–2.

Kyle Haviland was tardy because he remained in the locker room for a one-on-one with Stoughton. He almost refused to practice. "I was taking off my shoulder pads," he says. "I came this close to taking off my skates. But I've gotta keep an open mind."

It becomes official at the end of practice.

"Today we're announcing that Jim Burton stepped down as coach of the Ice Bats," Blaine Stoughton tells the press. "It's a situation where I didn't think, and Jim didn't think, that the team was playing up to their capabilities. He came to me, well . . . actually last week, and he kind of felt us out and said, 'Hey, let's give it the weekend. Let's see what happens here and we'll make a decision Monday.' The guys, for whatever reason, just weren't responding. Jim's got a lot of character, and he's a great guy. It's just a mutual decision between all of us that Paul could give it a shot here, try to get the boys going."

Stoughton acknowledges that Burton has been working under difficult circumstances, what with all the injuries, suspensions and call-ups. "There is a little bit of an alibi," the general manager says, "but there's no alibi for hard work. The last few games, the guys never competed. I think they need more of a vocal guy. Someone to provide a little more direction, and maybe a little more discipline."

The players are stunned. Sure, Burty had told them after the Morque trade that struggling teams usually go through a three-step process. "First they warn you, then they trade a player, then they fire the coach," Ryan Anderson remembers. "When he said it, I didn't really think it was going to come about."

But after the long meeting and longer practice, the reality has hit them. They know it's just a part of hockey. Most of them have already been through two or three coaches at the junior level. They have to put their energy into playing well for the current coach, rather than crying over the fired one.

"I love Burty," Ryan Pawluk says. "He's one of the best coaches

I ever played for. It's a shock. But I think he made a personal choice and put the team in front of himself. I think Lawly's gonna inflict a little bit more discipline on some guys."

"Maybe Burty didn't discipline us enough," Tim Findlay echoes. "He let some guys run around and get on their own schedules, and that shows a little bit on the ice. You gotta have all 20 guys on the same page. It wasn't that they didn't want to play for Burty, but some guys were getting a little out of hand."

"I think we're all upset," Jeremy Thompson says. "It's our fault that Burty isn't the coach anymore. We basically let him down. Sometimes, with a players' coach, guys get complacent. They maybe don't work as hard as they might when they have a coach that can be a drill sergeant."

In front of a TV camera, Erickson sounds the only note of skepticism. "They decided to make a change," the goalie shrugs. "That's their decision. They're the owners. But we're missing our two leading scorers, and with a young team, you need a guy like Burty to teach these guys. I don't know if it was the best move, but it's not for me to say. Maybe this has been brewing for a while, I don't know. It's none of my business. It's a lot easier to get rid of a coach than it is to replace 18 guys."

"It's something we felt was necessary," Lawless says. "The team was a sinking ship. We lost a lot of games we should have won. I think we have the manpower and the talent here to win a championship, and I think Jim Burton had a lot to do with that. It's not going to be one individual that's going to do it. If these guys win the championship, I'm not the hero."

"Why go from one rookie coach to another rookie coach?" broadcaster Mark Martello wonders.

It's a valid question. If the owners wanted to make a serious change, it might have done better to look outside the organization. Who knows what the players' comfort level would have been with a complete stranger, assuming that person had real autonomy. Lawless will do his share of kicking ass and taking names, and as a former goal-scorer, he has a real connection with the younger forwards. But he's also a an ex–Ice Bats player, a glad-handing charmer—he calls everybody "Big Boy"—who, as owner, likes nothing more than to pass out the drink tickets and share a bar stool with the boys.

On the bright side, the players don't perceive him as a member of the brass. When it comes to hockey decisions, Stoughton is the scapegoat. When it comes to money decisions, it's the other partners. Lawly is the friendly front man, a goodwill ambassador to both the fans and the players. It's funny to remember him huffing and puffing during training camp, and being unwilling to play more than one game in December when the team needed him. He has always avoided those long road trips. He won't be able to now.

THE MAN HIMSELF faces the day with dignity and humor.

"This'll be good for your book, eh?" Burty says to me wistfully.

Everything about the scenario suggests that Burton was forced out. At best, he made a gracious exit before the owners could act ungraciously. The question is not did he jump or was he pushed. The question is why was he at the precipice at all?

On the record, the ex-coach toes the party line. It was a joint decision. "That is accurate in this situation," Burton says. "I talked to Blaine before the previous weekend. I told him if it doesn't turn around, let's do something, because I've tried everything I know. I put every ounce of energy I had into it. I had exhausted everything that I could, trying to make them win—other than going on the ice and shooting the puck myself.

"It's a tough situation," he continues. "Ownership didn't want to lose, and I didn't want to lose. I was always a team player when I played, so I thought that the way to do things as a team player was to try something different. I didn't want to take the chance that this thing wouldn't turn around without at least trying something."

So quitting is his final tactical adjustment?

"That's right. My last card up my sleeve. I hope it works."

Burty admits that he may have been too easy on the squad. "They're like my kids. I feel for them, maybe to a fault. Maybe I killed them with kindness. But as a coach, you learn.

"I think they feel that they let me down," he adds. "And at times, possibly, they did. They didn't do everything they could've to keep me employed, so they should feel a sense of responsibility for what's happened here. I actually asked the team if they thought it was me. But being the nice guy that I am, which is really a fault as a coach, I don't think they would have said it was my fault even if it was. I don't think I was a bad coach. I felt that I was . . . I was as good as I knew how to be. I think I taught them a lot. I'm not going to lie to you. I'm disappointed. But I'm still a part of it."

Burty is still part of it as assistant general manager—technically, a job he already had, at least in terms of the work he did. Still, if the title reeks of the standard "reassignment" that happens to any fired coach, that isn't entirely the case. Burton doesn't have a guaranteed or multi-year contract, so the team isn't obligated to keep him on.

"I always thought when a coach got fired you had 24 hours to get out of town," he jokes. "I'm grateful for the chance to stick around and help out, to be a part of what I started."

In the big picture, sticking around means there's a position for him next year, perhaps in Austin, but more likely with the WPHL expansion team the Ice Bats owners are starting up in Arkansas.

For the players, this bitter pill is easier to swallow with Burty still around. "If he had packed up his bags and left, it would have been a lot more disappointing," Ryan Pawluk says. "But he's still gonna have a lot to do with the team. If we win, he's gonna feel just as proud because of all the work he put in for the first three-quarters of the season."

Coincidentally—if you believe in coincidence, that is—the day of Burty's exit is also the day of the team picture. Looking at the shot, it's hard to tell what's really on the players' minds. Certain guys appear brooding or angry, but that's just the way some players look when cameras are around.

Ryan Pawluk grins like he's in high school. Chad Erickson sticks his tongue out. Darrin MacKay wears his old number 12 instead of a coach's jumpsuit. At the end of the second row, standing next to Eric Seeber, is head coach—for all of 20 minutes—Paul Lawless. Jim Burton is nowhere to be found.

thirteen
THIS SHOE IS MADE
FOR STOMPING

FOR ALL THE DRAMA around the coaching change, the daily banality of hockey must go on. The weekend comes. The wake-up call is heard and answered. The Bats begin the Lawless era.

The fans are just as energized as the players. Signs at the arena are voluminous. Behind one goal, homemade posters bear the legends "King Kungle," "All Hart and No Fear" and "Shootouts? We Don't Need No Stinkin' Shootouts." Banners raised over the players' entrance by the booster club remind them, "Never, ever, ever give up" (the motto of late, legendary college basketball coach Jim Valvano), as well as "100 percent of the pucks you don't shoot don't go in" (quoting Wayne Gretzky).

Before his debut, Lawly asks Eric for throat lozenges instead of gum. The new boss is a yeller—he'll need them. He is also active with the chalkboard, diagramming breakouts and defensive coverage between periods when things get a little shaky.

"It's been a long time," Rob Hartnell says, 20 minutes before the Bats wrap up a victory over Waco. "Just do it. We don't have to talk about it."

The Bats take it 4–1. Jim Burton, who'd waited for the lights to go down before slipping through the stands and up into the press box, is there at the locker room door afterward with congratulations. "The guys earned it," Lawless says. "The two and a half days I've had them, they've worked their rear ends off for me. We have a system and we're gonna stick with it. We didn't change a thing all night. The second effort was there, and morale's very high right now. But one game doesn't make a season. It's one out of 14 that we want to win."

Lawless's most valuable first-night lesson? Leather soles might be the mark of a finely crafted dress shoe, but they're of little help when you're walking on ice. Before the Bats earn triumph number two by beating Central Texas, Lawly goes to the local DSW outlet for a pair of rubber-soled black lace-ups.

Then the team buses it to Shreveport for what has become a ritual flogging on Mudbugs ice. The Bats go down 3–0 in a matter of minutes, regain their composure to make it 3–2, but trail 4–2 by the end of the second.

"I'm minus three," Andy Ross laments. "Are you kidding me?"

"We haven't won a game trailing after two periods all season," Kyle Haviland says. "That's bullshit. That says we're not a character team. Everybody thinks we're not coming back. So let's do it."

Meanwhile—shades of Jim Mullin—Chad Erickson is eating a Snickers bar, washed down with his fourth Pepsi of the day.

"What does my diet matter, I'm not playing anyway," the goalie says. Between periods of the previous contest, he sat in Gunner's office reading *The Hockey News*, isolated from his teammates.

Lawless had said he would make a "night-to-night decision" on the starting goalie, but that decision has been to play Christian Soucy three times in a row. It seems unfair, and maybe even petty considering Erickson's comments about the Burton firing. But it's also true that, given his four-month layoff, Soucy needs the work. "The IHL doesn't send a guy to Austin to have him sitting on the bench," Lawless points out. "That's part of the deal."

The Bats lose to Shreveport 8–3. Many a locker door is

slammed. At the Texaco convenience store outside Hirsch Coliseum, a guy notices the bus.

"What are you?" he asks Kyle Haviland.

"Half a hockey team," Havs replies.

NEXT MORNING, the Bats return to Austin for an afternoon matchup against El Paso, the fourth game in four days. "As far as I'm concerned, last night is in the books," Lawless says. "We beat ourselves. We were running around in our own zone staring at the puck. I don't even need to show you the tape because it's so fuckin' obvious."

The Bats bounce back, eking out a win over the Buzzards 4–3. They do so without Ryan Pawluk, who woke up (after a 6 A.M. arrival from Shreveport) to find a message on his answering machine telling him to get to the airport and join the Aeros in Las Vegas, pronto. In Pawluk's absence, Joe Van Volsen picks up the offensive slack with a natural hat trick, and Rob Hartnell gets the shootout winner.

The reunion with Chris Morque is uneventful. Jeremy Thompson, asked if he would "go"—get into a fight—with his former teammate, cracks, "I'll just go wide on him."

It's a bittersweet day for Morque, but he's happy to be part of the defending WPHL champions. He is also not surprised by Burton's fate. "You can't undermine your coach like that and expect him to have any power with his players," he says. "I think Jim saw the writing on the wall. He knew what was coming. I think this was cooked up a lot longer than two weeks ago. I think this was cooked up about six months ago, to be honest with you."

The Bats' 3–1 start under Lawless can be compared to a presidential candidate's poll numbers immediately after the inaugurating convention, or an obscure rock band's record sales following an appearance on *David Letterman* or *Mike Bullard*. It's a spike, a boost, a temporary ray of sunshine.

For Austin, the next four games are more like business as usual—a loss to Shreveport, a loss to Lake Charles, a win over Monroe, a shootout loss to Central Texas.

"Who's in the doghouse?" I ask Haviland after one defeat. "Who isn't?" he counters. A different defenseman has been scratched every night. With various forwards coming off the injury list, the numbers game is heating up again.

"It's getting a little scary," Chris Haskett says.

"I worry about it every day," Keith Moran admits. Now that he's made it this far, he'd like to finish. Moran knew where he stood with Burty, earning the coach's respect over a period of several months. Now he has to make himself stand out all over again.

Of course, neither Haskett nor Moran will argue about losing out to the team's best player. Tim Findlay has been skating in practice, slowly, no pads, wearing a backwards baseball cap instead of a helmet. Now he's at 100 percent—better, in fact. "I asked the doctor, if I get into a fight and I get punched in the eye, is it going to do any damage?" Findlay says. "He said it's not going to do any more damage than it would to my other eye. It's actually stronger than the other one."

"Sure, *now* he comes back," Jim Burton says to me, with a light-hearted, joking-but-not-joking tone, after Findlay's first appearance.

The assistant general manager is also responsible for the Ice Bats' latest newcomer. Fans who bother showing up early for warm-ups are immediately abuzz about the fresh body wearing number 15, a lumbering giant with a long goatee, no front teeth and a leonine mane of hair. Bruce Shoebottom's plane landed in Austin at 5:30 P.M. He was on the ice an hour later.

"See the new guy?" Ryan Pawluk asks me. "He's a fucking Neanderthal."

He looks like a member of Metallica, I suggest.

"James Hetfield!" Pawluk enthusiastically agrees. "I gotta go tell the guys!"

Angie Craig, an off-ice official who is also Brett Seguin's girl-friend, notes that "Shoe" strongly resembles the guy in the Minnesota Vikings logo as well.

In the dressing room, Shoe issues a disclaimer. "I'm old, slow, out of shape and not exactly healthy," he says. "But I'll chip in any way I can. Bear with me, because I wasn't that good when I was young."

In fact, he's played at a higher level than anyone on the baby-faced Ice Bats team. Shoe's stint as a Boston Bruin was intermit-tent—just 35 games over four seasons—but he was still a cult favorite among the die-hard fans. The defenseman's stat line in his final NHL season says it all: 1 game, 0 points, 5 PiMs.

He had a much more productive career in the AHL and IHL. In 1986–87, he topped 300 PiMs as a Fort Wayne Komet. Burton was a teammate.

"I noticed his name in USA *Today* around December," Shoebottom says. "I wasn't too sure it was the same guy. Ended up giving him a call and talking to him." Shoe was back home in Maine, trying to get in shape. "I figured I might as well play in one of the better cities. I might just call him every December 31, so I can get out of New England for January, February and March."

Shoe became somewhat notorious in the Central Hockey League as a member of the Oklahoma City Blazers. In 1994, the Blazers were in a first-round playoff match against bitter rivals Tulsa when Shoebottom, already in the penalty box following a fracas, came out for more when an Oiler taunted him. Only problem is he barreled over the penalty box attendant. The Tulsa cops became involved, hitting him with pepper spray and a choke hold. League officials failed to take significant disciplinary action, but the local D.A. had assault charges pending for several years. Shoebottom countered with a personal-injury lawsuit, arguing that his ability to play was affected.

Shoe's career has been limited since the incident. He managed seasons of 22 games and 38 games for the San Diego Gulls, helping them take the West Cost Hockey League championship twice. The second time, he had 288 PIMs in what was essentially half a year.

"I got him from the California Penal League," Burty jokes.

In addition to providing veteran leadership, Shoebottom will try to do the job that Morque used to: play tough, solid, simple defense, especially in front of the net. Rose and Riley are too young and too small to fill that role. They're not bad players, but as Chad Erickson notes, Morque is basically a number-two or number-three defenseman. Rose and Riley are more like fifth or sixth.

Shoe's arrival prompts a full renovation of the Ice Bats defense. Just before Burty's resignation, Ken Ruddick was scratched for one game and chose to leave the team soon afterward. But Keith Moran saves his job by moving to the blueline. He'd taken the odd shift there in recent weeks, most notably in New Mexico. The first time, Burty was desperate for more offense. The second time was the night the coach chose to make an example out of the regular blueliners. He did well enough that Jeff Kungle took Lawless aside and suggested that the club could really benefit from Moran's work ethic and ability back there. Moran also caught the attention of his teammates when he paired off with Rob Hartwell in a little practice spat.

"I've gained so much respect for Keith," Ryan Pawluk says. "He's the utility man. He puts his hard hat on, goes to the rink, plays wherever they want him, plays his nuts off. I'm surprised we don't see him in net."

As a New England native, Moran gets a gigantic kick out of hearing MacKay call out the defense pairs: "Moran, Shoe, you're up next." His friends back home start e-mailing him questions about the Bruins. "Ask Shoe what Ken Linseman was really like," one wants to know.

It takes but a single shift for the Ice Bats crowd to start up chants of SHOE! SHOE! By his second game, someone has strung up footwear to a stick, waving the contraption like a flag. By then, Shoe has switched his number from 15 to 31—the goalie-sized jersey fits him better.

With creaky knees and a laundry list of other ailments, Shoebottom isn't the most mobile guy in the world. When Lawless puts him down low on the power play, an innovation inspired by the Dallas Stars' use of Derian Hatcher, the Bats forwards complain that whatever oomph he provides as a crease-crasher is negated by the fact that he can't chase down the puck.

Everyone is *really* shocked when Lawless puts him in the shootout versus Central Texas. "I've got a move," Shoe had muttered. And wouldn't you know it . . . he almost scores.

Whatever the condition of his legs, Shoe can still do damage with his fists. When he has to, that is—few opposing players really want a piece of him, which means more freedom for guys like Findlay and Pawluk. Having someone play that role is necessary; Thompson and Anderson will fight anybody, but they aren't really heavyweights. Mike Jackson's health is more important than his willingness to brawl. With all the bad mojo of the last few months,

Kyle Haviland has lost his mean streak. Not to mention that any time one of those four go, suspensions follow. Adding Shoe is like getting a player with an extra set of fouls in basketball.

"The main thing I can teach these young guys is that winning is the only acceptable option," Shoebottom tells *Austin City Search* writer Philip Billnitzer. "At this level, the only time people want your autograph is right after the hockey game. The only other time they'll want it is when they want you to sign a bill or invoice."

THE BATS FINISH OUT the season as a homeless hockey team. March is rodeo time at the Travis County Exposition Center. A crowd of 7,346 comes out to see the final home game. For the year, 216,776 fans visited the Bat Cave, roughly the same WPHL-leading figure as last season. (The number actually rose by approximately 17,000, but the home schedule was three games longer.)

If the club is going to get itself in order before the playoffs, it will have to do so in seven straight road tests. "These are the biggest games of the year," Tim Findlay says.

After the shootout loss in Central Texas, the team goes back to Shreveport one last time. Findlay endures the seven-hour trip half-naked—he sunburned himself in a tanning bed, and spends the whole ride applying and reapplying aloe vera.

The importance of tonight's game is not too hard to figure. The Bats have never won here. The Mudbugs, on a 9–0–1 tear, have already clinched a playoff berth with 83 points (as has Fort Worth, with 86). Austin is third, with 75 points, and can guarantee its postseason appearance with a victory.

On paper, finishing second is not important because of the Bat Cave's booked-up status. But the Mudbugs loom as a possible playoff opponent. Such a series would go down easier if the team didn't have to read the phrase "the Bats have never won in Shreveport" in every postseason preview. And the most important thing is for the club to win, period—to pick up momentum regardless of who is in the way come playoff time.

Speaking of momentum, there's less of that on the Bat Bus now that Ruben's back behind the wheel. Dave was reassigned after he accidentally left his West Texas highway patrol warnings in the glove box. When Ruben turned them over to Star Shuttle, Dave got hit with a lot more than "a minor that should have been a major." Just as the refs never listen to a player's excuses on the ice, the bus company bosses were unmoved by Dave's insistence that he didn't mean to go so fast, that low tire pressure led to faulty speedometer readings.

It doesn't take long for Shoebottom, instantly ensconced in the last row of the bus, to notice Ruben's glacial pace. "Hey, there's a dog pissing on the rear tire," he says.

Despite his safety-first velocity, it is not the driver's night. Halfway through the trip, Ruben lists slightly to the left, and the bus is nearly leveled by a semi.

"RUBEN!" 10 shaken players yell at once.

"Too hot?" the bus driver replies.

At 5 A.M., he actually nods off, the bus jerking suddenly toward the shoulder, then back into the lane.

Paul Lawless decides he'd better stay awake for the final hour of the trip. He beckons me to join him in the front row, the idea being that our conversation will keep Ruben semi-conscious. Since I've been playing voyeur while these guys put their bodies on the line all season long, I guess it's the least I can do.

Lawly reminisces about playing in Italy. During games, one fan would pass the players shots of grappa. He talks about his NHL experience. He was a first-round draft pick—taken before the likes of Dave Andreychuk and Pat Verbeek—who never fully blossomed.

"He wasn't exactly a student of the game," Mark Martello joked after Lawless first took over. "He was probably the kind of player who got coaches fired."

Meaning, someone with a lot of talent that's never fully harvested, so the coach gets blamed. Lawless was a Hartford Whaler for five seasons, with Blaine Stoughton assisting on his first professional goal. He still holds the Whalers/Hurricanes record for most points in a single night, scoring six against Toronto in January 1987. The Whalers traded him to Philadelphia in 1988; he played a total of 34 games for three different NHL teams in three different seasons after that. Then came Europe and the IHL.

Lawless actually began last season in Cincinnati but chose to join the Bats about six weeks in. He's not quite Mario Lemieux, but Lawly's presence as player/owner increased the team's market-ability. Fans related to the novelty of his position as well as the "former NHLer" angle. He also scored his share of goals.

Now, as coach, Lawless is looking forward to the Mudbugs match-up. At long last, the team will deploy all five of its top-scoring forwards. Pawluk, Findlay, Ross and Hartnell are four of them, and now Brett Seguin is back. With all the bike riding he did during his month of inactivity, Pig might be in better shape now than he was before.

After a lovely "O Canada" and "Star-Spangled Banner" from 660 children gathered in Shreveport for the Texas/Louisiana/Arkansas Choir Festival, the Bugs strike first on an unchallenged shot that hits net well wide of a slow-to-react Erickson, playing his second straight game because Soucy is in Houston. 1–0 Bugs.

The Bats respond with pressure, getting chances but not rebounds. But then they can't even manage to get a line change— Shreveport spends nearly three minutes in the Bats zone.

"We're pissing into the wind if we think we can stop these guys with half a fucking team," Lawless says. "Guys gotta start showing up."

"Man, they sure know how to drink beer in juniors," Gunner says. "But they don't teach you team defense."

Lawly ducks into another room to call Stoughton on his cell phone. Tomorrow is the trade deadline. The Bats still need an offensive defenseman so much so that Findlay is manning the point on power plays. And there's a guy in Amarillo who might become available. This makes Rob Hartnell nervous. "I played for their coach in juniors," Hartsy had said. "He would want me." Truth is, all the Ice Bats not named Tim Findlay or Ryan Pawluk are nervous.

"Half the team is playing, half the team isn't," Lawless tells the general manager.

In the second period, Hartnell and his third-line comrades go to work. Shoebottom starts things with a hard point drive. Mud-bugs netminder St. Pierre goes down, and Thompson's turnaround rebound shot goes wide. But Thompson stays with it, heading for the boards and sending it hard around to the opposite corner. Richard Uniacke gets it toward the net with Thompson and

Hartnell going. They both poke at the puck, and Hartnell gets the goal. Who says dump-and-chase isn't fun? Score: 1–1.

But minutes later, Erickson gets tied up behind net ever so briefly. As the puck heads for the side boards he gets back in time to stop the initial shot but has no position and can't cover. Former Ice Bat (for all of two games last season) Rob Hyrtsak skates around Erickson's prostrate form to put it in the empty net.

As Findlay, Pawluk and D.J. Mando got ready for the subsequent draw, Bats fans—about 20 made the trip—can't help but think how when the Ice Bats were unstoppable, it was mostly because the kids came through with timely goals.

Findlay knows it: "I had a strange feeling we were going to score on that shift," he says later. "I don't know why."

It takes all of 12 seconds. After the headman pass from Ryan Anderson and a crosser from Pawluk, Findlay blows by Shreveport defender Jim Sprott at the blueline. With Mando as a decoy it was two-on-none, and Finner doesn't miss those. He buries it in the top corner to make it 2–2.

"Hey Sprottsy, nice move," Darrin MacKay yells at the face-off.

"Sprottsy says he's going to kill you," Andy Ross says when he returns to the bench.

Soon thereafter Shoebottom and the Bugs' Trevor Buchanan fight, lamely, with the tough Buchanan (a 200 PIM guy) mostly clutching.

The turning point of the game is at hand. But it's not the kind of thing anyone likes to see. Uniacke and Thompson are digging for the puck in the corner when Kevin Barrett slams Uniacke from behind and skates away. Ten seconds later, Thompson is raging on Barrett. While the crowd cheers for blood, it is literally spilling over by the boards—Uniacke is unconscious. Eric Seeber frantically waves for assistance as a chill goes over Austin's bench.

Emotions boil. Several players on both teams are ready to get out of hand, but the officials, and Andy Ross, do a good job of peacemaking. Ross is aware that there's a major penalty to capitalize on if the Ice Bats stay cool.

The tally ends up with Barrett getting five minutes for fighting and five for charging, with a game misconduct. Thompson gets five for fighting but also gets the instigator penalty, with a game misconduct as well. It's a shame, because J.T. had been playing one of the best games of his injury- and suspension-shortened season. Now he'll be suspended again, but with no regrets.

"I can't really remember what happened," he says after the game. "I just saw blood everywhere, and I snapped. I wanted to hurt the guy."

Ryan Anderson, who says that he was in tears out on the ice, gets 10 minutes for his efforts.

So with more than half the game left, the Bats are down to seven forwards and, for 10 minutes, five D. Plus, Shoebottom is still serving a major. Shorthanded against Shreveport, just the way Austin likes it.

Uniacke is helped off the ice, blood pooling around his eyes and over the top half of his sweater. The biggest concern, a neck or spine injury, has been ruled out.

After two squeegees and a shovel turn the ice back to white from red, the Bats wait out Thompson's minor and take advantage of a three-minute major power play. Kungle puts one on net from up high 30 seconds in, and Hartnell gets a piece of it, making it 3–2 Bats. But the rest of the man-advantage goes by with no score, and then those pesky Mudbugs bust a three-on-one to make the score 3–3.

All the emotion and momentum is up for grabs again. Hartnell takes it back. He gains the zone with Findlay, who attracts two defenders. Rob feints to the right, weaves to the left and top-shelfs it: 4–3 Bats. Hartsy has his third hat trick of the year.

Back in the locker room between periods, the focus is on Uniacke.

"Is the kid okay?" Gunner, who is cleaning the blood out of Uni's helmet with a towel, asks Eric Seeber. "He didn't crack his skull?"

Darrin MacKay says that all he could think about was the two friends of his who are in wheelchairs because of hits from behind.

It would violate basic notions of natural justice if the Bats don't win this one. Nothing needs to be said. Before the team gets back on the ice, Uniacke comes out of the training room, a pillow-sized ice pack on his head.

The Bats stay strong in the third. While the Bugs seem deflated by the fourth goal, the Bats stick to D, and Erickson is terrific late. Early in the third, Keith Moran, back at forward for the moment, leads a three-on-one. Moran feeds Hartnell going in, then Hartnell flips a beautiful pass over the defenseman's stick, which Moran collects and puts high, giving him (because there was a late Shreveport goal) his second game-winner against the Bugs. Findlay adds another for a 6–4 final in front of 8,591 disappointed Shreveport fans.

"It was good for us to pull together behind Richard," Rob Hartnell says. "It was a gutless hit, and I think the guys went out and played hard and got what we deserved. Thank God he's all right."

Uniacke turns out to need fewer stitches than all the blood suggested. He does have a concussion.

"Watch this," Gunner says, turning toward the rookie.

"Too much of a prima donna to pack your own bag?!" the equipment manager barks.

Uniacke looks surprised for a second—he's too dazed to register much emotion—but then he realizes Gunner's busting balls like always.

The team takes a vote to skip the usual casino stop and head for home. The emotion of the victory was sufficient drama for the night. Van Volsen and Moran double up so Uniacke can have his own row for the bus ride. The concussion is minor enough that he's able to focus on a magazine for part of the trip.

"I'm fine now," Uniacke says. "It's the first time I don't remember anything from getting hit in the head."

Lawless reveals that he got hit in the head once in juniors. "The swelling never went down," he jokes.

Thrilled with the win, the coach buys beers for everyone. Then he takes the cardboard from a 12-pack and tapes it over the speaker above his seat. "I must have the only Bose speaker on the whole bus," Lawly gripes. He is craving sleep.

Eventually, an argument over bedtime versus movie-watching becomes a full-scale war. The front of the bus wants to rest. The back of the bus is eager for entertainment. They still have beers. When a clearly agitated Kyle Haviland makes his way up the aisle to commandeer the VCR, Tim Findlay intervenes.

"Calm down, Havy," Finner says. "You'll wake up Ruben!"

fourteen

SHOT THROUGH THE HART

Despite a 7 a.m. bedtime coming off the road, Kyle Haviland couldn't help himself. He woke at the stroke of noon and there it was: the dreaded answering-machine light.

"I thought, 'Oh shit—where am I going?'" Haviland says. "I checked my messages, and it was Burty."

False alarm. All Burton wanted was Derek Riley's phone number. Riley, Jason Rose and Chris Haskett had been dealt to Waco for Rob Schriner, the woeful Wizards' best player and former coach.

"I was like, 'Don't do that to me, Burty!'" Haviland says.

Elsewhere in the Riata complex, Rob Hartnell rolled out of bed. It was 12:30, and his machine was undisturbed.

"I thought, 'I made it,'" Hartsy says. "I've never really fit into any one role with this team, but coming off a good game and a big win, I figured, hey, things are coming together. I was happy."

The phone rang at 12:32.

"It's Blaine," Darrin MacKay informed his roommate.

Just as he had predicted, Hartnell was going to the Amarillo Rattlers. But not for the high-caliber offensive defenseman many Bats had hoped for. Nope. The Ice Bats player who'd scored a hat trick 14 hours earlier—the guy with five game-winners in Austin's last eight wins—was dealt for "future considerations."

Hartnell is depressed and dumbfounded.

"I think I've gone above and beyond the call of duty for this team," he says. "I took a huge pay cut to come here. I'm not a big drinker. I'm not a troublemaker. I'm a good dressing-room guy. I train harder than anybody. I had to play a role that I don't like playing, going out and stirring it up, having every guy on the ice wanting to kill me. But I did it because I knew it was a piece of the puzzle for this team. I was blocking shots, taking punches in the face to get a key guy off the ice. All the shit that helps you win.

"I don't know what the hell they were thinking, to be honest with you. You can't really try to figure Blaine out because he fucking doesn't have a clue what he's doing. Obviously, he's known for his good trades. So fuck him.

"I don't know . . . it's disheartening. It's hard. I want to kill him, of course, that's my first reaction. But all I can do is keep a positive attitude and go and bust my ass for Amarillo and help them make the playoffs."

From management's point of view, Rob Schriner is an offensive upgrade, a veteran with a natural scoring touch. The team also has a hotshot rookie coming in from Europe for the playoffs. Between those guys and the money paid to Shoebottom, there wasn't roster space or cap room for Hartnell. In their mind, they needed more offense, even at the expense of Hartnell's grit and spirit.

What of the hat trick the night before?

"Bad timing by us," Stoughton concedes. But he'd already decided to make the move a week ago. Because the Rattlers' post-season hopes are still alive, the general manager could not pry loose something major in return. Stoughton says that the guy the Ice Bats wanted may end up as a player-to-be-named. "It depends on if they make the playoffs this year, and if they re-sign him for next year," he says. "We'll see what happens with their team."

The general manager talks of needing veteran leadership, but there's no way Schriner can provide more than Hartnell does. His former Waco colleague is an offensive threat, but the Ice Bats already know firsthand that if you pound the guy, he goes away. Schriner has 24 goals in 30 games since stepping down as coach, but Hartnell's 18 over the last 33 are no less impressive, especially considering their different roles.

"From what I hear, they don't believe I'll be there for them in the playoffs," Hartnell says. "Now they'll never know. I know I can produce in the playoffs. I was willing to play any role they wanted me to play. Did they think I was gonna complain if I was the 10th forward? If I had to sit the odd night? I wasn't gonna complain. I loved it here. I would have done whatever they asked me to do, same as I've done all year. I would have kept stats. But I can't really say to them, 'Hey, I don't want to go, I want to stay here.' They're telling me they don't want me.

"They forget we're human beings, and we have feelings. It makes it hard. We're a commodity. It kind of conditions you to be heartless—you know that you can never make strong ties in a city."

All the Bats are baffled. As a third-line player with first-line skills, it made a certain amount of sense that Hartnell could be dealt. But for nothing in return?

"It's a really shitty trade," Tim Findlay says.

"Obviously, on the personal side, I'm disappointed for him," MacKay says. "But I'm also disappointed for the team, because I think we could use him. A 30-goal scorer who can play any position, the power play and the penalty kill? I definitely think he's an asset. Plus he's a good guy. Sometimes you'll get players on a team that don't get along with everyone. That wasn't the case with Harts. He got along with everyone, from the office staff to the players. And down the stretch here he scored 20 goals in two months.

"But what can you do?" MacKay concludes. "You just kind of have to go on."

"I don't think the guys are happy with the move," Hartnell says. "But they also realize that's hockey. Tomorrow they'll wake up, and it'll be like I was never here."

THE POST-TRADE PRACTICE is uninspired.

"Who am I going to catch a buzz off of today?" Lawless wonders. "I'm thinking Roscoe."

Sure, a fair amount of beer was laid to waste on Sunday. But more than that, the team's collective mind is elsewhere—out the rink door and down the hall, where Rose, Riley, Haskett and Hartnell are packing their equipment.

Ten minutes in, Lawless puts his foot down.

"Okay, we can practice like this for an hour and a half or we can fucking practice hard for an hour," the coach says. "I've got all day. It's a beautiful day, but I don't fucking care. At least fucking do the drills right."

The Bats muddle through. In the locker room at Chaparral, where the team is again basing itself with the rodeo in town, Lawless unlaces and talks about the deal.

"Hartsy was the unfortunate fellow that got the shaft," he says. "It wasn't that he couldn't play. He was a good guy. It's just one of those ugly things of hockey—a numbers game. You've got to look at the big picture. If we weren't trying to make our club stronger we wouldn't have gotten rid of him."

He dismisses the idea that team chemistry could be affected. "Let me put it this way. If one guy makes a difference on a hockey team, then we're in deep shit. I don't worry about chemistry. Chemistry is winning."

THE NEXT GAME is in Odessa, a seven-hour journey. The Bats are in the middle of a long road trip, fighting for their playoff lives. But because there are no games the day before or the day after, the owners decide not to spend any money on hotel rooms.

The bus leaves at 9 A.M. There are two drivers, because it would be illegal for one to go more than 12 hours on a same-day trip. Both of them are unfamiliar; after the last Shreveport swing, Ruben is never seen again.

In the *Austin American-Statesman* sports section that's being passed around, an article about spring training mentions how major league baseball requires each of its teams to dress four veterans in every game. Otherwise, they would all sit out the bus trips—most of which are a whopping two hours.

The bus is a symphony of bedhead. If he had hair, Brett Seguin would have it worst. The center stumbles onto the bus a little after nine, blaming his alarm clock.

"Didn't even take a morning piss yet," Pig complains.

"You just know he was checking the road atlas to see where Odessa is," Chad Erickson says.

Thirty minutes out of town, the bus stops to pick up Stoughton, saving the GM the trouble of driving out to Chaparral.

"What the fuck is he doing here?" Erickson mutters in the back. "Stay home and count your money."

It's not clear why Stoughton is along. Does he think his presence will have a salutary effect, or is it meant to add additional pressure? Does Lawless need help coaching? Or does he just want to watch the game?

The guys up front get the VCR going with *Goodfellas*. You haven't lived, or at least this Jewish writer hasn't, until you've heard a bunch of white-bread Canadians shout out "*Mazel tov!*" in unison as Ray Liotta and Lorraine Bracco step on a cup in the wedding scene.

"Why'd you have to put this movie on now?" Erickson gripes. "Ten hours to go and you put in the only good movie. I want to go to bed."

He needs the rest. Since Soucy went to Houston, Chad has been the only goalie. For an emergency back-up, they've got a local men's leaguer, Scott Erfurth, who is driving on his own. The Bats played one game against Central Texas with no number-two target at all. Under those circumstances, Chad was happy to take slashing penalties against his favorite Stampede forwards, practically daring the ref to toss him.

"Hope my trick back doesn't act up in warm-ups," he kids today.

Erickson is not a happy camper. That he finds himself playing every night while Soucy is in Houston (where he was just named IHL goalie of the week) just makes it more insulting that they benched him in the first place.

"When Paul took over, he called me in his office and said, 'You know, just because Soucy's here doesn't mean you're not gonna play,' " Erickson says. "I have no problem with not playing. But if that's the way it's gonna be, tell me that's the way it's gonna be.

Have enough guts to come to me and say it. If I'm playing bad, come and tell me. It's my eighth year pro—I can handle it. I think I deserve a little bit of respect, just to be told what the situation is." Erickson grew up in Warroad, Minnesota, six miles from the border. "We had 13 cable channels, and three of them were Canadian." Warroad, the only American town on the Lake of the Woods, is known for three things: the Marvin Window factory, fishing and Christian Brothers. Or, as the chamber of commerce puts it, "Windows, walleyes and hockey sticks."

Erickson's dad works for Marvin. The window company is responsible for much of the town's infrastructure, while Christian Brothers, the hockey equipment maker, took care of everybody's hockey needs. "That town got me and a lot of other players where we are today," Erickson says. "As dull as it is sometimes, if it wasn't for Warroad I wouldn't be playing. Our ice time was free, and I never had to buy my own equipment, except for skates."

High school hockey doesn't get any bigger than it is in Minnesota. Some NHL observers believe the league failed there the first time because most folks would rather watch teenagers. Erickson's Warroad squad went to the state tournament twice, putting themselves up against schools with bigger student bodies than the population of their whole town. "We were the sentimental favorites," he remembers. "We'd have our letter jackets on, and when everyone saw that you were from Warroad they'd be rooting for you."

Erickson played three years at the University of Minnesota–Duluth, then signed with the New Jersey Devils, who'd taken him in the seventh round of the 1988 draft. The last denizen of the Meadowlands to wear jersey number 30 before Martin Brodeur, he played exactly two games for the parent club, going 1–1.

"Every guy who ever laced up a pair of skates should be able to play one NHL game, just to say he did," he says. "It was an amazing experience."

People inevitably ask him, did you slam the door on anyone famous? Erickson's moment in the spotlight was even better than that. "Mark Messier scored four goals on me," he admits. "I got him where he is today."

"Chadly" has bounced around the minors ever since, uncertain what life after hockey holds for him, though he does plan to wrap up his business degree one of these days. He also got married before the current season. Wife Holly watches every home game from high above the cage the Bats defend once, giving her a straight-on, across-the-ice view of Erickson for the other two. Her body language during the team's many shootouts pretty much defines the phrase "on edge."

All in all, Erickson is a pretty straightforward guy . . . for a goalie. "I've been told that by a lot of people—that I'm the most normal goalie they've ever run into," he allows. Meaning, he doesn't vomit before games or talk to goalposts or ignore his teammates in the locker room (unless he's cranky).

"Honestly, we're all a little bit crazy to be standing in front of a vulcanized rubber puck that comes at you 90 miles an hour," he says. "But then, I'm the one with all the pads on. And I don't have to skate up and down the ice and get slammed into the boards. So who's the crazy one?"

What's more, ex-goalies often seem smarter or more articulate than their skating counterparts, whether they end up as coaches, color commentators or lawyers-turned-front-office bureacrats. It's sort of like being a catcher in baseball: the vantage point allows you to soak up every aspect of the game.

"As a goalie, you see everything develop," Erickson says. "You get a good idea of how the game is played. I think if every forward would play goalie for one or two days, he'd realize how difficult it is or how many more opportunities he had to score. It'd probably make them better players. They'd realize what's hard to defend.

"As a goaltender you try to determine where the guy's gonna shoot," he continues. "You try to find out what's the toughest shot and try to push him toward that. Maybe you take a little bit away so he'll have to make a harder play. He looks up and sees you're covering his favorite shot, so then he's like, 'Well, now what do I do?' There's a lot more thought process in it than people think. It's not like we just dive around and run into a puck." That's particularly true of Erickson, who lets his positioning do the work for him.

Prior to joining the Bats, Erickson was with Birmingham of the ECHL. It was a little different going down a couple of levels after being with an NHL club. And it was a lot different going down below the Mason–Dixon Line. "I had heard all these stories about how it was just a goon festival. I went down not knowing what to expect," he says.

At Erickson's first ECHL game in Knoxville, the "Star-Spangled Banner" singer botched the same line of the anthem three times in a row. Eventually, the crowd bellowed out the words for him . . . at which point the guy revealed that he had a $50 bet with his buddy that he could get the whole arena to sing along. "I just went, 'Ah, what am I getting myself into here?'" Chad remembers.

Despite such antics, the Coast was a particularly good league back then, the only AA outfit around. "There were a lot of guys that had moved up the ladder," Erickson recalls. "Now the boom down South has afforded hundreds of players the opportunity to continue playing. If this league hadn't started, I'd have been done two years ago. And I think this level is better for the fans, because the game is more exciting. Unless you get two of the best teams in the league, NHL hockey is pretty dull—you get 15 shots on goal. That's embarrassing. Whereas down here you get goals, you get fights."

During the course of his minor league travels and travails, Erickson played 10 games for the Cincinnati Cyclones of the IHL, which is why Lawless and Stoughton ended up recruiting him. In the inaugural season, Erickson equaled his platoonmate John Blue's effort but rarely got credit for it, because Blue had a stronger NHL pedigree (with the Bruins and the Sabres) as well as a fan-friendly name. ("Bloooooooooooooo," the home crowd always chanted . . . even when Chad was in goal.) But Erickson was the team's best player in the otherwise crappy postseason, earning him the right to return this year as starter.

Or so he thought. If it weren't for Soucy's injury, he probably would have been traded in the fall. Now he's wishing he had been.

Erickson's performance this year has been excellent, but not extraordinary. Defensively, the team in front of him has been brutal on occasion. At the same time, there haven't been many games in which the Bats were thoroughly outplayed but won because of goaltending. Ironically, Erickson would have benefited greatly from a steady partner—someone who would not only share the load but also force him to elevate his play. Even now, with Soucy here but not here, you can see Chad's intensity has risen because he's playing with a grudge.

Soucy is a brilliant goalie. It just doesn't feel like he's a member of the team. He's been MIA for four months, choosing to rehabilitate his injury back home in Vermont because, at the time, it didn't look like he'd play again this season.

The Bats' only Québecois—he's a native of Gatineau, a couple of hours north of Hull—Soucy is a product of the University of Vermont. A few of his college friends caught a game recently and were disgusted by the brawls that are a fact of life in the WPHL. (Fighting is illegal in the NCAA, but that doesn't mean there isn't bad behavior—Vermont is the school that cancelled its entire 2000 season due to rampant hazing.)

Soucy's hunter-green Jeep Grand Cherokee is the nicest car in the Bats' parking lot. From 1993 to 1996 he was in the Chicago Blackhawks organization, an undrafted free agent who played exactly three minutes in the NHL, plus three seasons with Indianapolis of the IHL.

Lawless and Stoughton's feelings about team chemistry are clear. If Soucy hasn't been fully absorbed into "the room," that's partially the players' fault. But it's unfortunate that Erickson, often a vocal leader, and a symbolic one between the pipes, has been stripped of both pride and status. That he's angry, and has isolated himself to the point of being disruptive, hasn't helped.

"My head's not really been in it for the last few weeks," Erickson acknowledges. "I probably have to apologize to the guys. I haven't been the same person."

"He's gross," Ryan Anderson says. "But I respect him for not hiding his feelings. You don't want to whine or be selfish, but you can't take it lying down. And he's got a great point. He's what, third in the league in wins? He's done everything for us. He's mad and he shows it."

"I've played hard for them for two years, and I don't think they could've found anyone to do a better job," he concludes. "If they didn't think I was any good, they should have done something with me months ago. But I was the best that they could find back then."

fifteen

PLAYING OUT THE STRING

THE BUS EXITS Interstate 10 and makes its pit stop in Junction, Texas. This particular junction of Junction is home to a Dairy Queen, a Phillips 66 convenience store and the Come and Get It Cafe.

Dairy Queen it is. Guys order up Beltbuster burgers. Anderson hits the jukebox, selecting Ace of Base and Kenny Rogers. Keith Moran stays healthy with a couple of bananas, though he has to employ a *Five Easy Pieces*–type routine to get it.

"You have banana splits, right?" Moran reasons.

Today's lunch topic is Todd Harris. The defenseman has been nursing a groin injury and taking loads of guff for it—the guys do not respect his tolerance for pain. One night, apropos of all the players who bug the trainer, Gunner suggested to Eric that he put a lock on the treatment-room door.

"Harry would just get a key," Seeber replied.

Riding Harris is a daily routine. "Softest guy I ever played with," Tim Findlay says. "If I had his body I'd be a first-round draft pick."

"If I had that body for one night, I'd wreak havoc," MacKay agrees.

Harry has further endeared himself by refusing a trade to Waco, thus sealing Rose's and Riley's fate. The peanut gallery is merciless on this subject.

"Yeah, Waco wanted me, but my groin, y'know . . ." one guy satirizes.

"Waco offered six players for me, but Blaine didn't think it was enough," says another.

"I heard it was eight."

They kid because they're frustrated. The guys up front can't get anything done on the power play because nobody feels threatened by the point men. Ruddick's gone. Harris doesn't hit the net enough to scare anyone. Trading day brought no help. Also, the offensive defenseman from Europe that Burton had lined up for the playoffs took a $5,000-a-week offer to stay overseas.

The situation is so desperate that Burty considered putting on the skates himself. He talked with Findlay about it, getting the kid's hopes up, and also received the go-ahead from his wife. Eric Seeber gave him a shot for his knees that made them feel great. But after practicing for a couple of days, he could barely walk.

I was as disappointed as the team that this scenario did not play out. I told Burty that if he got back on the ice and led the team to a championship after being fired, Tom Hanks would play him in the movie for sure.

The team is in Ector County by 4 P.M.

"I left my legs on the bus," Keith Moran says. A few guys get a game of parking lot hacky-sack going to loosen up. Others go off in search of coffee, maybe a little food. Already, everyone feels like crap, the consensus being that the Dairy Queen lunch was the worst pregame meal of the season. Following it up with additional bus time was no fun either.

Over coffee at McDonald's, Darrin MacKay admits that he figures the Bats will go down in the first round of the playoffs.

"I think we play with a lot of heart. But we're certainly short of that team chemistry that we're gonna need if we want to win the championship," he says. "And then the owners will bitch and moan and say the team didn't try hard enough and didn't do what it was supposed to, when they knew all along our D wasn't good enough." Keith Moran had said the same thing—that the team just didn't have enough toughness or D—as long ago as January. Now he's on the blueline.

At the coliseum, back-up rent-a-goalie Scott Erfurth reports for duty. He's a Chicago native who played for Marquette University and made a brief attempt at going pro. "In those days it was pretty much the ECHL or nothing," he says. He tried out for Johnstown, "and that was basically it. Thanks for your time, see you later. That was 10 years and 40 pounds ago."

He is not looking to make a comeback. "I just hope Chad stays well," he says. "If we're up by eight goals with three minutes left to go, I'd be more than happy to go in there."

After first working in the golf business, Erfurth now sells hockey gear in Texas, Oklahoma, Louisiana, Mississippi and Arkansas, representing companies like CCM and Christian Brothers. He was able to come to Odessa ahead of the team and do a little sales work. Business is booming.

"Everywhere a team goes, you can count on something being built, whether it's inline or an ice rink, in the next year or two years. That makes my job easier. Right now, I have 23 professional teams in my territory. Next year it'll be 29."

If the point of Erfurth's temp gig is a free close-up seat for an exciting hockey game, someone owes him money. There is nothing to see on this dreary Tuesday night.

"They've got a special promotion," MacKay says, trotting out an old one. "Dress as a blue seat night."

Tonight's crowd aside, Odessa, the high school football–crazed town made famous by H.G. Bissinger's *Friday Night Lights*, has embraced hockey with gusto. Crowds of 4,000 to 5,000 people have been coming to the coliseum, a venue where Bats computer guru Casey Weaver saw Elvis in 1976, on a regular basis. Some in the community have even laced up skates. There is actually something called the Permian Basin Youth Hockey League—a particularly incongruous appellation, something along the lines of, say, the Yellowknife Beach Volleyball League.

The team's logo is a cuddly, mock-ferocious rendition of the mythical beast the jackalope—a furry, antlered creature, part jackrabbit, part antelope—that's said to hop around the West Texas plains when no one's looking. It has been honored twice by *The Hockey News* as the best logo in lower-level minor pro.

Odessa is also home to one of the nation's most successful junior college basketball teams, a program that has produced, among others, UNLV and New York Knicks player Larry Johnson. The last time the Bats were here, I spent some time in the stands with the current team. Judging from their cell phones and Rolexes, some of them may be ticketed to follow in L.J.'s footsteps.

Despite such innocent questions as "Does the penalty carry over to the next period?", the hoopsters had an intuitive grasp of the action on the ice. "It's like we can't pass over half court," one player explained after an offside call. "There's no icing on a power play," he confidently declared at another point. When the Bats had a goal waved off after a hard-charging, multiple-rebound sequence, they'd all seen enough *SportsCenter* hockey highlights to recognize the call: "He was in the crease! He was in the crease!" they exclaimed.

Odessa's next loss eliminates them from the playoffs. They are also trying to avoid the WPHL cellar. At least they have something to play for. The only other potential drama is that Jim Mullin is their goalie, having been traded to the Jacks when Soucy's return rendered him unnecessary. He'll be looking to do in a game what he didn't do against the Bats in practice.

"We didn't travel all this fucking way not to win this thing," Lawless says.

It's the most cheerful thought the coach will have all night. Because of his unexpected presence, I figure it'd be good for me to grab a spot on the bench again . . . and this time I brought a suit and tie. Lawly's only concern is that I'll catch him cursing way too often.

Can't imagine why.

First period: "We're fucking standing still. We're fucking standing still. Fuck me!"

And: "What's with the fucking flamingos?" Translation: Why aren't guys keeping their heads up?

"I hope they have strippers or something between periods,"

Darrin MacKay says, "because there's nothing entertaining about this game."

The only good thing is it's moving quickly. No scraps, no whistles. No shots, no checks. No defense, but no goals in spite of that. No spirit, no desire. "That's what happens when neither team wants to play," Mac points out.

Second period: "This is fucking bullshit now. We're fucking playing to their level. It's a fucking disgrace."

Ross and Shoebottom go hard into the Odessa zone. The Bats' newest number 31 meets its previous number 31 in a heavy crash. Mullin's bum shoulder pops out. He skates off to the dressing room without a moment's hesitation.

"Way to drive the net, Shoe," Lawly says with a laugh.

"There goes our chance to score on Jimmy Two-Legs," Keith Moran laments.

In the third, the Bats go on a power play and don't even set up in Odessa's zone. It remains a crappy 0–0 game.

"I'll let you guys decide who's up," Lawly says. "Just let me know." It's hard to tell if this is a calculated motivational ploy or genuine disgust.

Finally, dangerous Odessa forward Sami Laine gets his 50th of the season. It's 1–0 Jackalopes. Lawly claps his hands together repeatedly as the guys come off the ice. It is not a "rally the troops" gesture, but, rather, sarcastic applause.

As the third period ticks away, Ross asks Lawless if he wants to call for a stick measurement in an attempt to get a cheap power play. The coach says no. In his mind, the Bats don't deserve the chance to win.

"He was pouting," Roscoe says later.

But with Erickson pulled for an offensive face-off with 59 seconds left, Findlay scores. He and Van Volsen and Pawluk dance all the way to center ice. Gunner is actually jumping up and down. His Odessa counterpart bangs the glass in anger.

"Now we fucking take two points, boys," Finner says. "Get something out of this fucking mess."

The shootout goes nine rounds without a score. The Bats are shorthanded at forward. (Haskett: traded. Hartnell: traded.

Jackson: suspended. Schriner: not yet arrived.) Todd Harris is up.

"Take a slapper!" the Bats players yell at the bench.

Instead, Harris skates to the left circle. Goaltender Billy Pye pokes it away. But the rubber's still sitting there, so the defenseman whacks it. Game over.

"Fuck, that was pretty," Harry exults as he comes back to the bench.

Thing is, rebounds are not allowed in shootouts. Pye pokechecked the puck, and everybody but the referee knows it. Rick Girhiny is going nuts. The crowd is throwing paper cups. But this one's in the books.

"Worst hockey game I've ever seen in my life," Lawly says, declining to comment further.

MEANWHILE, in his first game with Amarillo, Rob Hartnell scores four goals and is named WPHL player of the week. He has 31 goals for the season. Andy Ross owes him a hundred bucks.

Fans have been calling the Bats' front office, saying they won't come to games anymore because of the trade.

"Who in the organization had the BRAIN FART to trade away Rob Hartnell????" one fan wonders on the Internet, before bleakly assessing the club's current state.

"From my limited knowledge, what I see is we have a problem with defense, offense and basic skills . . . What does that leave???? Not much except to keep LOSING . . ."

The worst part is, it turns out Stoughton's talk of "future considerations" or "a player to be named later" were bald-faced lies. Hartnell was traded straight up to Amarillo, for $2,000 cash. The WPHL office confirms that the Rattlers do not owe the Ice Bats anything more for him. Hartnell's 27 goals were worth nothing more than a week's salary for one of the four owners.

"We traded Hartsy for a roll of tape and a water bottle," reports Mark Martello during one of his game broadcasts.

"Maybe he was fucking Blaine's wife," one fan suggests. *"There's no other explanation."*

Then there was this open letter to Blaine Stoughton from rabid fan Marilyn Wesson.

"In your interview on the radio last night you came across as an egotistical, cold-hearted SOB. *How dare you act like you were doing Hartnell a favor by trading him rather than waiving him? . . . Rob may have had a slight slump, but he had risen to the place of one of the leaders of the team. On the other hand, did it ever occur to you that perhaps the Bats did not* NEED *one of these new players that are coming in?. . .Has it ever occurred to you that the talent is already there? . . .*

"Darrell Royal, former coach of the Texas Longhorns, is a legend in college football. One year, he was faced with the dilemma of whether to go to his second-string quarterback when his first-string quarterback was faltering. He made the statement, 'I'll dance with the one who brung me.' He understood what loyalty was all about. I don't know, or really care, where you come from, but people here in Texas understand what loyalty is all about. In case you haven't noticed, fans don't wear the names of coaches or general managers on their backs at games. They wear the names of players . . .

"Too bad we can't trade or waive general managers and owners."

THE REMNANT of the Bats' season is no more inspired than the Odessa game. The team beats Waco in a similar display of apathetic hockey. Out on the town the next night, a drunk Mike Jackson walks up to Lawless. He tells the coach that no one on the team has any heart except for him, and that they are going to lose in the first round for sure.

"Problem is, he may be right," Eric Seeber says.

The next day, Jackson makes the mistake of showing up late for practice (something about confusion with his girlfriend over who had the car keys). That earns him an involuntary hiatus, from that practice as well as the next day's.

Meanwhile, there's a rumor that the team will have to go back to Odessa and replay the shootout. Because the rules were improperly applied, instead of it being simply a bad judgment call, the league has intervened. The word is, if the game somehow affects playoff seedings, there would be another lunch stop at the Dairy Queen. Odessa's coach is insisting that if it's the difference between his team finishing fifth or last, he wants to replay it. But the league doesn't go for that. The plan is to send back just the goaltenders and a handful of players to continue the overtime period. Fortunately, it never happens.

On the final weekend of the regular season, the Bats lose to Central Texas, then lose again in Lake Charles. On the latter trip, both Stoughton and co-owner Daniel Hart are along, grabbing bus rows for themselves while the players double up. The three owners put in a fair amount of time at the casino—several Bats say that the only reason Lawly didn't have a hangover at the game-day skate is because he was still tipsy.

The team has no emotion and less execution. The power play is struggling, so in Lake Charles the coach tries playing a couple of forwards on the point—and the Ice Pirates score shorthanded twice. "Do you want to play on the power play?" Ryan Pawluk says to me as he heads into the locker room. Somehow, I find it flattering rather than insulting that my lack of hockey ability has become a point of comparison for the team's lowest moments.

On the bus ride home, the VCR goes out. Three different players mess with the wiring but can't get it to work.

Lawly steps in. "Just do what you did all night," he says, shooing the players aside. "Just relax."

Lawless gives the thing a whack and the TV comes to life. It's his best coaching move of the week.

The back of the bus clamors for more volume.

"Lawly says he can hear it just fine!" Ryan Pawluk replies.

The good news is, the Bats' lackluster performance has earned them fourth place, putting them in line for a desired first-round match-up with Fort Worth. The two teams play each other on the last day of the season. A win wouldn't put the Ice Bats into third, but a Fort Worth loss could elevate Shreveport to the top. Austin would like to avoid the Mudbugs for as long as possible, so, essentially, they want to tank the game.

"Imagine what it would be like if *both* teams really, really didn't want to win," D.J. Mando speculates before the game. "Like, really didn't try."

Watching one team play like that turns out to be bad enough. Fort Worth wins it 5–1. The Bats are ready for the playoffs.

sixteen

THE REAL SEASON

ONE HOUR BEFORE the Bats take on the Brahmas in Game 2 of their first-round series, the most curious sight around the Austin locker room is Andy Ross, clean-shaven. During the regular season, Ross's facial hair fluctuated like that of any other player. But this is the playoffs, when razors are few and far between and the team with the longest collective beard is the Cup winner.

"After my performance last night . . ." is Ross's explanation. The Bats lost Game 1, and Paul Lawless hadn't exactly made a secret of the fact that Roscoe's defensive lapse led to Fort Worth's crucial go-ahead score early in the third.

"Ninety-five percent of the team played well," the coach said.

Prior to the game, Lawless talked about how there were three different seasons in hockey—before Christmas, after Christmas and the playoffs. Before Christmas, the Bats' scorers were so dominating that nothing else mattered. After Christmas, those same stars were often injured or called up, and the team's defensive shortcomings were exposed. But everything is bass-ackwards now—that one breakdown aside, the Bats got impressively sturdy D throughout Game 1, but couldn't find the net. They lost 3–2, scoring the second goal in garbage time.

The same hockey team that looked so flaccid a week ago played smart and strong, with solid positioning and a total effort throughout. It's as if the Wizard of Oz visited the locker room beforehand, doling out heart, brains and courage wherever necessary. Players who never said a word all season spoke up. Guys who never gave a hit all year banged away. Hot-blooded penalty attractors stayed cool. Dipsy-doodle forwards dumped and chased. Pursuing the President's Cup is a powerful form of behavior modification.

If you had told the Bats they would play that well while grabbing seven power plays and allowing just 23 shots on goal, the players would have anticipated a postgame celebration. But the power play did less than nothing, and the Brahmas were just a little better.

Now Austin has to win Game 2. There's no way the Brahmas, the team with the WPHL's best record, a club whose coach and key players already own three championship rings from other leagues, will blow a 2–0 series lead.

"Are you ready for the last Ice Bats road game of the season?" devoted fan Victor Diaz asks me during Game 2 warm-ups. Considering all that's happened this year, his cynicism is justified.

"You guys know what to do, so let's fucking do it," Lawly says in the dressing room before the game. He's absolutely right—and thus a full-blown speech really isn't needed.

But the owner-turned-bench-boss is guilty of under-coaching in other areas. "Why didn't your team practice?" a Brahmas fan asked a Bat this morning, having witnessed Austin's brief, let's-get-loose game-day skate on the heels of the Brahmas' more complicated session.

"We still don't have a system in some situations," D. J. Mando marvels.

Mando is a healthy scratch in this series, and it's hard to argue with that move—the six-foot-four rookie, expected to combine natural offensive skill with hard-nosed physicality, hasn't shown enough of either. But Lawless is also sitting out Richard Uniacke, who averaged over a point per game and carried much of the Bats

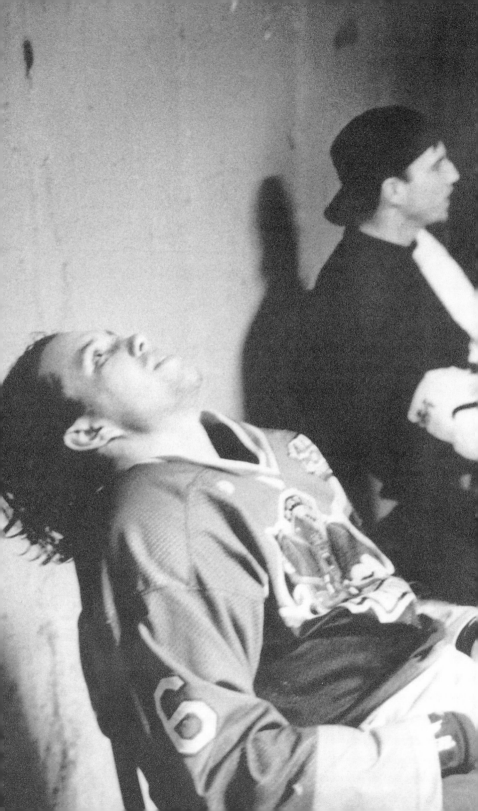

offense, mostly as Ryan Pawluk's playmaker, during Seguin's and Findlay's absences. Uni was a favorite of Jim Burton, but Lawly thinks he's soft. There's also a story going around that on the center's first night as a Bat, Lawless lectured him for drinking Budweiser instead of Miller (Miller being the team's most important sponsor, as well as Ed Novess's employer). At the time, Uniacke had no idea who Lawless was and gave him lip.

The two players in the stands allow room for Curtis Fry, who came over from Austria on the last weekend of the season, slipping his five-foot-seven frame into the very same number 16 sweater that used to be Rob Hartnell's. "We trade away one four-foot fucker and get someone even smaller," Gunner gripes. The Bats' other extra part is Bruce Shoebottom—instead of dressing 10 forwards, Lawless is going with seven defensemen. Fort Worth is a big, nasty team, with six guys in triple-digit PIMs and one defenseman checking in at six-foot-two, 270 pounds. Shoe is meant to be an intimidating countermeasure.

That's all he's good for. The grizzled veteran reinjured his knee last weekend and can barely walk. He's getting by on pills and needles. Andy Ross watches Shoe limp across their living room and asks him what the hell he's thinking, soldiering on at this stage of his career. "Gotta play," the washed-up warrior grunts. He can't skate, but he might be able to stay on his feet long enough to beat the crap out of somebody.

Tonight, Shoe gets in his night's work early. In warm-ups, he uses the head of Brahmas forward Stephan LaRocque—a whiny but dangerous 51-goal, 275-PIM agitator—for target practice, shooting a puck at him from across the redline. The enforcer is assessed with a 10-minute misconduct to start the game and never takes a shift. To get from the bench to the locker room between periods he has to use his stick as a quasi crutch. But the message has been sent.

Game 2 is much like its predecessor, with both teams playing smart, tough, close-to-the-vest hockey. After two periods it's 0–0. Once again, an excess of Brahma penalties fails to lead to the palace of Austin goals. "Fort Worth has the short-man advantage," Bats fan Carl Phinney snorts during one sequence.

Around five minutes into the third, the Bats get the break. Rob Schriner knocks the puck ahead from deep in his own zone. Seguin is there at the blueline but can't quite reel in the high, hard rubber. As the puck bounces back toward the slot, Schriner swoops in and heads up right wing. Seguin joins, and on the two-on-one chance Schriner weaves toward center a bit, makes as if he might try a five-hole shot from the right side and instead puts it high to the left. Pandemonium! (Well, as much pandemonium as 40 faithful Austinites, in town to support their team, can generate.)

Then the Brahmas tie it up with a goal that Lawless and his players thought was kicked in. "We must look like bitches, because we keep getting fucked out there," Ryan Anderson says.

Everybody is upset, but they can't let it get to them. There is still more hockey to be played. Overtime. Sudden Death. Postseason. Best thing in sports. Every rush into the offensive zone has the potential of a Final Four buzzer beater, a bottom-of-the-ninth World Series home run and a Super Bowl Hail Mary, all at once and at all times. The Bats had said on many occasions—11 unfortunate shootout losses, to be specific—"Hey, they don't have shootouts in the playoffs. Overtime will be ours."

"Well," Kyle Haviland says, "here it is."

"Someone's got the winner," Darrin MacKay implores. "Who is it?"

The dressing room goes quiet. This is solemn business. The guys no longer have the luxury of saying things like "We were pleased with the effort" or "We had our chances; the goals will come." If the Bats go down 2–0 in this series, odds are good that when the goals do come, it will be under a hot July sun, with macadam and Rollerblades underfoot.

As penance for his Game 1 gaffe, Roscoe is off the power play and his usual spot with Seguin, joining a checking line with Jeremy Thompson and Joe Van Volsen. Naturally, he turns out to be the hero. He doesn't score the game-winner—he isn't even on the ice when it happens. But he bears as much responsibility as anyone for the Bats' 2–1 win, drawing a rare OT penalty by going hard in the offensive zone. Attacking the perimeters with Van Volsen, Roscoe barely beats his guy and heads for the net, switching to his backhand for a shot as the D-man takes him down. His effort, and perhaps a certain amount of theater, forces referee Ron Morgan's hand to go up for the first time in over 30 minutes (not counting offsetting calls).

With Findlay playing the point and Mike Jackson taking a pounding down low, the Bats work their first successful power play. The first 90 seconds or so pass with nothing more than chances, but then Findlay collapses toward the slot, with activity in front. The rookie star gets a rebound past Fort Worth goalie Rob Laurie—your basic ugly playoff goal.

"The biggest goal of my life," Findlay says afterward.

THE SERIES MOVES to Austin. Jeremy Thompson, who scored that big one on the road against El Paso in last year's playoffs, believes it's his turn to shine once more.

With all his suspensions and injuries, J.T. missed 33 games this season. He managed 222 penalty minutes but only one goal, and that was in November. On the way to the rink before Game 3 he tells Jeff Kungle that tonight, he's got one in him. So what if he's told Kungle that a dozen times before?

"Don't put on a show," Lawless says in the dressing room before the face-off. The standard admonition when playing hockey in front of home fans. Don't be pretty or fancy or entertaining, just good. "The show we'll put on is at the end of the fucking game, when we have one more fucking point than they do."

Again, it's quiet. The stakes are high. The guys really stay within themselves, building focus. "We know what we gotta do out there," Pawluk says.

Tonight, 6,186 Austin fans are attending their first home game in five weeks. They get their money's worth and more in the form of another tight-checking contest with few mistakes—and even fewer offensive fireworks. The Austin power play continues to stink it up.

After two periods, the Brahmas lead 1–0. Considering the Bats haven't won a single game all year when trailing after two, things look bleak. But the effort is there, and so is Christian Soucy. The enigmatic goalie has been so hot that it's no longer possible to feel sorry for Chad Erickson, though there's no doubt Chad would have raised his game as well, and he never had this kind of defensive commitment in front of him.

Soucy manages plenty of stops without support. He gloves and/or covers at least a dozen nerve-wrackers. He gets tiny little pieces of dangerous point-blank chances. He frustrates the Brahmas enough that they miss a few gimmes. They say it's better to be lucky than good, but it sure doesn't hurt when you're both. There is one incredible, split-second sequence where Soucy goes from out of the net completely to down with his skates in the air to sprawled horizontally across the goal mouth.

Still, Brahma Rob Laurie has the edge. At least, he does until late in the third period, when Keith Moran (playing forward after Curtis Fry leaves the game with a concussion) corrals a puck at his own blueline and flips it across to Rob Schriner. It's an 80-degree day in Austin, and the ice is porridge. The disc takes forever to get to Schriner, and when it does, it's a little behind him. Schriner busts a stunning pirouette to get the puck, and after rotating the full 360 degrees, heads up right wing. It was a brilliant move, but now that Schriner is almost to the corner with no help, it doesn't seem like anything will come from it.

Laurie thinks so too—he is even more surprised than the deafening crowd when Schriner sends a wide-angle slap shot high to the short side. It's 1–1 Bats, with 5:05 left in regulation. Schriner now has a goal in each of the three postseason games. Way up in the press box, Blaine Stoughton smiles.

Kyle Haviland takes a between-periods piss and enters the locker room clapping hands. "All right! I feel good!"

"The place went apeshit," Pawluk says, referring to the crowd's reaction to Schriner's goal. There are no cynics among the Ice Bats faithful now.

"The last time I heard an ovation that loud was in Chicago Stadium," Darrin MacKay offers.

"Fucking-A, this is fun," Havy exults. "Somebody's going to score. Who's it going to be?"

"We need the tally, boys," Lawless says. "We gotta create traffic in front of this guy. You guys are all fucking goal-scorers. Improvise. Find a way."

"We deserve it, boys," Ryan Pawluk says.

"It's our rink—fucking right we deserve it," Haviland proclaims.

And soon enough, after eight minutes of uneventful overtime, here's Jeremy Thompson after all. He's streaking down the ice with Andy Ross, both of them going as fast as they can, which isn't very. Still, they're ahead of the nearest defender, and under the circumstances, no one can afford to be picky about scoring chances. Thompson has already blown a few opportunities tonight. As ever, his gusto puts him into great position, but his lingering aches and modest skills leave it at that. Score here, though, and no one will remember anything but this moment.

So there's Ross and there's Thompson and there's no one near them and *Aaaah-aaah-aaaaaaaah* . . . They enter the slot and Ross waits a beat, nice and easy, nothing but time, Laurie certain he's the shooter, just get it over there and *Mmmmmhhhhhhh!* There's the pass and there goes the puck, and the crowd has stored up enough CO_2 to fuel a thoroughly disillusioned *Ohhhhhhhhhhhhh!* but the puck doesn't skip over Thompson's blade and it doesn't get knocked away by the caught-up defenseman and *Ah . . . ah . . .* J.T. flicks his hands toward the gaping net, not too soon and not too late, and his shot's not wide, and it's not high, and *Ah . . . ah . . .* If Laurie doesn't defy all laws of physics and flexibility, the only thing that's going to stop this puck is twine . . . SCORE!

That's the sound. Cue Gary Glitter! HEY! HEY! Jeremy Thompson gets his second goal of the year! Bats win!

J.T. is not just a prophet—he is also the Ice Bats's all-time leader in the category of game-winning playoff goals. Suddenly, the Fort Worth Brahmas are the ones who have to get the next one on the road, lest their work visas and free apartments and discounted greens fees disappear before the snow has melted in Saskatchewan.

IT ALL GOES BAD from there.

A few minutes before Game 4 warm-ups, Paul Lawless is practicing his golf swing in the office. He is certain there won't be a Game 5 in Fort Worth tomorrow afternoon. "He already has a tee time," Gerald Stoughton tells me. "That's how confident he is."

Tonight the Bats hand the Brahmas a 2–0 lead, but then the

offense purrs for the first time in a month, scoring the next two goals to seize all the momentum. With less than a minute remaining in the first period, Mike Jackson, Tim Findlay and Ryan Pawluk cycle like they did back in October, making it 2–1. Then, with less than a minute remaining in the second period, Jake and Findlay cash in a five-on-three power play with Roscoe getting dirty in the slot. It's 2–2.

As usual, Kyle Haviland leads the charge into the third. "We come out buzzin' here and they're done," he declares. "They're finished."

"They can't play with us," Brett Seguin says. "We've got another notch, though."

"Let's put it away now," Pawluk says.

"Deflate their balloon," Roscoe offers. "Give that second and third effort."

"It all comes down to desire," Haviland finishes.

It all comes down to one face-off. And Austin's frazzled power play.

Findlay and Seguin team up for the go-ahead goal just minutes into the final period, and the Bats protect the lead through a couple of nail-biting penalty kills. Stephan LaRocque sets up one of them with a melodramatic dive, treating the ref to a command performance of "Mommy, Send in the Trainer," then going back on the ice with Fort Worth's PP unit.

The Bats kill off that one too, but the Brahmas tie it up at even strength midway through the period. Then, with just four minutes to go, Brahma Adam Robbins is exiled to the box. Fort Worth coach Bill MacDonald ordinarily might have been furious, but in this series, putting Austin on the power play has yet to truly hurt his team.

This time, it helps. Austin's PP woes have been more complicated than the lack of goals, or even scoring chances. Puck control and breakouts have also been problematic, so much so that the Brahmas blithely send in two forecheckers on penalty kills. That pressure forces a face-off in Austin's defensive zone, something that should never happen with the extra man.

And something Brett Seguin wishes never happened for many months to come. Seguin loses the draw clean to Chris Albert, and Fort Worth point man Mark O'Donnell snaps the puck by Soucy before the goaltender can react. It's 4–3 Brahmas. The Bats can't exploit the remaining power play (surprise, surprise) and Fort Worth adds an empty-netter.

Lawly heads straight for his office and slams the door. Christian Soucy looks sad. Others try to put up a brave front.

"Big deal—we play one more fucking game," Jeff Kungle says.

"We're a younger team," Ryan Anderson offers, meaning the Bats will have the fresher legs now that the series has reached its limit.

But before Game 5 is played, those legs spend three glorious hours on the Bat Bus. Five months after its first-night breakdown in Ellinger, the trusty old vehicle responds to an 85-degree Texas day by shorting out the air-conditioning. A cranky, sweaty, dehydrated Ice Bats team arrives at the Fort Worth Convention Center just 90 minutes before game time.

Before the bus left Austin, Andy Ross and Kyle Haviland were worrying out loud about the possibility that they might have to start paying rent in two days. This doesn't exactly qualify as positive thinking.

In the dressing room, it's Gunner Garrett who delivers the closest thing to a Knute Rockne moment.

"C'mon gentlemen, it's in your fucking hands now," the equipment manager bellows. "You can play soft and go home tomorrow, or you can play hard and play again on Wednesday. You guys make that decision."

"We need all 18 tonight, boys," Andy Ross says.

"We've got a close-knit bunch of guys here," Kyle Haviland states. "The opportunity to play with good friends doesn't happen often. Fuck, let's prolong this season!"

"Not a whole lot to be said, boys," Paul Lawless offers. "We can fucking do it."

They do it for 38 minutes. By the time the next 22 have passed, it no longer feels like either team could have won the series. It no longer matters that both teams played equally hard. It just feels like the better team won.

First the Bats wear down: by the middle of the game, four of the team's seven defensemen are injured in some way, including Shoebottom. After sitting out the last two games (in favor of

Mando, with Lawless continuing to shut out Uniacke), Shoe has taken one final injection. "Good as new," he tells Roscoe, flashing his crooked, toothless grin as he limps on by.

"Some guys are day-to-day," Eric Seeber says. "Shoe is shift-to-shift."

As for the rest of the blueline corps, Ryan Anderson took a puck to the face in Game 4. Keith Moran has a bad wrist and can barely grip his stick. Todd Harris has a groin injury, and is . . . well, just being Harry, the way his teammates see it.

"If guys really can't play, get their gear off," Darrin MacKay demands after the second period. "I don't want them out there."

Anderson can barely talk. He says that when the puck smashed into his jaw and knocked him to the ice, all he could think about, while also trying not to swallow his teeth, was the way his dad used to yell at him when he was a kid: "Don't ever let me see you laying on the ice! You lay on the ice, I'll come and drag you off!"

Anderson got up under his own power. Now he has to listen to Harris moan. "The guy won a championship, but he can't play hurt in the last 20 minutes of what could be the season?" Ryan wonders.

The Bats are hanging on. It was 2–2 late in the second, but Fort Worth got one a couple of minutes before the buzzer, giving the Bats something to think about in the locker room.

"Hey guys! They're the ones that are tight," Lawless booms, desperately trying to keep his team's bodies and spirits alive for one more frame. "We just have to win this period. Let's take some chances."

"C'mon boys, dig deep," Ryan Pawluk says. "Dig deep. Here we go."

And there they went. Before the Bats can gather up their wits, Brahma Chris Albert applies the hammer with back-to-back goals just minutes apart. It's 5–2. The game is over, except for the sideshow.

Which is this: with around eight minutes to go, Tim Findlay gets his stick up, catching Ryan Pawluk in the face, leaving him bloody and broken-nosed. Talk about symbolism. Meanwhile, referee Ron Morgan doesn't even see that Pawluk was down, prompting Lawless to toss a roll of tape at the official. Though the

Brahmas had nothing to do with the injury, Morgan finally gets around to making a call (which is negated by Lawly's unsportsman-like conduct penalty). When the Austin coach lofts another roll of tape, Morgan catches it with one hand and gives the ejection sign with the other. It takes a few more minutes, with Ross and Mike Jackson bemusedly skating back and forth between the ref and their coach, before Lawless finally leaves the ice. For five minutes, Darrin MacKay makes his professional head-coaching debut. A series, and a season, that began so promisingly, ends in shambles.

"I think that's the best hockey we played all year," Jeff Kungle says. "We have nothing to be ashamed of. We played as hard as we could and certainly gave them a run for their money."

A true statement, but also an indicator of just how skewed the Ice Bats season has become. Back in November, Austin was sup-posed to be as good as any team in the league, not just scrappy youngsters who might make life difficult for better teams. Blaine Stoughton even admits that the team's youth movement failed, never mind whether it was motivated by economics, as most be-lieve, or by hockey factors, as the general manager claimed back in October.

"Our philosophy was to get younger and try and develop kids for the next level," he says. "We might have went a little too far. We've got some good young kids, but do you win a championship with that? Fort Worth, they've got a lot of guys that aren't going anywhere, but they know how to compete at this level."

The acquisition of Schriner proved to be important. Teamed with Seguin, he was the closest the Bats came to replacing Binnie. But Curtis Fry, Hartnell's ostensible replacement, never adjusted to his new team, having spent the whole season playing the softer, big-ice game of the European leagues. Certainly Hartnell, or Uni-acke for that matter, couldn't have contributed any less.

Stoughton also acknowledges the team's lack of an offensive defenseman was devastating, especially on the power play. Young or old, the Bats are more talented than Fort Worth. If the pp is even slightly better than 3–30, Austin probably wins another game. And they only needed one.

That onus could be on Paul Lawless, who didn't conduct a single power play practice the entire series, even though it had been equally unreliable the last month of the season. But Lawly believed the struggles were a matter of hard work, rather than the execution or Xs and Os. Brett Seguin agrees, noting that it's hard to practice a power play against your own team, because everyone knows what both units are trying to do. "I think a lot of coaches on this level just say 'Let's put our five best guys on the ice and they'll figure out what to do,'" Seguin says.

Jeff Kungle has a different perspective, though he puts it in his usual tactful way. "I've been around teams where we used to practice the power play a lot," the captain says. "And those teams, I think, are the ones that have done better."

Whatever else went wrong for Austin, everybody agrees the series ended in Game 4—if not when Fort Worth scored the winner, then when they tied it.

"3–2, 10 minutes to go, if we could have scored another one there, the game is over," Stoughton says. "You only get one kick at the cat."

"That play bothered me for a long time," Seguin will say a few months later. "During the series I was probably 90 percent on my face-offs. I was really confident that we were gonna beat those guys. To have that happen in a split second, it was like, oh my God. I felt like I let down the 18 other guys. That pretty much summarized my whole season."

So it's 9:50 p.m. on a Sunday night, and a small throng of fans surrounds the bus as the players, dejected but stoic, load up their gear. A few of the guys disperse right there, catching a ride back to Austin with friends or family. Others pass up that opportunity, choosing to be part of the team for a few more hours, to hurtle down the darkness of I-35 one final time.

Copious drinking, accompanied by Denny's take-out, is all that's left on the agenda. Ryan Anderson even picks up a gallon jug of convenience-store wine. The last night of the season deserves something special.

The mood on the bus is a mixture of disappointment, denial,

relief and pride. "It takes a special group of guys to win a championship," Anderson says. "Obviously we didn't have what it takes."

Lawly comes back and mingles. He can be one of the boys again. He talks about how hard it was for him and Blaine to just stand by and let Burty do his job while they were struggling. It was a helpless feeling. Then they acted on it.

Sitting nearby, Brett Seguin suggests that Burty asked too much of certain guys, that he wanted the players to do things beyond their talents. For example, he asked Ryan Anderson to try to fake out the first forechecker before breaking out of the defensive zone. Anderson, by his own admission, is a player who's better suited to a simple first pass, or to ringing the puck around the boards.

Anderson says he liked Lawly as the coach. "I was surprised how well he took to it, to tell you the truth. He actually enjoyed himself." Now the Kid will head back to Bowsman for another summer, a 23-year-old who already owns a house. He says that for all the ups and downs, this was a good season, and a bang-up group of guys. He specifically mentions Keith Moran, saying he never imagined that he, a high school dropout, would pal around with a college kid like Keith. Moran, of course, had expressed similar sentiments.

A small rumble emerges from the rear. "I'm gonna hit the kid with the sunglasses," Bruce Shoebottom threatens.

He's referring to Tim Findlay, who's a little too cool for the room in his Nike beret and Oakley shades. The guys have been ribbing Fins about it all day, but now Shoe, fueled by booze as well as painkillers, completely wigs, walking up to Findlay's seat and actually slugging him on the head.

Ryan Pawluk is disgusted. "Yeah, he was in the Show."

Nursing his wound, Findlay says this was the best year of his life. He loves Austin. He says he could see himself raising a family here, though who knows what the future holds for him, in life or hockey. This morning, Findlay, kidding around with Gunner as usual, asked him if equipment managers in the IHL griped about their players as much as he did.

"When you get to the I," Gunner replied, "you can send me a postcard and tell me."

"Next year," Findlay said. If not, he figures he'll pursue his dream at the U.S. minor level for three or four more years. Then he'll either go to Europe, where there can be good money for a player of his caliber, or shut it down.

Things get silly fast. Disposable cameras flash off every 30 seconds. Jeff Kungle rubs Brett Seguin's bare head. Andy Ross smokes on board for the first time all season. Why not, especially since the vent is open, thanks to that broken A/C.

"The bus," Keith Moran observes, "is drunk."

And there's more where that came from. If everything times out right, the guys will get to the rink at 1 A.M., leaving them just enough wiggle room to get to Pearl's, a bar and restaurant not far from the apartments, for a round of Naked Road Hockey, the gin-and-lemonade concoction that is the team's intoxicant of choice.

"The first guy who gets there, order a hundred of 'em," Mike Jackson says.

"One at Pearl's, a dozen at home," says Seguin.

There is no more hockey. The cliques and rivalries and conflicts, the bad trades and the coaching change and the tension with the owners—it all melts away for now. The bus is no longer carrying the Ice Bats. All that's left are "the boys," 20 friends who have lived through six bitter, glorious and crazy months in the WPHL. Another season gone.

r

epilogue

INSTANT KARMA

EIGHT THOUSAND–PLUS FANS packed the Travis County Expo Center for the third annual Western Professional Hockey League All-Star game in January 1999. It was a marvelous experience for almost everyone involved. Tim Findlay was selected as a starter for the second straight year, and Ryan Pawluk made his first appearance. Jim Burton joined them as a coach, having led the expansion Arkansas Glacier Cats to the best record in their division at mid-season. As expected, the former Bats coach went from assistant general manager in Austin to main man with the Cats. He was thriving, which came as no surprise to the Ice Bats faithful.

Nope, the surprise had come a few months earlier. Before the season began, Blaine Stoughton traded Findlay and Pawluk to Arkansas.

Findlay's rights fetched three players who never wore an Ice Bats sweater. (They moved on to other leagues or demanded trades to other teams.) Stoughton said he did the deal because it was in Tim's best interests, as Arkansas (which is to say, Burty) offered him a two-way slot with Kansas City of the IHL. Once Findlay moved to Little Rock, it was inevitable that his friend would follow. Pawluk's rights attracted a pair of serviceable defensemen. The trades would have been lousy by any standard. But since Stoughton and his partners also owned the Glacier Cats, they were a blatant conflict of interest. And Stoughton's comments about the IHL affiliation turned out to be another not-quite-truth—Burty had connections in K.C., but Findlay was not signed to an actual two-way contract, and he never spent a minute with the Blades (though several Arkansas goaltenders and defensemen did).

The WPHL would later institute a rule prohibiting transactions between teams with common owners. But they didn't have one at that point, partly because it was the league's first dual-owner situation, and partly because the Wiffle knew that if Findlay and Pawluk couldn't play for Burty they would bolt for another league.

One thing was certain: they didn't want to be in Austin. The Bats spent the summer after my season on the bus in hockey limbo, barely scraping up a team. Lawless chose not to return as coach, and there was no Burty to take care of recruiting. Gerald Stoughton assembled the makings of a decent squad, and finally, at the end of August, his older brother found a bench boss in Al Tuer, an ex–Cincinnati Cyclone teammate and former NHLer.

Tuer, a career sub-.500 coach in five seasons with the WHL Moose Jaw Warriors, initially turned down the job. He changed his mind when Moose Jaw cut him loose. At long last, the Bats would have an authoritative, fire-breathing outsider to give the squad a little discipline. Stoughton even awarded Tuer the larger dressing-room office that Jim Burton never got to occupy.

So half a season goes by, and here's Burty, coaching in the All-Star game. And here's the Ice Bats, a last-place club. Even with the game on Austin ice, the host team isn't good enough to merit more than the mandatory single All-Star player.

On his squad, Burty has not just Findlay and Pawluk, but also Monroe Moccasin Rob Hartnell. Over the summer, Hartsy asked for and received a trade from Amarillo to Monroe, as Mocs coach Rob Bremner was an old Western League compadre. Like previous Stoughton-exile Rick Girhiny, Hartnell wears the "C" for his new team. At that point in the season, Findlay, Pawluk and Hartnell had a combined 67 goals, more than the total for Austin's top six scorers.

The Windsor Kids accounted for two goals and two assists in the All-Star game. Unfortunately, Burty's mischievous plan to skate them on a line with their good friend Hartnell fell through. Hartsy suffered a herniated groin during the Fastest Skater skills competition, and only played a token 20-second shift.

Though he was booed wildly by the home crowd, Burton remained as gracious as ever. And why not? This was a redemptive moment for him, though he couldn't really gloat about it: he still worked for the same guys who fired him the first time. "I've kind of proven them wrong and proven them right," he says.

With his bread still buttered by the Bats brass, Burton would only discuss Findlay and Pawluk in broad, albeit easily decipherable, terms. "I don't know what to tell you about the trades," he says. "I know what kind of players they are, so I wanted them. And if the Ice Bats had wanted them that much, I wouldn't have gotten them."

"So is it fair to say that if you were the coach of the Ice Bats this year, we'd be watching those guys play in Austin?" I ask him.

"Absolutely," he replies. "You can bank on that one."

I had already interviewed Burty earlier in the season as a post-mortem for this book, traveling to Little Rock to watch the Glacier Cats beat Austin 8–3. He said that one of the challenges he faced with Findlay and Pawluk was keeping them hungry. It's easy for minor league players to get comfortable when their dreams don't come true quickly. Just look at the previous season's Bats.

"Some of those guys could have potentially made it to the NHL, but obviously their physical attributes held them back," Burton says. "So then a guy will realize, 'Hey, no matter how good I get I'm not quite big enough, and I'm not quite fast enough. So I'll score 35 or 40 goals a year, make a little bit of money, and have some fun.' There's nothing wrong with that, but I don't want those kind of players."

"We had some guys who were kind of on their own agenda," Tim Findlay says. "They cared more about living in Austin and having a good time than playing hockey. Everybody on the team saw that. I like to go out as much as the next guy, but I don't want to be in the Western Pro League for the rest of my life. I work on things that are gonna help me be a better hockey player, not things that are gonna make me more social."

Even though he still works for them, Burty concedes that the Austin owners didn't treat his charges well. The attitude seemed to be that since Austin was the best market in the league, and one of the most livable cities in all of minor pro, the team didn't have to do its players any favors.

"But players at this level, all they really want is a pat on the back and a few niceties," Burton says. "Mike Jackson put it best. He said, 'Hey, I've played a lot of different places. They've all got free golf for hockey players. They've all got three or four good bars. Just because you're giving me Austin, that means nothing.'"

Burton, Findlay, Pawluk and the Glacier Cats continued winning in the season's second half. Things in Austin got even worse. Al Tuer's hard-ass tactics worked initially—he even got Andy Ross to quit smoking—but wore thin fast. His defense-oriented squad failed to shut down opponents and wasn't really tough, just ill-tempered and penalty-prone. "They've got nothing but slugs and hammers," Burton said after the Arkansas win I witnessed.

Ryan Anderson became Tuer's whipping boy, harangued in practice and out of uniform for games. Tuer made players like Ross, and even Keith O'Brien, feel like they had to fight to earn his respect. After one particularly ugly game, the coach himself got into a brawl with Waco counterpart Todd Lalonde. Finally, in late February, he flipped the bird at a group of Ice Bats fans who'd gone to see their dreadful team play a meaningless road game. Gerald Stoughton finished out the season as head coach.

There was no playoff hockey that year at the Bat Cave. There was in Arkansas, though the Glacier Cats were surprised by Hartnell and the Moccasins in the best-of-three-game wild card round.

Meanwhile, over in the western division, the San Angelo Outlaws became the Wiffle's feel-good club. The Three Amigos were riding high again, but the team owed most of its success to goaltender Chad Erickson.

Erickson was traded to the Outlaws as the "future consideration" from the Todd Harris deal. Instead of retiring, which he'd
seriously considered, the goalie seized his opportunity to be the Man,
posting a 31–14–3 record with a .917 save percentage in the regular
season. He then took the Outlaws all the way to the President's Cup
finals. They were trounced there by a loaded Shreveport club, but in
the previous round, Chad prevailed over the highly favored, somewhat familiar Fort Worth Brahmas.

In hindsight, "I probably didn't handle it very well," Erickson
says of his late-season benching as a Bat. "But I didn't think it was
fair for me to play there for two years, and then they go and do that.
In this league, we're playing for the fun of it. You just want to be
treated well. The tough thing about it is that both Paul and Blaine
were players. We thought they would have been a little more sup-
portive. How do you expect to play your best hockey when you
know the owners are second-guessing everything you do out there?"

And how do you play your best hockey when one of those owners is the coach? Erickson is one of several players who suggest
that Lawless only took over because "it was something for him to
do. He had no real responsibilities. It might have been different if
Paul had the intention of staying for the next year. But it was just
so they could say his name over the PA.

"Jimmy is one of the best coaches in the league," Erickson continues. "We played with injuries and call-ups and a pretty tough
schedule. Then when we go on a little bit of a slide they decide to
get rid of him? I didn't think it was right, and I said that. If that's
part of the reason I got frustrated, that's fine. I can live with that."

THERE WOULD BE good times for Austin hockey fans again, but
not until later in 1999, when Stoughton, Lawless, Novess and Hart
sold the franchise to Houston businessman John McVaney. Mc-
Vaney hired Brent Hughes and Ken McRae, former NHLers and
former Houston Aeros, as head coach and assistant coach, respectively. In April 2000, the Bats finally won the first playoff round in
franchise history.

By then, the bottom was falling out of the WPHL's best-laid
expansion plans. Burton's Glacier Cats made it to the second

round that season but went out of business before the next one. Original Six team Waco shut its doors in the middle of the 1999–2000 campaign, and franchises in Abilene, Texas, and Alexandria, Louisiana, also didn't make it. In January 2001, Central Texas went under, playing its last-ever game against the Bats.

Five months later, the WPHL announced a merger with the Central Hockey League. Because the CHL name has been around in some form or another since the 1960s, that is the banner under which the league now operates. Former WPHL teams in Austin, Corpus Christi, Lubbock, San Angelo, Fort Worth, Odessa, El Paso, Amarillo, Albuquerque and Bossier–Shreveport will now battle with CHL clubs in Oklahoma City, Tulsa, Wichita, Memphis, San Antonio and Indianapolis. Other Central League cities in the southeastern U.S. moved on to other leagues or out of hockey entirely, while the WPHL bade farewell to Lake Charles, Monroe and Tupelo, Mississippi.

Despite the backdrop of economic uncertainty, 2000–01 was another fine season for the Bats. After a two-year exile, Brett Seguin returned to Austin and dazzled, leading the team in scoring with 95 points while earning his fifth straight All-Star nod. Brent Hughes was thrilled to have him. "He never takes the night off," Seguin's new coach said. "He has a burning desire to win, and he sees the ice so well. He's like Gretzky out there."

He was also a more dedicated player. Two weeks before the playoffs I went to practice and was surprised to find him pedaling away on the exercise bike afterward.

"You know why he's on there?" Gunner Garrett said. "To work up a thirst."

"I haven't had a beer in three weeks," Seguin retorted. That dry spell happened to coincide with a 16-game point streak.

Gunner, Seguin, Jeff Kungle and Ryan Anderson are the final remnants from the Ice Bats' first two seasons.

"Skinny" (they just can't call him "Kid" anymore) came away from his Al Tuer experience the better, blossoming into a veteran leader after Brent Hughes put an "A" on his sweater and took him off the blueline. Anderson is never going to be a pretty player, but the move transformed him from a beatable defenseman into an effective and annoying checking grunt. After averaging close to 250 penalty minutes in his first four seasons, Skinny had 110 in the most recent one. He had a combined 17 goals in his last two seasons, after averaging just one per year the first three. There were actually times when Hughes wouldn't let him fight—he needed Skinny on the ice.

It's all gravy to Anderson, who has also won the team's "Fan Favorite" award three times. Coming out of juniors, there's no way he could have ever pictured himself getting ready for his sixth pro season. He didn't even think he'd be a hockey player.

"Well, I was gonna play," he says. "I just couldn't wait to play bush league, where you have the beer right beside you during the game. I'd get my kid to carry the beer to me: 'Oh, that's a good boy. Good boy.'"

afterword

"THE KID" STAYS IN THE PICTURE

RYAN ANDERSON FIGURED he was washed up at 26, the victim of a rule that turns minor-league hockey into something out of *Logan's Run*. In that classic sci-fi flick, reaching 30 meant your life was over. In AA hockey, the situation's much the same. In the name of "player development," teams are permitted to sign only a certain number of guys with a certain number of games under their belt. Whether you're a star who scores his age or someone like "Skinny" who the fans have bonded with for years, there's always someone younger looming, a player who can do 80 percent of your job for 60 percent of your salary.

This "veteran's rule" is the reason guys like Rob Hartnell and Andy Ross left other leagues for Texas to begin with. But by 2001, in the wake of the Western Professional Hockey League's merger with the CHL, the Ice Bats had the regulation too: each club could carry only five players with 230 games or more professional experience. The figure rose to 260 in 2002, but in a sport where healthy players rack up 60 to 70 games per season, either is a tiny number.

So after five great years in Austin, Anderson figured that was it.

He and his fellow grunts—the fighters, anonymous defensemen and stonehanded "character" types who are an important part of every team, but hardly irreplaceable—were out the door. "It's hard for guys like us," he said at the time. "Those five players are going to be pretty talented, you'd think."

You'd think. But 1500 miles away in Windsor, Tim Findlay was just as worried. It didn't matter that he was still only 25 years old. It didn't matter that he had 40-plus goals for three straight years. It didn't even matter that he'd just played in the AHL for 27 games— the Louisville Panthers sent him packing to make room for players under contract with the team's NHL parent.

"The coach even told me, 'you're one of my best forwards right now,'" Findlay remembers. "Looking back, I didn't even realize what I had. You get called up, go from one team right to another and you don't even realize, holy shit, I'm a half-step from the NHL!" He was occasionally reminded of that fact, when playing in the old Philadelphia Spectrum against the Phantoms or putting practice pucks by Roberto Luongo. He also roomed with Rocky Thompson, Jeremy's older brother.

But in the end, Findlay was sent down to Port Huron of the UHL. He began 2001–02 back with the Border Cats, got traded to Fort Wayne, then returned to Port Huron—all moves that never would have happened if he hadn't been a so-called vet. He finished out the year with Flint—ironically, the team he didn't want to play for as a rookie. The Generals coach liked him, especially when he continued to work hard and stay positive after sitting out some playoff games. But by training camp 2002, the numbers still were not in Findlay's favor.

He got on the phone to Texas, but the Ice Bats had their roster set. So did Amarillo, where a former Arkansas teammate was assistant coach. Finally, Odessa said he could come down. But Findlay had gotten used to playing close to home, and he and Jenn Theriault had gotten married in July. He looked at his wife of three months, thought about loading up the car for a 25-hour drive, and "that was that," he says. "I called it a career."

It helped that Findlay's uncle offered him a solid, well-paying job as an operator at a local food-processing plant. And on the side, he's replaced sticks and pucks with a Fender Telecaster and a home-recording set-up—music was always a big passion, and he wishes he'd seen more bands during his time in Austin.

"I've got my feet planted, and hopefully we'll be buying a house here soon," Findlay says. "I don't regret the decision [to quit hockey], but it's crummy—the veteran rule was probably the demise of my career. The number should be 500, or 600. The Central Hockey League and the United Hockey League, they're not really developmental leagues."

This is absolutely right. The ECHL continues to be the primary pipeline to both the AHL and, in less dramatic but still consistent fashion, the NHL. The CHL has made great inroads with its AHL affiliations, but the league's primary business is entertaining fans, not shaping the best players of tomorrow. Youth should be served—as Findlay and Ryan Pawluk proved themselves, new players often work harder, the fans enjoy the freshness, and most coaches would rather teach and mold a kid who may yet have something else ahead of him rather than a set-in-his-ways vet. But the rule is really about money—experienced players make more, owners want to pay less.

In truth, there's only one kind of player the CHL develops with any sort of regularity, and Findlay is proof of that as well. You get better. Maybe you get a shot at the next level. But in the end, you're right back where you started, so you either hang 'em up or become one of the oldsters. Findlay, occasionally critical of his veteran teammates' ways back when his ambition was still raw, knows that now.

"I thought they were crazy at the time," he says. "I wanted to go balls-out and be an NHL superstar, while those guys were just playing out the string. But I came to realize there's more to being on a team than the games. You should enjoy the cities, enjoy what's going on around you, find a balance between the two."

THINGS WORKED OUT a lot better for the ostensibly less-talented Ryan Anderson. Despite Skinny's fears, Brent Hughes never wavered on the fan favorite's status in 2001. "He's earned the opportunity to play on this hockey club, for what he's done here for five years," the Ice Bats coach said then. "What he does inside this dressing room, what he does in the community, all his hard work and effort, it's huge." But in 2002, the Bats asked him to come to training camp without a contract. He'd have to make the team. Hughes figured Anderson was part of Austin now, that he loved the city too much to go who-knows-where just to play another year or two.

He figured wrong. It wasn't necessarily a bad decision by the Bats, hockey-wise. But Skinny had the last laugh. He landed with the Orlando Seals of the Atlantic Coast Hockey League, a first-year, six-team circuit like the WPHL of old. The Seals set up Anderson and his girlfriend in their own apartment (the Bats would have required roommates), and Orlando's coach, former NHL/IHL stalwart Stan Drulia, gave Skinny more responsibility and playing time than he'd ever dreamed of.

"I wanted high-quality guys," Drulia says. "All I heard about Ryan was how good a guy he was, and how well he was liked by the fans in Austin."

Although Anderson had grown into a leadership role with the Bats, he has a more commanding vibe in the Orlando dressing room, where nobody knows he used to be "The Kid." Skinny still remembers being that first-year naif, looking up to veterans Andy Ross and Kyle Haviland. Now he is them. "He takes control of the dressing room, really keeps the guys in there on their toes," Drulia says.

"Can I say wisdom?" says Anderson, when asked what he brought to the table, "Does that sound right coming out of my mouth? All of a sudden players were looking up to me, asking my advice."

Early in the season, the Seals were getting blown out by the Cape Fear Fire Antz, 8–2, with all the line brawls you'd expect from such a hopeless effort. With eight seconds left, so many guys were in either the box or the showers that Orlando had just Anderson and one other player on the ice for one last D-zone faceoff. The opposing goaltender, two zones away, was resting on one knee. The puck dropped. *What the hell*, thought Skinny as he drew back his stick, and, you guessed it: "He shoots, he scores!"

"We'd just been beaten 8–3, and the two of them celebrated like they'd won the Stanley Cup," Drulia remembers. "Skinny put his hands in the air, skated by the bench, put his hands down, skated back to center ice, put his hands back up, went to the other team's bench. We got on the bus, and I said, 'Okay boys, we're watching the video of this one. . . .' The only thing we watched was that goal. Those are the kind of circumstances that bring a team together."

The Seals went on to take the ACHL championship, winning every single playoff game. After losing in the finals his last year as an Ice Bat, and losing well before then every other season, Skinny got himself a ring. "It was unbelievable," he stammers. "It wasn't even real. It hasn't clicked in at all. It's everything that you ever wanted it to be."

"Usually [in the off-season] you're sitting around going, I can't believe how the year ended," Anderson observes. "This year it was like, do we get to play anybody else?"

Meanwhile, Brett Seguin and the 2002–03 Bats fell in the finals yet again. He and Skinny have outlasted all the other players from this book. "It's weird," Anderson says. "Pawluk and Findlay, you'd think those guys would be playing forever, and at a higher level. People get better offers or better things to do. You start to move on. But for people like 'Pig' or myself, the hockey, the guys, the bus, it's the hardest thing to walk away from. It's just been our lives. We're probably in for a pretty rude awakening when it's all over."

"Hockey's kind of a fantasy world," Findlay echoes. "You're playing a game, the money's coming in every week, you don't worry about real issues. I feel bad for a lot of guys, and I guess I was one of them, who came right out of juniors and didn't finish their schooling and went right to pro. They're making five or six hundred dollars a week, living paycheck to paycheck, going to bars. Even in Austin, Pawly would say to me, 'Fins, one day we're gonna have to be doing something else,' and I'd be like, 'Awwww, I'm gonna play hockey until I'm 35.'"

"But it was a great five, six years. I think about it every day."

May 2003

appendix
WHERE ARE THEY NOW?

(Note: Statistics do not include playoff games.)

TIM FINDLAY · *Center*
GP: 50   G: 42   A: 32   PIM: 8
After two seasons in Arkansas with Jim Burton, Findlay made some headway on his dream, signing a contract with the Florida Panthers–affiliated Port Huron Border Cats of the UHL. He split the 2000–01 season between Port Huron and Louisville of the AHL, registering 3 goals and 11 assists in 27 games at the higher level. But after spending the 2001–02 season with the Flint Generals, he retired. Tim married Jenn Theriault in the summer of 2002 and went to work for ADM Agri-Industries.

RYAN PAWLUK · *Wing*
GP: 65   G: 36   A: 60   PIM: 51
Pawluk played one season in Arkansas, then struggled the following year in the ECHL. Partially reunited with Findlay in 2000–01, he was a point-per-game player for the Border Cats. He now runs

his own business, Lakeshore Landscaping and Canadian Natural Stone, near Windsor.

ROB HARTNELL · *Center/Wing*
GP: 67   G: 33   A: 17   PIM: 217 *(combined stats, Austin/Amarillo)*
Hartnell left the Moccasins when Brian Curran returned to Monroe in the fall of 1999, this time as head coach. Rob then played for Idaho of the WCHL, but continued to be bothered by the injury he suffered at the 1999 All-Star game. Now married and a full-time Boise resident, he has left behind the oil fields to work for one of Utah Jazz owner Larry Miller's car dealerships.

CHAD ERICKSON · *Goaltender*
GP: 51   GAA: 3.45   SPCT: .899
After taking San Angelo to the 1998–99 President's Cup finals, Erickson played two more seasons for Tulsa of the CHL. He lost his Oilers gig to future Ice Bats goalie Matt Barnes, and he and wife, Holly, ultimately returned to Minnesota.

CHRIS MORQUE · *Defenseman*
GP: 70   G: 6   A: 22   PIM: 196 *(combined stats, Austin/El Paso)*
The deposed Ice Bats captain won the 1997–98 President's Cup with the El Paso Buzzards. He was then traded to Odessa, where he played two seasons before heading home to North Dakota.

JEFF KUNGLE · *Defenseman*
GP: 62   G: 5   A: 31   PIM: 27
Jeff Kungle spent the 1998–99 season playing in Germany. He returned to the Ice Bats the following year, reclaiming the "C" for two more campaigns. Now married to Lisa and the father of one child, he works for Pound's Photographic Labs in Austin and remains associated with the Bats as an assistant coach.

TODD HARRIS · DEFENSEMAN
GP: 64   G: 9   A: 31   PIM: 54 *(combined stats, Austin/San Angelo)*
Harris was left unprotected in the 1998 WPHL expansion draft and chose to retire. He is now a firefighter in Victoria, B.C.

JOE VAN VOLSEN · *Center/Wing*

GP: 29   G: 10   A:7   PIM: 12

Van Volsen was left unprotected in the expansion draft and subsequently played three seasons for the Tupelo T-Rex, who grabbed him before Burton could. He was voted the WPHL's second-most underrated player in 2001, and has spent the last two seasons with the Fort Worth Brahmas.

RICHARD UNIACKE · *Center*

GP: 32   G: 14   A: 20   PIM: 13

Also left unprotected, Uniacke became Jim Burton's first pick in Arkansas. The center opted to play overseas, then joined the Glacier Cats for the 1999–2000 season, scoring 69 points in 70 games.

CHRISTIAN SOUCY · *Goaltender*

GP: 11   GAA: 3.46   SPCT: .899

Soucy reunited with Jim Burton on the 1999–2000 Arkansas team, then played two seasons for ex–El Paso coach Todd Brost on the UHL Elmira Jackals. He spent 2002–03 in Anchorage, Alaska, playing for the Aces of the WCHL.

BRIAN FAIRFIELD · *Goaltender*

GP: 1   GAA: 4.29   SPCT: .800

After leaving Austin, Fairfield played just two games in the QMJHL. He never returned to the professional level.

DARRIN MACKAY · *Wing*

GP: 39   G: 1   A: 7   PIM: 18

MacKay once again reentered the workforce in Calgary, though he spent the first part of the 1999–2000 season playing in Amsterdam.

KEITH MORAN · *Defenseman/Wing*

GP: 54   G: 7   A:8   PIM: 10

Moran spent the summer of 1998 in Europe and has since worked for Fidelity Investments and current employer AT&T—just like he planned it all along.

JEREMY THOMPSON · *Wing*

GP: 36   G: 1   A: 7   PIM: 222

Thompson played a couple more seasons in the ECHL and UHL. He also worked as a linesman and referee. He and his wife, Jennifer, had a daughter, Faith, in May 2001. She wasn't born in Texas, but she wasn't born in Canada either. The Thompson family now calls Red Deer home. Older brother Rocky remains in the Florida Panthers' system, spending the 2002–03 season with the AHL's San Antonio Rampage.

TROY BINNIE · *Center/Wing*

GP: 19   G: 14   A: 13   PIM: 22

Binnie's Oakville, Ontario–based business, Touchwood Home Improvements, has evolved from a decking company (because its owner was always busy in the winter) to a full-service renovations and construction firm.

KEN RUDDICK · *Defenseman*

GP: 32   G: 5   A: 21   PIM: 28

The on-again, off-again offensive D-man played four seasons for three different teams in the ECHL and UHL. He rejoined the Bats at the 2001 training camp but didn't make the team; the same thing happened with Orlando of the ACHL in 2002. He has also played in Germany and Great Britain.

MIKE JACKSON · *Wing*

GP: 40   G: 7   A: 17   PIM: 186

"Jake" returned to Austin for the 1998–99 season, then retired because of a lingering shoulder injury. He has filed a medical malpractice suit against the Bats' ownership group and the doctor from that era. He splits his time between Ontario and Texas, frequently attending Bats games with his little daughter, Meadow.

CHRIS HASKETT · *Center*

GP: 58   G: 4   A: 5   PIM: 69

Haskett played three games for Macon of the CHL in 1998–99, then returned to Canada, where he attended and played hockey for the University of Western Ontario.

D.J. MANDO · *Wing*
GP: 35   G: 8   A: 7   PIM: 53
Mando went on to become a pretty good player in the ECHL, though injuries limited him to just five games in 2000–01. He has now retired.

JAY HUTTON · *Defenseman*
GP: 3   G: 1   A: 1   PIM: 4 *(combined stats, Austin/Waco)*
Hutton is now a police officer, as well as a linesman in the OHL. He met Marilyn Manson at a recent Ozzfest concert.

KEITH O'BRIEN · *Wing*
GP: 8   G: 0   A: 2   PIM: 15
"O.B." has worn five different numbers for six different Ice Bats teams, skating in 58 games from 1998–2003, including five playoff contests. He remains "on call," but spends most of his professional energy as a salesman for a company called Meeting Maker.

KYLE HAVILAND · *Defenseman*
GP: 60   G: 2   A: 9   PIM: 170
Haviland left Austin for Topeka of the CHL, serving as the team's player/assistant coach for a season-plus before losing his roster spot to another veteran player. He then skated for Lake Charles, and managed a hockey shop in that city with Bobby Wallwork. He is now married with one child and living in the Detroit/ Windsor area.

ANDY ROSS · *Wing*
GP: 59   G: 27   A: 37   PIM: 60
"Roscoe" returned to Austin for the next two seasons, but by the time the team's fortunes changed, he was no longer capable of top-line play. He finished his career with the Corpus Christi Ice Rays, chipping in four goals in seven playoff games after managing just five for the Bats and Rays combined in the regular season. He is now back in Philadelphia, where he works for a company that appraises school-district buildings and has more youth-hockey coaching offers than he knows what to do with. His dad is still pissed about the smoking.

BRETT SEGUIN · *Center*
GP: 53   G: 22   A: 46   PIM: 34
Brett Seguin joined Haviland in Topeka for two seasons before returning to the Bat Cave. He is Austin's all-time leader in goals, assists and points (passing Ross in all those categories). In 2001–02 he centered what became known as the "STP Fuel Line" and finished second in the CHL scoring race, one point behind linemate Dan Price. He became the Ice Bats' captain in 2002–03. He and his wife, Angie, live in Austin year-round.

RYAN ANDERSON · *Defenseman*
GP: 69   G: 1   A: 7   PIM: 309
Ryan was the only player in the history of the WPHL to play all five seasons with a single team. He played a sixth in Austin before joining Orlando of the ACHL, where he has once again settled in as a key character player and huge fan favorite.

OTHERS
Jim Mullin, Corey Fletcher, Bruce Shoebottom, Derek Riley, Rob Schriner and *Jason Rose* all retired.

Curtis Fry continues to play hockey in Germany and Austria.

Rick Girhiny hung up his skates in the spring of 2000. His number 7 was retired by the Odessa Jackalopes.

Mark Martello went on to work for the Lousiana Ice Gators, the Shreveport Mudbugs and the Chicago Blackhawks (hosting the NHL team's pre- and post-game show). He was last spotted with the Junior A Bozeman Ice Dogs.

Blaine Stoughton owns and operates the Tween Lakes Motel in Dauphin, Manitoba. His brother Gerald remains an occasional fixture at Bats games.

Paul Lawless suited up for another 40 minutes as an Ice Bats player in 1998–99. He is now vice-president of development for the Cincinnati Cyclones, which moved to the ECHL after the IHL went under in 2001. Lawless's number 13 has been retired by the Cyclones; he also served as interim head coach toward the end of the 2001–02 season.

After Arkansas, *Jim Burton* spent the first half of the 2000–01 season out of work when a WPHL expansion team in Tucson, Arizona, went out of business before it ever played a game. He then became head coach of the ECHL's Lynx in Augusta, where he forged an affiliation with Wayne Gretzky's Phoenix Coyotes. However, in a bit of Ice Bats deja-vu, Burty was kicked upstairs to general manager early in the 2002–03 season. "I got to learn more about business in one year than I would have in a long time as a coach, but if I was thinking I was being groomed to go to the next level, it was certainly a backwards step," he says. "After five years of coaching at this level and a year of GMing, there's not a whole lot left to learn. You're either ready and someone wants to take a shot at you or maybe you want to do something else. It's just like anything, you want to get to the NHL, and you can't if you don't get out of this level."

Finally, although players, coaches, owners, fans and even leagues come and go, *Gunner Garrett* remains the Ice Bats equipment manager. The 2003–04 season will be his eighth in Austin.

ACKNOWLEDGMENTS

IT TOOK A LOT of manpower to make this book. So much, in fact, that I'm sure I'd be better off thanking nobody, 'cause someone always gets left out. So I apologize to that person or persons in advance. Meanwhile, my gratitude goes out to:

The original WPHL powerbrokers: Rick Kozuback, Brad Treliving, Duane Lewis and Steve Cherwonak.

The old Ice Bats ownership group: Daniel Hart, Edward Novess, Blaine Stoughton and Paul Lawless. Because every story needs a villain. Seriously, there wouldn't be hockey in Austin without them, and I couldn't have done this book without their cooperation.

That goes double for Jim Burton. Burty, as drama, it was certainly "good for my book" when you got the boot. But you still should have been there to finish what you started.

Mark Martello. Especially because his preference for sleeping on the floor allowed me my own row on the bus.

Other denizens of the Ice Bats office past and present: Norma Jean Gallegos, Jim Bond, Richard Floco, Scott Shaunessy, Lee Bryant, Kim Bohn, Marie Vedder, Matthew Payne, Jason Bruzzone, Danny Foreman, Mark Jones, Kenneth Tait and Clint Shuman. Eric Seeber and Gunner Garrett for tolerating my presence in "their" locker room. And current media guy Glen "Sharky" Norman deserves his own sentence as well.

Paula Jensen, and everyone at the Zamboni Company. Mr. Frank Zamboni's invention is synonymous with the great game of hockey. Since its title trades on that symbolic currency, I hope my book does it justice.

Heather Dunn, Craig MacDonald, Myrrah Pardini and Sarah Marmion, for interview transcripts. Joe Drape of the *New York Times*, Amy Hettenhausen and Ian Tennant of the *Austin American-Statesman* and Phil Billnitzer of *Austin City Search*, for articles that helped fill holes in my own reporting.

Faith and Terry Elkins at *Just Hockey* and Tom Schettino and Lou Lafrado at *In the Crease* (www.inthecrease.com), for publishing my work during the writing of this book. Josh Daniel and Greg Curtis at *Texas Monthly*, for their involvement in that first-ever Ice Bats story. Evan Smith, for the *Texas Monthly* article as well, and for overall rabbinical tasks. David Humphrey, Camille Wheeler, John Agee, James Wangemann, Art Moore and Danny Douglas at the *Austin American-Statesman* and Matt Thompson at *Austin360*. Props to Richard Martin at *Seattle Weekly*, and Larry Carlat and Bill Crandall at Rollingstone.com. And thanks in advance to any magazine editor who starts giving me work again, especially the ones who've already heard me say "I'll be done with the book and back at it soon" more than a couple of times.

Chris at The Management Group in Santa Fe (and Robert Baird for the office chair). Lorna at Vacations West. Leo and Sargit Toews and Barb and Tom Posmituk in Qualicum Beach. Martye Cohen and the once and future Susie Parker for Miacomet Road.

Jeff Salamon gets a second assist for being an old friend of Jeff Z. Klein, who gets the first one for leading me to my agent, David Johnston of Livingston-Cooke. He made this book happen after agents in my own country tried to talk me out of writing it.

Rob Sanders at Greystone/Douglas & McIntyre had faith that this thing would transcend the category of "hockey book" even when I wasn't so sure. Thanks also to Leanne Denis, Nancy Flight,

Peter Cocking, Chris Labonté, Lucy Kenward and Susan Rana, and thanks in advance to Kelly Mitchell and Bob Pipe for all the work we are doing together by now. And the President's Cup for editing goes to Brian Scrivener, who was helpful, funny, tireless, clever, overworked and (most of all) patient in getting this thing out of me.

Darren Carroll. It was my great luck that a photographer of his talent and experience happened to lock onto the same subject as me at exactly the same time. Darren, I hope you'll agree this book is better than a master's thesis any old day.

Patty Trimble, Victor Diaz, Gene Wohlfarth, Mike Rice, Mitch Cooper, Sara Hurley, Marilyn Wesson and Carl Phinney, for camaraderie on the road and arguments on the Internet. I could probably write a whole other book about Texans who love hockey. A special mention for my very favorite Texas hockey fan, Susan Shepard. And thanks to Nathan Jones for research assistance, Casey Weaver for (im)moral support, Gray Moore of KXAN for video footage, Shelly Kanter for photos, Kim Powell for the original ZR Web site and Rusty Reid for Version 2.0.

Leah Wilkes believes this book affected her life adversely in some way, so I'll humor her with gratitude here. Michael Krugman couldn't be less interested in hockey, so thanks for reading this far. And, of course, much love to my mother, Marilyn Cohen, my little sister Sarah Cohen and my bigger little sister Julie Cohen San Clemente.

Finally, thanks to all the Ice Bats players who were part of this story. It wasn't always pretty, but hey, that's hockey. And on behalf of Austin puckheads everywhere, bravo to John McVaney, Brent Hughes, Ken McRae, Craig Jenkins and Marc Carlson for returning the Ice Bats to respectability in less time than it took me to finish this book.

JASON COHEN
Austin, Texas, June 2001

PHOTO IDENTIFICATION

Page ii, Andy Ross; p. vi, Rob Hartnell; p. 6, Ryan Anderson (seated); p. 32, an unidentified Lake Charles Ice Pirate; p. 48, Ken Ruddick; p. 64, Ryan Anderson; p. 78, Rob Hartnell and Central Texas Stampede goalie Larry Dyck; p. 91, unknown; p. 106, Mike Jackson; p. 129, Chris Haskett (right) and Stephan Desjardins; p. 143, Jason Rose (patient) and Kelly Cunningham (doctor); p. 154, Brett Seguin; p. 170, Paul Lawless; p. 181, Joe Van Volsen; p. 192, Christian Soucy; p. 203, Ken Ruddick; p. 213, Jason Rose (left) and Andy Ross.

ABOUT THE AUTHOR

Jason Cohen first wrote about the Austin Ice Bats for *Texas Monthly,* where he is a contributing editor. He also writes regularly for *Rolling Stone, Spin* and *TV Guide* and is the co-author (with Michael Krugman) of *Generation Ecch!* He lives in Austin, Texas, and can be contacted via www.zambonirodeo.com.